The Conservative Party

The Conservative Party

Edited by
Philip Norton

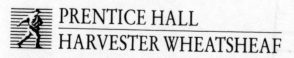
PRENTICE HALL
HARVESTER WHEATSHEAF

LONDON   NEW YORK TORONTO SYDNEY TOKYO SINGAPORE
MADRID   MEXICO CITY MUNICH

First published 1996 by
Prentice Hall/Harvester Wheatsheaf
Campus 400, Maylands Avenue
Hemel Hempstead
Hertfordshire, HP2 7EZ
A division of
Simon & Schuster International Group

Typeset in 10/12pt Times
by Dorwyn Ltd, Rowlands Castle, Hants

Printed and bound in Great Britain by
T.J. Press (Padstow) Ltd

Library of Congress Cataloging-in-Publication Data

The Conservative Party/edited by Philip Norton.
    p.   cm.
    Includes bibliographical references and index.
    ISBN 0–13–374653–4
    1. Conservative Party (Great Britain)–History. 2. Conservative
Party (Great Britain) I. Norton, Philip.
JN1129.C7C5747 1996
324.24104–dc20   95–50139
                                                CIP

British Library Cataloguing in Publication Data

A catalogue record for this book is available from
the British Library

ISBN 0–13–374653–4

1 2 3 4 5 00 99 98 97 96

Contents

Preface

The Conservative Party has a history of political success spanning more than a century. Despite its longevity, it has attracted relatively few texts providing a rounded overview of its history, beliefs, organisation, support and policies. There are books on each of these different facets, and a considerable number on some of its individual leaders, but very few that try to bring the facets together in a way that explains the Conservative Party to the student of politics.

An earlier book that did seek to provide an overview was *Conservatives and Conservatism*, published in 1981, which I co-authored with one of the contributors to this volume, Arthur Aughey. I have been conscious of the need for some form of successor for some time. A great deal has happened to the Conservative Party since that book was published. The era of Margaret Thatcher's leadership, just beginning when *Conservatives and Conservatism* was published, came to an end more than five years ago. The Conservative Party, in office for a longer continuous period than any previous Conservative administration, faces new challenges under her successor.

This volume is designed to combine depth with breadth, putting the Conservative Party into its historical context and providing a clear picture of the party today. That entails identifying explanations of Conservative success – why it has been the most successful political party in the era of mass politics in Britain – and why the party faces political difficulties in the 1990s.

In editing this volume I have been fortunate in being able to call on the services of a number of distinguished scholars. I am grateful to them for their contributions and for the care which they have taken in preparing their chapters. Despite other demands on their time, they have been diligent in meeting deadlines. Chapter 4, on the party's beliefs, draws on an earlier publication of mine, 'Conservatism', published in Michael Foley (ed.), *Ideas that Shape Politics* (Manchester University Press, 1994) and I am grateful for permission to reproduce that material here. Clare Grist of Harvester Wheatsheaf/Prentice Hall has been a pivotal figure in getting the volume under way and her usual efficient self in seeing it·through to publication.

Philip Norton
University of Hull
November 1995

Notes on contributors

Arthur Aughey is Senior Lecturer in Politics at the University of Ulster.

David Denver is Senior Lecturer in Politics at the University of Lancaster.

Justin Fisher is Lecturer in Politics at London Guildhall University.

Andrew Gamble is Professor of Politics at Sheffield University.

Philip Norton is Professor of Government at the University of Hull.

Philip Tether is Senior Lecturer in Economics and Public Sector Studies at Humberside University.

David Willetts is Member of Parliament for Havant.

The party in perspective

Philip Norton

The Conservative Party constitutes the great enigma of British politics. We know a great deal about some parts of the party and much has been written about its individual leaders. Several forests have been felled to produce the pages written on one leader alone, Margaret Thatcher. Some good works have been published on the history of the party. Robert Blake's *The Conservative Party from Peel to Churchill* (1970) – updated in 1985 – is an outstanding example. There have also been several substantial volumes on Conservatism, drawing together the basic beliefs of the party or providing a particular interpretation of the party's philosophy. Some leading figures within the party have put pen to paper to sketch the direction in which they believe the party should be going. Psephologists have variously analysed and explained Conservative success – or lack of it – at the ballot box; yet very few works have appeared that draw the strands together and give us a clear understanding of the Conservative Party in British politics. The sum of the parts (adumbrated in a magisterial survey by Ball, 1994a: 727–72) is very much greater than the whole.

The need for a work that looks at the Conservative Party in the round is essential. The party is the most successful party in British history; it has been an important force in British politics for more than a century and a half; it has been the 'in' party in British politics for more than a century; it has outlived the collapse of the other principal non-socialist party, the Liberal Party, and it predates the formation of its contemporary rival, the Labour Party, by more than 60 years. No other party in Britain, or Western Europe, can match its record.

Furthermore, it remains a party of government. On occasion, notably in 1906 and 1945, it has appeared to be destined for political oblivion only to bounce back and become again the party in government. It set a new record in twentieth-century British politics by winning, from 1979 onwards, four consecutive general elections. It produced a leader – Margaret Thatcher –

who dominated British politics and who served as Prime Minister for 11½ years, a record unequalled in the era of mass politics. From the late 1970s onwards it appeared to be the dominant force in British politics, forging a new political agenda and forcing its opponents to respond to what it was doing.

Yet what, for many commentators, is puzzling is why it remains a party of government, indeed the party most frequently in government. It is a party that has its roots in a predecessor party (the Tory Party) based on landed interests, that emphasises hierarchy and eschews the notions of intraparty democracy and equality, and yet which has remained *the* leading party in Britain in the era of mass politics. What makes any political party successful is an important question. It appears especially important in the case of the Conservative Party, given its long periods in government, as well as intriguing, given its nature and history.

Trying to explain why the Conservative Party is as it is, and why it is so often elected to office, is far from easy. Conservatives themselves are not prone to reflect on why they are as they are. They are as they are, and they are more concerned with the practicalities of life, and of learning from experience, than they are with abstract reasoning and reflection. That feature of Conservatives is itself important, as we shall have cause to see. Scholars who look at the Conservative Party with little sympathy for that feature often have difficulty getting to grips with its nature and the basis of its success. They certainly have difficulty in agreeing why the Conservative Party has proved so successful. A variety of explanations has been offered. Some of the explanations are persuasive and a few are close to bizarre.

The purpose of this volume is to contribute to an understanding of the Conservative Party through drawing together analyses of the various elements that collectively make it what it is. It identifies the principal explanations for the success of the Conservative Party and, informed by the explanations that appear the most persuasive, brings together descriptions and analyses of different facets of the party. By looking in some detail at where the party has been, what it has done, what it stands for, how it organises itself, where it gets its support from and the stances it takes on issues of public policy, it is possible to have a better understanding of the Conservative Party as a central political actor in the British polity.

Such a task is affected by the time at which it is undertaken. In the mid-1990s the Conservative Party occupies a remarkable position. It is the most enduring political party in British history. It is the party of government. It is also remarkably unpopular, having reached sustained and unprecedented lows in the opinion polls. The party confounded the pollsters by winning a general election in 1992 but within months of doing so had slumped in popular support. During the early part of 1995 it regularly trailed the Labour Party in the opinion polls by more than 30 points. Its leader reached an unprecedented low point in popular esteem. The last time the party had managed to retain a seat in a by-election was February 1989. A belief that the party would be consigned to the political wilderness at the next general election was widespread, including among party supporters and some Conservative Members of Parliament.

We thus have the task not only of providing historical depth but also of seeking to identify the cause of the party's present problems. Why is Britain's most successful party, the party returned at general elections continuously since 1979, experiencing what appear to be deep problems in the 1990s? Is it going through a period similar to previous periods in its history, from which it has emerged triumphant, or are its present travails without precedent?

The Introduction and Conclusion provide the two sides of the intellectual sandwich. The Introduction sketches various explanations of Conservative success. The Conclusion draws out explanations of why the Conservative Party faces an uncertain future. The chapters between provide the meat. Part 1 draws out the history and beliefs of the party; Part 2 looks at how the party organises itself, who comprises it and what they do, as well as identifying the sources of the party's funding and electoral support; and Part 3 looks at the party's stance on public policy, focusing on economic, foreign and social policy as well as the party's stance on the union of England, Scotland, Wales and Northern Ireland. The material embodied in the three parts contributes to an understanding of why the party has been where it has been, and where it is now. It also provides the basis for considering its future. Can one ask simply whither the future? Or do the events of recent years suggest that the 'h' should be dropped from whither?

Explanations of success

Why do people proclaim themselves to be Conservative? Why have so many people been prepared to vote the Conservative Party into power? Several explanations of Conservative support have been offered. They can be grouped under six headings: the psychological, the sociological, the ideological, the political, the instrumental and the coincidental.

Psychological

Three explanations fall under this heading. One is the psychology of fear and the second is the psychology of greed. The first derives from fear of the unknown, of seeing change as a threat. The fear is one well expressed by a leading exponent of British Conservatism, Lord Hugh Cecil, earlier this century. In his book *Conservatism*, published in 1912, he asked:

Q   Why depart from the known which is safe to the unknown which may be
    dangerous? None would be so mad as to run the risk without much search and

scrutiny. And this means perplexity, effort, confusion of mind, weariness. Why not let it alone? Why be weary instead of at rest? Why rush into danger instead of staying in safety? (p. 10)

For those who dislike or fear change, who prefer the known to the unknown, then the natural preference is for the political party most committed to the present and most wary of change.

The second explanation derives not from fear of the unknown but rather from greed or selfishness. This explanation has been offered most recently by a philosophy professor, Ted Honderich. Arguing that the various tenets of belief espoused by Conservatives are not sustainable on grounds of logic, he writes:

> The conclusion to which we come is not that Conservatives are selfish. It is that they are nothing else. Their selfishness is the rationale of their politics, and they have no other rationale. They stand without the support, the legitimation, of any recognisably moral principle. It is in this that they are distinguished fudamentally from those who are opposed to them. (Honderich, 1991: 238–9)

The third explanation to fall under this heading is that of false consciousness (see Norton and Aughey, 1981: 273). People are unknowingly manipulated to support a party which does not represent their true interests. To Marxists, parties such as the British Conservative Party serve the interests of the capitalist ruling class and work against the interests of the proletariat. The main problem for such a party, according to Halliday, is 'how to conciliate the interests of the social forces *it represents* with those of the social forces which *support it*' (cited in Miliband, 1973: 168n). Such parties devise ways to dress themselves in the 'ideological clothing suitable for political competition in the age of "mass politics"' (Miliband, 1973: 168). The parties offer some ameliorative reforms and employ the language of classlessness. They benefit from constitutional structures, imposing top-down forms of control, and from the financial backing of capitalist interests. They are thus able to maintain the support of working class voters even though they pursue interests contrary to those of the working class.

There are several problems with these explanations. One of the most obvious, certainly as far as the false consciousness thesis is concerned, is the problem of empirical verification. The explanation does not present obviously testable propositions. That is, they are not easily amenable to proof or falsification. They have to be assessed on the basis of their plausibility. The false consciousness thesis has been challenged on the grounds that it presumes the ability of one particular group to determine, apparently universally and in accord with some scientific law, what is in the interests of all workers, regardless of the workers' perceptions of their own interests (Norton and Aughey, 1981: 273). What are we to make of a situation where proponents of this thesis assert that y is in the interests of the working class and members of the working class assert that z is in their interests? There is no way of providing an objective answer.

The fear and greed theses are also open to the objection that neither can provide an exclusive explanation for Conservative support. The thesis that people wary of change will vote Conservative is a plausible one, but by itself cannot explain why all those who vote Conservative do so. There have been periods when the Conservative Party has offered change rather than a simple maintenance of the *status quo*. The Conservative Party under Margaret Thatcher advocated and pursued policies that were innovative and wrought significant changes in the economic and social life of the nation. If those who voted Conservative in the 1980s did so out of fear of change then they must have believed that the other parties threatened even greater change than the Conservative Party, and thus we must have witnessed the most reluctant mass vote imaginable; yet we know that many people voted Conservative enthusiastically. Their enthusiastic support cannot be explained by this particular thesis.

The argument that Conservative support derives from self interest is also plausible. Many, perhaps most, people will tend to prefer their own interests where there is a conflict between personal interest and the interests of others, including sometimes the good of the wider community. Car drivers will often prefer driving to work rather than taking the environmentally friendly step of walking or catching a bus. Trade unionists will strike for higher wages even though the effect may be to generate inflationary pressures. What these examples show is that pursuit of one's own interests is not a feature particular to Conservatives. Indeed, self interest can be argued to be the basis of class voting. Honderich recognises this and thus argues that self interest is not confined to Conservatives but that it is the distinguishing feature of Conservatives because they have no motivation other than self interest. There are two problems with this argument. The first is Honderich's line of reasoning. He argues that the principles that Conservatives espouse are illogical and thus cannot be sustained, and that therefore all that is left is selfishness. This argument supposes that people cannot genuinely hold beliefs that are illogical or run counter to other beliefs. The fact that a set of beliefs is not internally consistent does not mean that they are not genuinely held, and there is substantial evidence to show that people can and do hold conflicting beliefs. The second problem is that there is empirical support to show that Conservatives are not motivated solely by self interest. A study of Conservative Party members published in 1994 found that members' stances on public policy could be explained 'by a combination of self-interested and altruistic motives, together with pre-adult political experiences' (Whiteley *et al.*, 1994: 159). To explain the extent of Conservative support we thus need to look at other explanations.

Sociological

There are several explanations that fall under this heading. The first is perhaps the best known and derives from a strong empirical base. This explains Conservative support in terms of class and class cohesion.

The class basis of British politics can be put succinctly: the middle and upper classes vote Conservative and the working class votes Labour. As David Denver shows later in this volume (Chapter 11), there is a substantial body of empirical evidence to show that class is, or at least has been, the most important predictor of voting behaviour. In the 1950s 70 per cent or more of middle class voters cast their votes for the Conservatives. In the 1960s 60 per cent or more of working class voters cast their votes for the Labour Party (Sarlvik and Crewe, 1983: 87). Peter Pulzer in *Political Representation and Elections in Britain*, published in 1967, penned a line that was to be for many years a staple feature of examination papers: 'Class is the basis of British party politics: all else is embellishment and detail' (p. 98). However, at the time the working class numerically outnumbered the middle class by a ratio of about two to one. The explanation for Conservative success was seen to lie, in part, in the cohesion of the middle class, with middle class voters voting more solidly for the Conservative Party than working class voters voted for the Labour Party.

This, however, can only be a partial explanation for Conservative support at the polling booths since it does not explain the failure of the working class voters to vote as cohesively as middle class voters. David Denver discusses (Chapter 11) the principal theses offered for why roughly one in every three working class voters during post-war decades cast their votes for Conservative candidates. These comprise cross-pressures, misperceptions of one's class, social deference, *embourgeoisement* and age of political awareness.

The first two – workers cross-pressured by other social forces or ascribing themselves to the middle class – fail to explain why other workers in the same situations do not vote Conservative. The other explanations have also proved problematic, but are worthy of comment given that at various times they have attracted considerable attention.

The social deference thesis is best described as both psychological and sociological. It explains Conservative support, or at least part of it, in terms of deference to social superiors. Robert McKenzie and Allan Silver, in *Angels in Marble* published in 1968, identified 'deferential' Conservative voters as those who saw 'the Conservative élite as the natural rulers of Britain – sensitive to her traditions and peculiarities and uniquely qualified to govern by birth, experience, and outlook' (McKenzie and Silver, 1968: 242). They found that 26 per cent of working class Conservatives that they interviewed fell into the deferential category and that a further 27 per cent occupied a mixed category (of deferential and secular).

Their findings thus gave some credence to the notion of social deference, but they served also to demonstrate the limitations of deference as an explanation of Conservative working class support. A plurality of their respondents (38 per cent) did not fall into the deferential category (they were classed as 'seculars' – a category to be discussed below under the 'instrumental' heading). Critics also noted that deference was not exclusive to working class

Conservative supporters, but was also to be found among some Labour (and middle class Conservative) voters (Kavanagh, 1976: 72).

McKenzie and Silver also recorded a decrease in the number of deferentials. It would seem plausible to hypothesise that the number will have decreased since, given an apparent erosion of class boundaries and a party led by leaders drawn from solidly middle class, rather than upper class, backgrounds. Certainly, the study of party members by Whiteley *et al.* would appear to provide some empirical support for this hypothesis. They asked party members if they agreed with the statement that 'it is best to leave government to people from the upper class'. 'A large majority of Conservatives disagreed with the statement; in this sense, therefore, they do not defer to people from an élite class background' (Whiteley *et al.*, 1994: 182). They found some difference between poor and affluent members, but the difference was not great. Although deference may serve to explain *some* Conservative support among working class voters it has 'not performed impressively' as a predictor of party choice by workers (Kavanagh, 1976: 72).

The *embourgeoisement* thesis contends that workers' identification with the working class, and with the Labour Party, has declined as affluence has increased. It was a product initially of the 1950s. As working class voters acquired homes, cars, telephones and refrigerators, so they developed the social and political self images of the middle class (see Abrams *et al.*, 1960). This process of *embourgeoisement* was apparent in the 1950s and the Conservative Party did increasingly well in general elections, thus leading to the hypothesis that the Conservatives were benefiting from more affluent workers voting for the party. The problem with this thesis, as David Denver records, is that it does not explain working class Conservative voting before the increase in affluence and, in any event, subsequent research showed that more affluent workers were more likely to vote Labour than were working class voters generally. As Butler and Stokes comment, 'if the Conservative gains of the 1950s were really the result of prosperous workers coming to think of themselves as middle class, these gains should surely not have been so abruptly swept away' (Butler and Stokes, 1974: 107).

The thesis based on the age of political awareness – the generational cohort thesis – is a time-bound thesis that need not detain us. Butler and Stokes argued that the failure of some working class voters to identify with 'their' party, the Labour Party, was the result of some older voters having come of political age before Labour was a principal contender for power. 'Given the extent to which party loyalties are transmitted in the childhood home, time was needed for historic attachments to the "bourgeois" parties to weaken and for "secondary" processes to complete the realignment by class' (Butler and Stokes, 1974: 185). With each generation, the incidence of Conservative support declined. As the authors recognised, there were other influences at work. The thesis provided only a partial explanation of Conservative support among the working class. Also, with each decade one would expect Conservative support to decline as older voters die. As David Denver shows, the thesis does not help to explain Conservative success in the 1980s, a period when Conservative support among workers, especially skilled workers, increased rather than decreased.

All class-based explanations also have to contend now with a waning of the class–party nexus. This is explained in some detail in Chapter 11. Social change has rendered the concept of class less relevant and, indeed, less easy to define. The two major parties can no longer rely on the support of their 'natural' class, at least not to the extent that they used to. Each party has witnessed a decline in partisan identification and voting support among its natural class supporters. Partisan identification, at least 'very strong' identification, declined in the 1970s. The 1980s saw Labour support among working class voters decline dramatically, with the party failing to achieve even half of the votes of the category. More skilled manual workers voted Conservative in 1987 than voted Labour. The Conservatives made no significant inroads among their traditional class supporters, and in the 1992 general election the swing against the Conservatives was actually greatest among the upper middle class. Although social class continues to structure party choice, it is no longer the stable anchor of party support that it was in earlier decades:

> British electors in the eighties were much less constrained in their behaviour by class or party loyalties than in the past. 'Will your anchor hold in the storms of life?' asks the revivalist hymn. In the eighties, the British electorate were *not* firmly anchored to parties, and their anchors would *not* hold in a political storm. (Miller *et al.*, 1990: 8).

Again, then, one has to look to other explanations.

Ideological

This heading can be taken to encompass two conflicting explanations. One is based on ideology and the other on the absence of ideology. The first ascribes Conservative support to citizens agreeing with the ideology of the party and voting accordingly. The other argues that the Conservative Party has no firm ideology other than that of winning elections and so will say whatever is necessary to get elected.

The Conservative Party, as we shall see in Chapter 4, has certain basic tenets of belief. It would thus seem plausible to argue that support flows to it on the basis of those beliefs, electors voting Conservative because they are in agreement with what the party believes in. There is certainly strong empirical evidence showing a link between ideology and party support. A panel-based study of voters in the 1980s found that 62 per cent of those who described themselves as on the right were undeviating Conservative supporters. Of those who described themselves as leaning to the right, 38 per cent were undeviating Conservative supporters. Similarly, 63 per cent of those who described themselves as being on the left were undeviating supporters of the Labour Party. Of those leaning left, 33 per cent were undeviating Labour supporters (Miller *et al.*, 1990: 35). The more recent study of Conservative Party members by Whiteley *et al.* turned up a similar relationship. 'It is clear from the distribution of opinions . . . that most Conservatives think of themselves as being on the centre-right within the Conservative party and within British politics as a whole' (Whiteley *et al.*, 1994: 141; see also Seyd and Whiteley, 1992 for the Labour Party).

There is thus a strong relationship and of the type that one would expect, yet the fit between ideology and party is not precise. There are those who regard themselves as being on the left, or leaning to the left, who are undeviating Conservative supporters. The numbers in the Miller study are not great (2 per cent of those on the left and 5 per cent of those leaning left) but are sufficient to demonstrate some lack of fit. Furthermore, there is no clear fit between party support and those who identify themselves as being in the political centre. 'Among those in the "centre" who lean neither left nor right there was no clear pattern of party loyalty nor of switching . . . And the switchers moved in all directions . . . – a "muddled centre" indeed!' (Miller *et al.*, 1990: 34).

Ideology, then, may provide a consistent base of support for the Conservative Party but it is not sufficient to explain all consistent support nor to explain significant changes in electoral behaviour. It does not explain Conservative success in the 1980s under the leadership of Margaret Thatcher. Although she generated a distinctive ideological approach, sufficient for it to be elevated to the status of an 'ism' (Thatcherism), claims that it brought about an ideological change among electors, party members and Conservative MPs are not borne out by the empirical evidence (see Crewe and Searing, 1988; Norton, 1990a, 1990b; Whiteley *et al.*, 1994). If anything electors became less, rather than more, Thatcherite in outlook in the 1980s (Crewe and Searing, 1988: 377). Electors voted Conservative despite Thatcherism and not because of it.

There are those who argue that the difference between electoral success and failure is attributable to the fact that the Conservative Party wears ideology very lightly indeed and that its only real guiding principle is winning general elections. According to a recent work, the party's success is attributable largely to 'the Conservative Party's recognition that the overriding purpose of political activity is the achievement of power' (Davies, 1995). The party therefore does whatever is necessary to achieve electoral victory. Dogma is eschewed in favour of compromise. The party comes together to show a united front, especially in the period before a general election. It engages in unsavoury political practices in order to stain the character of its opponents. If a particular policy, or a particular leader, looks like being a major electoral liability, then the policy – or leader – is jettisoned. Thus in 1990, when the combination of Margaret Thatcher and the poll tax appeared to jeopardise the party's chances of staying in office, the parliamentary party replaced Margaret Thatcher with a leader prepared to abandon the tax.

The contention that the party exhibits a strong will to win is difficult to dispute. As Robert Blake has succinctly observed, 'If you do not hold office you can do nothing' (Blake, 1995: 34). The party is willing to work hard to win office. In political terms it plays hardball rather than softball. However, this explanation is not sufficient by itself to explain Conservative success, a fact recognised usually by those who advance it. As we have seen, there is an ideological base to the party's support. That arguably provides some anchor in terms of the policies that the party is prepared to espouse. The history of the party also reveals that the will to win may not always win out over a major clash over a particular policy. As we shall see in Chapter 1, the party tore itself apart over the issue of free trade in the 1840s and again at the beginning of this century, on both occasions being forced into the political wilderness. The 1980s and the 1990s have also witnessed major clashes within the party over economic policy and the issue of European integration. Some party supporters have clearly been cross-pressured, wanting the party to win and yet not being prepared to suppress their strong feelings on the issue.

Political

The principal political explanation for Conservative success is that the party has managed to convey that it is a party of governance. This explanation embodies two elements. One concerns how it governs and the other concerns policies pursued in government, although – as we shall see – the two are intimately linked.

The first element may be explained in terms of statecraft. This, according to Jim Bulpitt, is concerned with the 'how' of politics, with the ways in which government is conducted – the ways in which the party is managed, in which a winning electoral strategy is devised, in which dominance is achieved in political debate and the way in which the party is able to demonstrate a competence in office (Bulpitt, 1986: 20–3). Competence is demonstrated not simply by the policies that the government adopts but by those it chooses not to adopt:

> In many ways . . . the important point is not which policies a government
> positively adopts, but rather which it rejects or avoids. Now this may be the result
> of ideological preference, but it may equally well be connected to problems of
> implementation. Parties in office will not normally pursue policies which they
> believe they will be unable to implement effectively, either because the opposition
> is so strong or because they cannot trust those supposed to execute these policies.
> (Bulpitt, 1986: 22)

A governing competence involves being able to make choices through weighing the problems of implementation, political pressure and ideological and other commitments. Bulpitt discerned in the Thatcher government a return to traditional Conservative statecraft, the government attempting to achieve some degree of autonomy in the determination of 'high policy' (Bulpitt, 1986: 29–39).

Statecraft, then, is concerned with choice and with recognising the limits of what is achievable. The second element is more substantive in that it derives from the policies pursued by government, especially in economic policy. By the manner in which it has governed, and by the policies it has pursued, the Conservative Party has managed to convey that it is a competent party of government. This is borne out by survey data (see Chapter 11). In the years from 1964 to 1992, the Conservative Party was almost invariably regarded as more competent in the management of the economy than the Labour Party (Sanders, 1995: 161). In terms of economic management, it is seen by electors as a safe pair of hands.

It is seen as a safe pair of hands particularly in relation to its opponents. This brings us to the other principal political explanation of Conservative success, namely – in Robert Blake's pithy assertion – 'the capacity of . . . opponents to shoot themselves in the foot' (Blake, 1995: 34). Opposition parties have espoused deeply unpopular policies or torn themselves apart at times propitious for the Conservative Party. The Liberal split over Home Rule at the end of the nineteenth century helped to drive Liberal Unionists into the arms of the Conservatives. The split between Asquithian and Lloyd George Liberals occurred when the Conservative and Liberal Parties were competing for the mantle of principal challenger to an emerging socialist party. The split in the Labour Cabinet in 1931 opened the door for a Conservative-dominated National government. Labour disarray in the 1950s and again in the 1980s helped bolster support for the Conservative Party. In the 1983 general election campaign, the Labour Party had difficulty in presenting itself as a credible party of government.

These political explanations appear especially plausible. They help to explain why Conservative governments have been returned to office, as in the 1980s, even though particular policies have not been especially popular. The popular perception has been one of a government knowing what it is doing and where it is going. On this analysis, therefore, the explanation for Conservative success in 1983 and 1987 rests more with Margaret Thatcher than it does with Thatcherism (see Norton, 1993: 32–3). She conveyed a sense of direction, of leading a government that knew what it was about and would deliver, yet at the same time avoiding or abandoning policies that could not be implemented. She faced opponents who had no such sense of what to do. The combination of these two variables in 1983 produced the largest Conservative parliamentary majority since 1935.

A failure of the Conservative government to convey that it is a competent party of government, especially in the management of the economy, has been seen as the principal basis of Conservative unpopularity in the period since

1992. Following the government's enforced withdrawal from the European exchange rate mechanism (ERM) in September 1992, the government's competence rating dropped dramatically (Sanders, 1992: 161–2). The combination of a government that failed to convey competence in managing the economic affairs of the nation with a revitalised opposition produced a dramatic lead for the Labour Party in the opinion polls. By early 1995, about 50 per cent of those surveyed in opinion polls were expressing their intention to support the Labour Party in a general election. Conservative support dipped below 30 per cent.

These explanations are powerful in terms of explaining Conservative electoral success. It is because of that electoral success that the Conservative Party is such an important body to study. However, the explanations are not necessarily sufficient for explaining all the support that accrues to the Conservative Party. There are committed Conservative supporters who will vote Conservative more or less under all circumstances. Survey data in the 1990s, when the party hit a low point of popularity, show that the party can rely on the support of at least 20 per cent of voters. The other explanations come into play in explaining the enduring and committed support of the party. However, the support of 20 per cent of electors is not sufficient to return the party to power in future general elections.

Instrumental

The instrumental explanation is that voters give their votes to a party that delivers on its promises. The supposition is that electors are not swayed by sentiment or tradition but rather will cast their votes rationally for the party that will deliver what they want. If a party delivers in office, then it will be rewarded by being re-elected to office.

This explanation may seem to be indistinguishable from the political explanation of economic competence, but there is a difference. Voters may distinguish between a competent party of government, able to manage the economy efficiently, and a party that can deliver particular benefits for them. Parties returned to office do have a record of carrying out manifesto promises and on an extensive basis (see Hofferbert and Budge, 1992), but the most important thing that voters apparently want government to deliver is economic prosperity. There is some debate as to whether electors vote on the basis of retrospective evaluation (rewarding a party for what it has done) or prospective evaluation (voting on the basis of what a party is expected to deliver). One study of the Labour Party in the 1980s, for example, placed particular emphasis on retrospective evaluation as an explanation for Labour's poor performance (Whiteley, 1982, 1983). Recent research points to prospective evaluation as more important in determining Conservative support than retrospective evaluations or the objective condition of the economy (Price and

Sanders, 1995: 451–71). Voters thus are motivated more by what they think the party will deliver than by their assessment of what it has delivered, although the latter may feed into the former. This might be described as the most instrumental, or rational, form of voting, not as a form of reward for services rendered but as a choice of the best possible future deal on offer.

Again, this explanation does not explain all Conservative support. The major research exercise that uncovered the importance of prospective evaluation also found, in line with other studies, that Conservative support varied according to age, class, region, housing tenure, gender and trade union membership (Price and Sanders, 1995: 470). Nonetheless, it is important in helping to explain Conservative success in the 1980s and Conservative unpopularity in the 1990s. According to Price and Sanders, 'a large part of the Conservatives' electoral success during the 1980s derived from their ability to generate a sense of optimism among sufficient electors in advance of the 1983 and 1987 general elections' (Price and Sanders, 1995: 470). Similar optimism was generated in the run-up to the 1992 general election (Sanders, 1995: 164). Optimism has not been a feature of the period since then.

Coincidental

The final explanation is that of coincidence, or luck. The Conservative Party has been in government when particular events have taken place that have boosted – or sometimes undermined – its support. This overlaps with the political in terms of the misfortunes of its political opponents. The misfortune of its opponents, coupled with particular historical events and being in office at times of world economic recovery, have put it in a position where electors see it as the best party to support. The party, it could be argued, was virtually saved from destroying itself by the advent of the First World War. Many, although not all, commentators believe the party was restored to political health by the outcome of the Falklands War in 1982. The party was in office during a period of international economic recovery in the 1950s and during an economic boom in the 1980s.

Luck is an important aspect of politics, for individuals as well as parties. However, while specific events external to the party – and over which the party may have little or no control – may have provided some boost to its fortunes (or served to undermine support), it would be difficult to sustain the argument that a string of external events has formed the basis of the party's electoral fortunes over more than a century. Indeed, there are analysts who question the impact of some of those events that are claimed to have provided a sustained boost to the party's fortunes. David Sanders, in particular, has been a critic of this 'specific events' thesis. His research, with other colleagues, suggests that the boost to Conservative fortunes provided by the Falklands War was short-lived and did not play a decisive role in determining the outcome of the 1983 general election (Sanders *et al.*, 1987, 1991; Price and Sanders, 1995). A similar short-term impact was produced by the introduction of the poll tax and Margaret Thatcher's removal as leader of the Conservative Party (Sanders, 1995: 158–9). This is not to say that particular events may not have some impact, on occasion a crucial impact, but rather that too much weight should not be assigned to them in seeking to explain Conservative support and the success of the Conservative Party as a party of government for more than 100 years.

Conclusion

We thus have some basis for explaining why the Conservative Party has maintained the support of a substantial proportion of voters for more than a century and why it has been the most successful party in British politics. There is no single, over-arching explanation. Although we give little credence to the false consciousness thesis and do not follow Honderich's perverse reasoning, we would not discard the principal explanations we have discussed. The earlier explanations – the psychological, the sociological and the ideological – are especially useful for explaining why there is an enduring body of support for the Conservative Party. The political and instrumental explanations (less so the coincidental) are powerful in helping us to understand why the Conservative Party has been elected to government on more occasions than its opponents. These explanations inform and are variously drawn out in the chapters that follow. They do not and cannot provide a complete explanation. Not all are empirically verifiable and a number are the subject of academic dispute; but they do go some way to help resolve the enigma that is the British Conservative Party.

PART 1

Party development

CHAPTER 1

History of the party I

Tory to Conservative

Philip Norton

The Conservative Party emerged in the 1830s. Its institutional antecedent is clear. It was the successor to the party of the landed gentry, the Tory Party. Indeed, the succession was almost of an apostolic nature: 'the party is dead, long live the party': not so much a new party as a party with a new name. The Conservative Party acquired the support and the intellectual baggage – what there was of it – of the Tories and was to add much more besides. In terms of its intellectual antecedents, they were varied and of more ancient lineage.

There is no precise date at which the Conservative Party came into being. There was no great meeting, or even a small meeting, to which its formation may be ascribed. No document was drawn up and agreed stipulating its organisation and its guiding principles. At the beginning of the decade, there was no body recognisable as the 'Conservative' party. By the middle of the decade there was.

Name

If one seeks the origins of the party in terms of its nomenclature the name 'Conservative' was discovered by Geoffrey Block (1964) to have been used by George Canning in 1824 but the most significant reference, prompting its more widespread use, was in the *Quarterly Review* in 1830. 'We now are, as we always have been, decidedly and conscientiously attached to what is called the Tory, and which might with more propriety be called the Conservative Party.' The name appears to have gained currency within a matter of months and by 1834 Sir Robert Peel was able to claim, in his Tamworth Manifesto, that he led 'the Great Conservative Party'.

Institution

If one looks for the origins of the party in institutional terms, several bodies embodying the name Conservative were established in 1832 and the years immediately thereafter. Various Conservative Associations, appealing to local notables and gentlemen, were formed: a Durham county Conservative Association and a Liverpool Conservative Association were set up in 1832 (Nossiter, 1975; Bulmer-Thomas, 1967: 77). Robert Blake notes the existence of an election fund, with Peel and the Duke of Wellington as Trustees, in 1835, with a similar fund existing in subsequent elections. 'But one would hardly date the origins of the Conservative Party in 1835, merely because of the fund' (Blake, 1970: 2). There are grounds, however, for seeing 1835 as the year in which the party was not so much formed but rather confirmed. Constituency Associations and registration societies (basically one and the same thing) were variously in existence by 1835 and that year saw the flowering of such bodies, the establishment of an election fund and the forming of the Operative Conservative Society in Leeds, 'which society', according to one of its founders, 'was the first that was established in the kingdom among the Conservative Operatives' (Paul, 1838: 8). The appeal to the skilled worker proved popular (see Tether, 1988). Within a year, 100 Operative Societies were in existence.

Issues and events

If one were to identify the origins of the party in terms of political issues and events, then the seminal event is the 1832 Reform Act. The issue of parliamentary reform had sounded the death knell of the Tory Party and necessitated a party that could respond to the changed circumstances. Peel's summons to assume the premiership in 1834 – on the recommendation of Wellington, who still had a claim to office – confirmed the transfer from Tory to Conservative. Peel's Tamworth Manifesto, issued to his constituents at the end of the year, articulated the stance of the party in relation to the new political situation. It constituted the first articulation of Conservative thought. Peel's brief tenure of office also established the party's claim to be a party of government.

The emergence of the Conservative Party may thus be ascribed to a four-year period between 1831 and 1835, but such an ascription is not to assert the foundation of a national party whose future was assured. In organisation, it was not wholly national. Politically, its future was far from assured. The Carlton Club, founded shortly before the 1832 Reform Act, provided a base for the central operations of the party but it was not until 1867 that the party acquired a formal national structure to encompass the voluntary associations. Although briefly in government for four months from December 1834 to April 1835, the party achieved a parliamentary majority only in the election of 1841, governing for five years until the issue of the Corn Laws split the party asunder. Not until 1874 was the party to hold office again with a parliamentary majority.

Ironically, at least from the view of the critics, the Conservative Party emerged, and then re-emerged, as a national party of government in the wake of the widening of the franchise. What may be termed the party's emergent period as a party of government was a long and tortuous one.

Wellington to Peel

Prior to the nineteenth century parties were not, in any institutional sense, organised. The term 'party' referred to a collection of men who were largely agreed upon a particular approach to government and enjoyed a certain common perception of the way of things. The labels 'Whig' and 'Tory' had emerged in the latter half of the seventeenth century, both initially as terms of abuse to denote supporters and opponents, respectively, of the Exclusion Bill designed to prevent James, Duke of York from succeeding his brother on the throne. The labels were applied to broad and far from cohesive groupings. The Tories tended to represent the landed interest and to be cautious of – or totally opposed to – change. Whigs were more disposed towards some change in the accepted ways of the nation and were more associated with the interests of trade. Such 'parties', however, were amorphous, lacking in both structure and cohesion. Some members of the political community carried party labels very lightly, if at all.

Nonetheless the labels counted for something, not least during general elections; election campaigns were partisan and not lacking in vindictiveness. The labels came to mean something in terms of the King's Government, with the eighteenth century witnessing the creation of 'party' ministries, one particular grouping finding the King's favour and using its position to deny patronage and influence to its opponents. The Whigs in particular enjoyed a period of hegemony; but there are dangers in pushing the terminology too far. It is indicative of the limited utility of party labels that the Tory Party at the end of the century should have its fortunes restored by a politician, William Pitt the Younger, who never called himself a Tory, and that the best Tory response to the French revolution was penned by the Whig, Edmund Burke. The terms 'Tory' and 'Whig' meant *something*, but not very precisely. Their meanings were mostly best known to those who wrapped themselves in them.

The first three decades of the nineteenth century were essentially Tory years, producing one of Britain's longest-serving Prime Ministers, the Earl of Liverpool (1812–27). Liverpool's government pursued a combination of repression (the Peterloo massacre of 1819, passage of the Six Acts) and moderate fiscal and penal reform carried out by some able ministers, notably William Huskisson at the Board of Trade and Sir Robert Peel at the Home Office. In the 1820s Huskisson displayed free trade instincts by getting duties reduced on various materials; Peel abolished the death penalty for more than 100 offences. Liverpool was succeeded, after a brief and confused interregnum (George Canning was briefly premier, bringing in Tory and Whig ministers, but died after a few months; Viscount Goderich resigned the office before

Parliament had met), by the Duke of Wellington, a national hero upon entering office, a figure of national hate when he left it. Wellington proved movable on a number of contentious issues, not least Catholic emancipation, but was destroyed on the rocks of parliamentary reform.

The industrial revolution had begun in the middle of the eighteenth century. Industry had expanded and become mechanised. Agricultural output had improved with the development of new production techniques, trade became more important and more organised, as did banking. There was a shift from the country to the towns. By the time Wellington had assumed the reins of office there was already a significant non-landed middle class and a notable body of artisans. Economic advancement, however, was not matched by political gains. Parliamentary representation was heavily skewed in favour of the rural counties. Parliament was dominated by the aristocracy and the landed gentry.

Pressure for a widening of the franchise and for a more equitable distribution of seats grew rapidly and was given impetus by unrest in a number of areas, both urban and agricultural, and by the French revolution of 1830, which was a spur to radical perceptions and action. For the Whigs, the 'outs' in politics, it was an issue which offered an opportunity to change the political structure and create the conditions that would allow them to be the party of government.

Wellington's stance on parliamentary reform was firm and unambiguous: he was totally opposed to it. To him, the nation had a constitution that was as perfect as one was likely to achieve. His stance left no room for compromise. Reform of the franchise, to him, was a non-issue. To others, it was most decidedly an issue and became a central one in the election of 1830. A defence of some of the more extreme examples of 'rotten boroughs' became increasingly untenable. For those who did have the vote the record of the ministry was mixed. The Tories failed to gain a majority in the election and Wellington's ministry was defeated when the new House of Commons met. A Whig government was formed under Earl Grey. Its first attempt to achieve passage of a Reform Bill floundered in committee. Grey persuaded the King to grant a dissolution and an election was held on the issue of 'the bill, the whole bill, and nothing but the bill'. The political mood of the time strongly favoured reform and that, coupled with the manipulative weapons that resided with the ministry, produced a large Whig majority. That majority was more than sufficient to ensure passage of the Bill in the House of Commons. The House of Lords rejected the measure, but eventually succumbed under the threat of the creation of 50 new Whig peers. Wellington recognised the inevitable and led the Tory absenters whose action made passage of the bill possible.

The Reform Act was not as radical as the Bill introduced in 1831. Fifty-six boroughs were disenfranchised, 32 member boroughs had their representation reduced to one member each and new seats were created in the more populous areas. The franchise was widened, resulting in an increase in the size of the electorate from a little under 500,000 electors to 813,000 (Conacher, 1971: 10). Although the changes were modest in quantitative terms – only one-thirtieth of the population had the vote – they wrought significant political changes. For the parties there was a need to come to terms with the new situation, both politically and organisationally. The electorate was now too large to be contacted and swayed solely on the basis of connection and the pull of the aristocracy. Politics were no longer confined to 'parliamentary circles and the drawing rooms connected with them' (Ostrogorski, 1902: 15). Not only had a new mass of electors been enfranchised, so too had a new class.

Any doubts that Tories may have harboured about the need to accommodate themselves to the new arrangements were dispelled by the general election of 1832. Held in December on the new franchise, it reduced Tory strength in the Commons to 185 seats – almost half the number it had in 1830. Those on the opposite side of the House numbered almost 500.

Wellington came to represent the unacceptable face of Toryism. He was an aristocrat, too closely tied to the old constitution. Sir Robert Peel was the son of an industrialist, he spoke with a provincial accent and represented a seat with at least a modest number of electors (almost 600). Despite, on a number of issues, having been no less opposed to change than Wellington – indeed, he accepted Catholic emancipation even less willingly than did the Duke – Peel came to be seen as coming closer to embodying the spirit of the age.

The organisational response to change came in the immediate wake of the Reform Act. By 1834 the name of the party by common usage was the Conservative Party and party associations of different hues were sprouting throughout the country, especially in the north-west. The opportunity for demonstrating a political response came, fortuitously, in 1834. In December the King dismissed the divided ministry of Lord Melbourne and turned to the Tories, now called Conservatives. Wellington was still, as the Tory ex-Prime Minister, leader of the party and had a claim to office, but he declined the King's invitation and recommended that Peel be appointed. Peel assumed the office and set about establishing the Conservative Party as a serious contender for the favour of the electors and not of just the monarch. He began preparations for the election contest, held the following month. Some degree of central co-ordination took place at the Carlton Club – 'It was there that F. R. Bonham, Peel's faithful henchman, had his desk, arranged for candidates, sought subscriptions, organised elections, and reported the gossip of the day to his master' (Blake, 1970: 137–8) – and an election committee and fund were established. At the same time Peel issued a 'manifesto' to his Tamworth constituents.

The Tamworth Manifesto reflected Peel's attempt to accommodate the Conservative Party to the conditions of the time: balancing the basic dispositions of the party with the prevailing political mood in order to attract the support of new electors without alienating the traditional constituency of the Tory Party. Rejection of the Reform Act was not tenable, while embracing change that appeared to threaten existing institutions would destroy the party's existing electoral base.

In the document, Peel made clear that he was by no means 'the defender of abuses or the enemy of judicious reform', citing in his support some of the measures he was responsible for as Home Secretary – 'the consolidation and amendment of the criminal law . . . the revisal of the whole system of Trial by Jury' – while, as Blake aptly notes (1970: 40), omitting reference to some of the more contentious reforms with which he was associated. The Reform Act he accepted as 'a final and irrevocable settlement of a great Constitutional question', utilising a phrase – 'final and irrevocable' – that demonstrated the quintessentially Conservative nature of his appeal. There was to be no reactionary stance advocating the *status quo ante* in respect of reform; now that the Reform Act was in place, it could be conserved. It was also 'final'. There were to be no more major disruptions to the nation's constitutional framework. This reflected an interesting conundrum for Peel, and one variously faced since by Conservatives: having opposed the Reform Bill on the grounds that it would necessarily lead to even greater and more dire upheavals, it was now necessary to argue that the measure, having been enacted, was final and would not and should not lead to further change.

As for the challenge levelled by Whigs that ministers must act in the spirit of the Act, he asserted that if that meant living in 'a perpetual vortex of agitation' and abandoning respect for ancient rights then he had no intention of acting in its spirit. If, however, it implied 'merely a careful review of institutions, civil and ecclesiastical, undertaken in a friendly temper, combining with the firm maintenance of established rights the correction of proved abuses and the redress of real grievances – in that case I can for myself and my colleagues undertake to act in such a spirit and with such intentions' (quoted in Blake, 1970: 40–1).

Much has been made subsequently of what was actually entailed by such sentiments, not least and more contemporaneously by Disraeli, but they served to provide an essential flavour of what the new party was about, to demonstrate to its landed supporters that established institutions were safe in its hands, while demonstrating to the newly enfranchised urban middle class that the new constitutional arrangements were similarly not under threat. In short, the party was neither radical nor reactionary. At a time of social instability, it was a stance of some significance.

The document helped confer respectability, although not office, upon the newly named party. In the election, the Conservatives improved their representation significantly, winning 279 seats. Their opponents won 100 seats more and so Peel's ministry could not long survive. The ministry resigned in April after losing a vote on the appropriations.

Everything, now, was in place for the Conservatives to assume the reins of office should their opponents fail. The party made further gains in the election of 1837 necessitated by the death of the King, its strength in the House rising above the figure of 300; and in 1839 it was denied office only by the intransigence of the new young Queen. (The Whigs were in disarray on a number of issues and resigned; as a condition of accepting office, Peel asked the Queen to replace the Whig Ladies of the Bedchamber with some Conservative Ladies – Victoria refused to do so and Peel declined office.) The disarray within the Whig ministry continued and in 1841 it was defeated on a vote of confidence. An election followed, with the Conservatives being returned with a majority of more than 70 over their parliamentary opponents. Support for the party was particularly strong in the English and Welsh counties (Stewart, 1989: 62). The first Conservative government in British history had been returned by the electorate.

Within five years the party was to be one with a glorious future behind it. The government – which in effect meant Peel – enacted a number of measures of reform. (The Cabinet included five former or future Prime Ministers and has been variously described as one of the most outstanding administrations of the century – but Peel, when he was not introducing reforms, meddled in the affairs of the various departments; on one occasion he introduced the budget himself.) Fiscal reforms in particular recognised the importance of trade, with a multiplicity of import duties being swept away: 750 duties were repealed as a consequence of the 1842 budget, a further 450 being swept away by the budget of 1845. In their place, income tax (previously a wartime expedient) was introduced. The Corn Laws, providing a protectionist barrier to the import of foreign corn until the domestic price reached specified levels, were modified. However, the ministry ran into trouble with its own supporters. The move away from protection was not uniformly welcomed. More significantly, Peel's Irish policy aroused bitter dissension. His attempts to deal with the problem included increasing the grant to the Catholic Maynooth Seminary and this, in particular, aroused the opposition of many Conservatives who remembered Peel's *volte face* on Catholic emancipation. The Bill to increase the grant only got through the Commons with Whig support (see Coleman, 1988: 69). Then came the final blow: famine in Ireland persuaded Peel of the need to repeal the Corn Laws. Peel carried the measure with Whig help, but it forced a rift between Peelite free traders and the (more numerous) protectionists within the party, a rift that was never healed. His opponents combined with the Whigs to defeat the ministry on a subsequent Bill – the Irish Coercion Bill – and Peel resigned. Peel and his supporters then went their separate way, standing at the subsequent election independently of the Conservative Party. The party, although continuing to win a substantial number of seats in elections, entered the political wilderness unsure of its direction.

Peel's failure, like that of Wellington, lay in the fact that he lacked the skills of governance. He took a stand on an issue, certain of its rightness, and made little or no attempt to incorporate perceptions of the prevailing political environment into his strategic thinking; indeed, in political terms, at the end of the ministry there was no strategic thinking. The parallel between Peel and his Conservative successor of 150 years later, Edward Heath, is even more striking. Both administrators and problem-solvers, they lacked the skills of parliamentary management. Both cold, aloof directors of government, the rightness of the issue determined what action each was to take. Both consequently dug themselves into political corners from which they could not extricate themselves.

Rebuilding the party

The Peelites in the House of Commons sat separately from the Conservative Party and in time disappeared from the political scene: some returned to the Conservative fold, others left politics, some – notably William Gladstone – joined the Whigs. The short-lived existence of this breakaway group nonetheless had profound consequences. For one thing, along with the Whigs, Radicals and Nationalists, it denied the Conservatives an overall majority in the House of Commons. For another, it rid the Conservative Party of much of its ministerial talent. In the Commons the party's principal figures were Lord John Bentinck, more at home on the turf than on the floor of the House of Commons, and Benjamin Disraeli, a flamboyant, overbearing Anglicised Jew. In the Lords leadership fell to an aristocrat with Cabinet experience, Lord Stanley – succeeding in 1851 to the title of the fourteenth Earl of Derby – who was recognised by Bentinck as the leader of the party. When in 1852 Derby formed a short-lived ministry it became known as the 'Who? Who?' ministry, from the Duke of Wellington's alleged response when Derby tried to tell him the names of ministers. Another consequence of the split was organisational confusion: in the election of 1847 the central machinery established by Peel was used to support Peelite candidates, although Peel himself failed to countenance an organised Peelite grouping or party.

Not only was the Conservative Party in a weak position to portray itself as the alternative government, it suffered also for a decade from the strength of leadership on the government side of the House. The years 1855–65 were the years of Palmerstonian dominance. In his robust defence of British interests abroad and opposition to reform at home Lord Palmerston – a former Canningite Tory who had left the party in 1830 on the issue of electoral reform – largely robbed the Conservatives of a significant political target at which to shoot.

The task for the Conservative Party was to regroup its strength and wait for an opportunity to prove itself. Neither proved easy. Although Derby was recognised as leader of the party, leadership of the parliamentary party in the Commons proved a problem. When Bentinck resigned in 1847, Disraeli was not an acceptable successor and the eventual solution was one of a commission of three (Disraeli included) to lead the party in the Lower House. When Disraeli was able, eventually, to claim the leadership, it was largely because no one could any longer deny it to him. That, however, was some way in the future.

The opportunities for the party to prove itself in government were few and those they had were largely wasted. Derby formed two short-lived governments in 1852 and 1858–9 (and declined office in 1855, when Lord Aberdeen's coalition collapsed), neither of which were used to much effect: in the first, Disraeli as Chancellor of the Exchequer introduced a badly received budget, too obviously favouring the interests of agriculture, and in the second the government introduced a Reform Bill that was too self-serving. For the party, the 20 years from 1846 to 1866 were largely barren of achievement and, indeed, it was a surprise to Derby that the party held together for so long with little more than group loyalty and personal attachments to bind it (Norton and Aughey, 1981: 106). Not until 1867 did the party make a significant mark on the political scene.

Palmerston's death in office in 1865 helped to release the radical tensions within the ranks of the Whigs and in 1866 the ministry of Russell introduced a Reform Bill to redistribute parliamentary seats and widen the franchise. The Bill split the Whigs and a sufficient number joined with the Conservatives to ensure its defeat. The government resigned and once again Derby was called upon to form a minority government. In office, Derby and Disraeli – with Derby being more the initiating force on the issue – introduced a Reform Bill that on the face of it was more radical than the defeated Whig Bill of 1866. The measure, in its final form, increased the electorate by 88 per cent (in the boroughs the increase was one of 140 per cent) and redrew the electoral map. It was a bold move, borne as much of immediate political perceptions as of principles or long-term calculations. It stole a march on the Whigs, it ensured a change in electoral arrangements that were less unfavourable to the Conservatives than the provisions of the 1866 Bill, it responded to political demands which could not long be staved off – 'there is', declared Derby, 'a genuine desire *now*' (Southgate, 1977: 157) – and it allowed the party to claim that it was not averse to change nor to the desires of the urban worker. The measure, passed with Whig support, was not sufficient to prevent electoral defeat in 1868, although the effects of constituency redistribution helped to soften the scale of the defeat (see Coleman, 1988: 136), but it did allow the party to generate the impression of being a party of government, of being a competent alternative to the then 'in' party. What Feuchtwanger (1968: 82) has described as Disraeli's 'justified gamble' may not have been responsible for the Conservative victory in 1874 and later elections but it may well have prevented the party from being denied victory and consignment to the dustbin of history.

The minority government formed by Derby in June 1866 survived for two-and-a-half years, though Derby himself served as premier for less than two of them. He resigned in February 1868 (he died the following year) and was succeeded by Disraeli. For Disraeli the wait had been a long one: he was already in his sixty-fourth year. Although the epithet 'an old man in a hurry' is ascribed to Gladstone, it applies equally well to Benjamin Disraeli. Disraeli was to lead the Conservative Party for 13 years – 8 from the House of Commons, 5 from the House of Lords as Lord Beaconsfield – until his death in 1881. In those 13 years he raised the Conservative Party to a new plane, both organisationally and politically.'

The Disraelian era

Disraeli served as Prime Minister from 1874 – when he was 70 years of age – to 1880. It was the only time he was in office with an overall parliamentary majority. Looked at in terms solely of the particular measures passed and the actions taken, the government was an able one, although not necessarily outstanding.

At home, a number of important measures of social welfare reached the statute book: foremost among them were the Acts regulating public health, factories, food and drugs and slum clearance, as well as trade union legislation that was to remain in force until well into the twentieth century. Abroad, there was extension of Empire – Disraeli endearing himself to the Queen by creating her Empress of India – and, most significant in diplomatic terms, the settlement of the Eastern Question at the Congress of Berlin, avoiding the danger of war and giving rise to one of Disraeli's many memorable phrases: 'Lord Salisbury and myself have brought you back peace – but a peace, I hope, with honour.' However, the measures of social reform, although important individually and collectively, were not – as Blake has observed – greatly different from those a Liberal government might have introduced and towards the end of the Parliament the government had to contend with a worsening economic climate and some minor colonial conflicts abroad. The record of the government was insufficient to keep it in office and in 1880 the Liberals under Gladstone were returned with a clear working majority of parliamentary seats.

In terms of the future wellbeing of the Conservative Party, the contribution of Disraeli – of which his ministry formed a substantial but not a total part – was profound. Disraeli was a romantic with little eye for detail and, indeed, with little consistency in his political opinions. There was no apparent grand design when he entered the leadership to ensure the future success of the Conservative Party; but the effect of what he did was the same as if he had had one. The principal transformation of the party under Disraeli's leadership was to make it a national party: national in its organisation and national in its electoral appeal.

The party's central organisation, in so far as it had any, was cast into disarray following the Peelite split of the 1840s. Disraeli turned some of his attention in the 1850s to improving the position and appointed his friend and solicitor Philip Rose to handle centrally the electoral management of the extra-parliamentary party; Rose became known as the party's Principal Agent, and the term stuck. In 1863 a Conservative Registration Association was formed. Central organisation, however, remained rudimentary. Elections were conducted essentially on a local basis, with candidates arranging their own funding.

What provided the imperative for change was the effect of the 1867 Reform Act. The sudden and massive expansion of the franchise meant that, in party terms, 'a system of centralisation became inevitable' (Seymour, 1970: 313). The electorate was now too large to be contacted – or corrupted – on an individual basis. Organisation was necessary if electors were to be reached and, indeed, if promises were to be made to them. The imperative of organisation was reinforced by the introduction of secret voting (1870), the outlawing of various corrupt practices (1882) and the further widening of the franchise in 1884, as a result of which a majority of working men enjoyed the vote. Party labels became increasingly important to an electorate less willing to discriminate on the basis of individual merit (or pecuniary inducements, now less freely available). Within Parliament the parties became more cohesive (Norton, 1981: 18–20); outside Parliament they became more organised.

The principal changes in Conservative organisation were the creation in 1867 of the National Union of Conservative and Constitutional Working Men's Associations (later the National Union of Conservative and Unionist Associations, known simply – and hereafter referred to – as 'the National Union') and in 1870 of Central Office, representing essentially the voluntary and the professional wings of the party respectively. From 1871 onwards there was some overlap between the two bodies – Central Office officials helped service the National Union – and both shared the same roof, features that have remained to the present day.

The National Union was formed largely on the initiative of Henry Raikes in order to bring together (and encourage new) working class Conservative Associations throughout the country and to help spread the Conservative message. At its first meeting the chairman explained that the purpose for which they were meeting was not to discuss party principles – 'in which we are all agreed' – but to consider the most appropriate form of organisation through which those principles may be made 'effective among the masses' (McKenzie, 1964: 151). Its beginnings were inauspicious and not all within the party (not least some associations, jealous of their independence) were anxious to see it succeed. What provided the basis for its success were the activities of the party's Principal Agent, John Gorst, who became joint secretary in 1871, and Disraeli's use of the organisation as the platform for major political addresses.[1] Previously Disraeli had confined his speeches to the House of Commons or his constituency. Recognising the changed political circumstances he addressed major rallies of the National Union, at Manchester in May 1872 and at Crystal Palace the following month.[2] The leader's speeches helped both to establish the position of the National Union and to provide the textual basis of what has been subsequently discerned as Disraeli's political creed.

The number of Conservative Associations affiliating to the National Union increased rapidly, from 289 in 1871 to 472 in 1875, and the Union embarked on an ambitious programme of disseminating literature throughout the country. However, its growth was stunted when the party was returned to office in 1874. Disraeli's interests turned elsewhere. 'From the moment he was returned to power with a majority, Disraeli put his faith in imperialism; and he unfortunately neglected the recommendations of the experienced managers of the party, who assured him that it would require greatly increased and unremitting efforts on the part of the Conservative organisation to win the next election' (Gorst, 1900: 153). While the party was in power the creation of the new Conservative working men's clubs – rapid in the years prior to 1874 – appears to have dried up (Tether, 1988: 29) and the National Union itself played little effective part in the general election of 1880. Not until the leadership of the Marquess of Salisbury did it enjoy a revival.

A similar history may be sketched for Central Office. Its origins lay in 1870, when John Gorst was appointed Principal Agent and given an office at 53 Parliament Street. He succeeded to the tasks which had been conducted previously from the Carlton Club, essentially those of electoral management, and from 1871 onwards served as joint secretary of the National Union. Gorst was a skilful organiser and made effective use of the National Union as the propaganda arm of the party. His good work, however, did not fully outlast him. He ceased to be Principal Agent once the party was returned to office in 1874; his successor failed to match his competence (Blake, 1970: 148–9) and in any event was overshadowed by the party's Chief Whip, who retained a coterminous and superior responsibility for electoral management. Disraeli ignored Gorst's unsolicited pleas to remove this onerous responsibility from the Whip's Office. A combination of the reduced competence of Central Office and the illness of the Chief Whip shortly before the election ensured that the party's electoral management in 1880 was less professional and effective than it had been six years earlier.

Disraeli thus bequeathed to his successors a party organisation that had an established base, but not one that was in the shape necessary if the party was to match the political activity of its opponents.

Despite the electoral defeat in 1880 Disraeli had, nonetheless, crafted a party with a much stronger electoral appeal than that which it enjoyed when he assumed the mantle of leadership. The transformation wrought by Disraeli was necessary to ensure the future success of the party, although by itself it was not sufficient: party organisation had to catch up with it and the party's opponents had to do what they became good at – dividing among themselves. Both conditions were to be met within five years of Disraeli's death.

The electoral appeal bequeathed by Disraeli lay in his having made the party a national one. Until his leadership the party relied heavily upon the same base of support – and to a large extent the tenets – of the Tory Party: it was still essentially a party of vested, primarily landed, interests with no obvious or extensive appeal to match that of the Liberals to the middle classes or the newly enfranchised worker. Little, if anything, had been added to the party's political creed since the Tamworth Manifesto. In his novel *Sybil* Disraeli had written: 'I have been told that the Privileged and the People formed Two Nations.' As leader, he set out to extend the party's reach beyond the privileged by creating 'One Nation'.

' The Disraelian creed rested on the trinity enunciated in his Crystal Palace speech in 1872: 'the maintenance of our institutions, the preservation of our empire, and the improvement of the condition of the people'. Each in its own way constituted a novel addition to Conservative thought. Although the maintenance of institutions was a central tenet of the Tory inheritance Disraeli made it more central to the needs of the time: he emphasised the defence of property. Defending property as a guarantee of liberty found a receptive audience among the propertied middle classes, increasingly wary of Liberal radicalism that threatened – or appeared to threaten – their new-found wealth and position in society. The Conservatives, defenders of established institutions, now stood as the guardians not just of the castle and the country estate but of the Englishman's home as well.

Improving the condition of the people entailed social reform of the sort that Disraeli's ministry introduced. Improvements were made when they appeared necessary, getting rid of palpable abuses. There was no social upheaval, nothing that would threaten the security of the propertied classes. Reforms were introduced in the spirit of Tory paternalism, those above the fray of industrial activity reaching down to secure the wellbeing of those toiling in the factories and the mills. It added a new dimension to Conservative appeal. As we have already observed, the reforms enacted by Disraeli's ministry were reforms that might have been introduced by a Liberal government; but that observation misses an important truth: the reforms were *not* introduced by a Liberal government, but by a Conservative one. Disraeli demonstrated that the Conservatives were able to attend to the needs of the workers. The Liberals no longer had any monopoly on the claim.

Disraeli's boldest move, however, was in associating the Conservative Party with imperialism. It marked a departure from the stance taken earlier by the party and, indeed, by Disraeli himself. When he attacked those who had looked upon the colonies 'as a burden upon this country', he failed to mention that he had previously been one of them. Indeed, he had coined one of the most memorable phrases in once describing colonies as 'millstones round our neck'. During the period of Palmerston's dominance the Conservatives had not been associated either with imperialism or the projection of British greatness on the world stage. All that changed in 1872 when Disraeli played the imperial card, associating the party with defence of the Empire and of Britain's interests in world affairs. The appeal merged into one sentiment: patriotism. 'No minister', declared Disraeli in his Crystal Palace speech, 'will do his duty who neglects any opportunity of reconstructing as much as possible of our Colonial Empire, and of responding to those distant sympathies which may become the source of incalculable strength and happiness to this land.' The Conservative Party stood for one nation at home and, in effect, now stood for one nation united on the world stage: 'Queen and country' was to make a far more effective rallying cry behind which Britons could gather than some appeal to pacifism or the niceties of arbitration. Empire was both a source of national pride and of national wellbeing: no longer a millstone but a source of 'incalculable strength and happiness to this land'.

Disraeli was thus able to portray the Conservative Party as one which posed no threat to the interests of the people at home, be it a member of the rising middle class or the newly enfranchised working class, nor to the interests of one nation abroad. It was a remarkable achievement. It provided the necessary base for success in an age of mass electorate. Nevertheless, as the results of the 1880 election demonstrated, it was not sufficient to ensure immediate electoral award.

That success required, as we have noted, organisational efficiency. It also required one further shove to ensure that Liberal electors switched their allegiance. That shove was given by a former Peelite Tory to whom Conservatives owe a debt of gratitude: William Gladstone. His policies, especially that of Home Rule for Ireland, served to drive a significant section of the Liberal Party, the Liberal Unionists, into the arms of the Conservative Party. Gladstone's radicalism was already a concern to many within the Liberal Party and his stand on Ireland confirmed their worst fears. For many the Conservative Party now offered a more congenial home.

Without Disraeli, and indeed without Gladstone, it is difficult to envisage what might have happened to the Conservative Party. Disraeli moved it signally in a direction that less visionary leaders are unlikely to have taken. He did so at a time when Gladstone was taking the Liberal Party away from the old Whiggish paths of Palmerston to a more radical – and rough – route that was to prove too demanding for many of his followers. Thanks to two elderly, unpredictable politicians – one a foppish romantic, the other a stubborn moralist – the foundations of the modern Conservative Party were laid.

CHAPTER 2

History of the party II

From a marquess to an earl

Philip Norton

The return of a Conservative government in 1886 heralded a century of Conservative ascendancy. During that century the party was out of office for only four significant periods of time – 1905–15, 1945–51, 1964–70 and 1974–9 – and on only one of those four occasions did it jeopardise its claim to be a party of governance. The contrast with the first 50 years of its history is stark: in those years, as we have seen, it achieved a parliamentary majority in only two elections, achieving re-election on neither occasion; its claim to be a party of government was jeopardised by the split of 1846 and reclaimed only by Disraeli more than a quarter of a century later.

The reasons for the Conservative ascendancy are to be found in the last 15 years of the nineteenth century, during the leadership of the third Marquess of Salisbury. Salisbury led the party for 17 years, serving for almost 14 of them as Prime Minister. During his tenure of the leadership the Disraelian inheritance was both consolidated and extended. The party was transformed from being the 'out' party in British politics to being, with one rare exception, the 'in' party. Disraeli gave the party a greater sense of purpose; Salisbury demonstrated the capacity of the party to govern effectively in pursuit of that purpose. The consequence was to be what Seldon and Ball (1994) have aptly called the *Conservative Century*.

The Salisbury era 1885–1902

Following the death of Disraeli, leadership of the party in the Commons passed to Sir Stafford Northcote and in the Lords to the Marquess of Salisbury. Northcote proved a lacklustre leader and was harried from his own side by a ginger group of four members ('the Fourth party') led by Lord Randolph Churchill. When in 1885 the Liberal government was defeated on an amendment to the Finance Bill and resigned, the Queen sent for Salisbury.

Salisbury governed for a few months until the 1885 Redistribution of Seats Act could take effect. An election was held in November of that year, producing a divided House of Commons: the combined strength of the Conservatives and Irish Nationalists matched the number of Liberal members. In the new year Salisbury's government was defeated on an amendment to the Address and Gladstone returned to office. Gladstone's tenure was short-lived. He introduced a Home Rule Bill for Ireland which he had personally drafted. Two members of his Cabinet resigned and, on second reading, the Bill was defeated by 343 votes to 313. Gladstone advised dissolution and in the ensuing election held in July 1886 the Conservatives emerged as the largest party with 316 seats; the Liberals were reduced to fewer than 200. With the support of Liberal Unionists the Conservatives were able to govern and, with the exception of the years 1892–5, Salisbury occupied the premiership until 1902 before handing on the mantle of office to his nephew, Arthur Balfour.

The consolidation and extension of the Disraelian inheritance during Salisbury's leadership was achieved as a result of three developments: the acquisition to the ranks of the party of the Liberal Unionists; the improvement of party organisation; and the record of the government.

The support of the Liberal Unionists

Gladstone's mission 'to pacify Ireland' split the Liberal Party irrevocably, although that was not apparent at the time: the rift with the Unionists within the party's ranks was expected to be a temporary phenomenon. Gladstone's policy, however, proved too much for them. The wider connotations read into Home Rule – a threat to property and to Protestantism – effectively scared the old Whig element within the party, and many within the middle class, into the arms of the Conservatives. It also induced a number of Liberal Radicals led by Joseph Chamberlain – who had turned against Home Rule – to change sides. Chamberlain was not alone among Radicals in having an imperialist vision and, given the work of Disraeli's ministry in the field of social reform, the Conservative Party now offered a vehicle through which municipal reform might be achieved. The Conservative Party acquired not only new support, it also acquired some very able (although not always controllable) individuals as well as a new dimension to its way of thinking. The Whig addition to its ranks emphasised the imperatives of wealth creation and individual liberty.

The improvement in party organisation

Conservative organisation was shown to be lacking in the election of 1880, not least compared with that of its opponents. Salisbury took a personal interest in improving the position and was assisted by some effective lieutenants. The years in opposition had been troublesome ones with Lord Randolph Churchill seeking to take over, under the rallying cry of 'Tory Democracy', the National Union. His challenge was a difficult but ultimately unsuccessful one: there was little substance to the notion of Tory Democracy and Churchill seemed content once his status in the party hierarchy was recognised. Salisbury, secure as party leader following his call to the palace in 1885, then presided over what has been called 'a golden age of Conservative organisation' (Bulmer-Thomas, 1967: 157). That golden age was the achievement of the triumvirate of Salisbury, Aretas Akers-Douglas, the party's Chief Whip from 1885 to 1902, and Richard Middleton, the party's Principal Agent from 1885 to 1903 (who in 1886 also became Secretary of the National Union).

All three worked harmoniously together, with Akers-Douglas and Middleton displaying remarkable skills of political intelligence: Akers-Douglas in knowing precisely how the House would vote, Middleton in predicting by-election results. The efficiency of party organisation was restored – lasting until the triumvirate ended in 1902 – and relationships established that were to remain features of the party throughout the twentieth century. The only major change during the early years of the twentieth century came in 1911 when the tasks of parliamentary management and control of Central Office became too onerous for the Chief Whip and a new post of Party Chairman was created.

The record of the government

Lord Salisbury represented in his thinking one particular strand of Conservative thought: Tory pessimism. He was, especially in domestic politics, opposed to change – he had left Derby's government over the 1867 Reform Bill – but was largely resigned to it. On one occasion he justified a particular provision on the grounds that it was the fashion of the day, and 'against fashion it is almost impossible to argue' (McDowell, 1974: 142). Such a stance did not presage inaction. The pessimist either forsakes politics altogether or gets on with the job of managing the inevitable. Salisbury took the latter course and, indeed, showed remarkable political acumen. He recognised the importance of organisation and was the first Prime Minister to seek a dissolution, in 1900, at a time that seemed electorally propitious for being returned to office. He helped to integrate the Liberal Unionists into the party fold by appointing some of their number to office (Chamberlain became Colonial Secretary) and he recognised the changing social structure of the party by advancing within government self-made and non-landed men such as W. H. Smith.

In policy terms the Salisbury government saw the flowering of the imperialist rose bred by Disraeli and in domestic affairs pursued measures of social reform that built upon the Disraelian achievements of 1874–80. Abroad, the Empire spread, with Africa being developed and Burma annexed; at home the Union with Ireland was vigorously defended. British imperialism was celebrated in 1897 on the diamond jubilee of Queen Victoria, Empress of India. In 1899 the Boer War rallied the country behind the national flag and divided the opposition; it also provided the basis for the government's electoral appeal in the 'Khaki Election' of 1900. Domestically, a wide range of reforming measures were carried to the statute book. The Local Government Act of 1888 created a structure of local government that was to remain for almost a century; a Coal Mines Regulation Act, an Agricultural Holdings Act, a Housing of the Working Classes Act and an Allotments Act were among other measures carried (see Bellairs, 1977). When Salisbury retired in 1902 – following peace in South Africa – he had a solid record of administration to his credit.

With the benefit of hindsight one can recognise the limitations of the Salisbury era. Robert Blake (1970: 163–4) has noted that the party's standing in the country was by no means consistently strong, with poor by-election results in particular, although Salisbury's government was hardly the only government about which that could be said. The measures of social reform did not constitute a coherent package of radical reforms sufficient to stifle support for the movement that was to emerge as the Labour Party; but that was to expect too much, both in terms of foresight and political disposition. In the context of the time, Salisbury – aided by disarray among his opponents – proved an effective Prime Minister, ensuring that the Conservative Party saw out the nineteenth century as the dominant party and a party of government. Combining political acumen with *gravitas*, Salisbury displayed the skills of governance. The skills, unfortunately, were not shared by all members of his family.

From strength to weakness 1902–15

Arthur James Balfour succeeded his uncle as Prime Minister and leader of the party in July 1902. His experience of the leadership – and that of his two successors – demonstrated that success and, indeed, the Conservative Party cannot be taken for granted.

Balfour got off to a bad start in office with an Education Bill that proved easy political bait for his opponents. Far worse was to come the following year. In May 1903 Joseph Chamberlain outlined a scheme for 'Imperial Preference', introducing duties that would discriminate in favour of the Empire and provide revenue that could be used to finance social reform. In October he opened a campaign to achieve his goal. It split the party wide open. Whereas the issues of the Union and of foreign wars could usually be relied upon to split the Liberals, the one issue that could still decisively split the Conservative Party was that of free trade versus protection. The battle was reminiscent of that over the Corn Laws. The Liberals united to defend free trade. On the Conservative side, two free trade members of the Cabinet resigned (as did Chamberlain in order to wage his campaign). They were later joined by the Duke of Devonshire. A young free trade Conservative MP, Winston Churchill, crossed the floor of the House. Balfour tried to achieve a compromise but failed; the two sides were irreconcilable. Over time, Balfour's utterances came more to favour imperial preference than free trade, a stand in line with the disposition of most Conservative Members. Imperial preference, however, found little resonance among the electorate, scared by the thought of expensive food. As well as this, other policies pursued by the government attracted popular opposition: the use of indentured Chinese coolies in South Africa was attacked on humanitarian grounds, the passage of a Licensing Act allowed the Liberals to equate the Conservative Party with the interests of the brewers and the government's failure to reverse by statute the Taff Vale decision (removing the legal protection which had previously been assumed to attach to trade union funds) detached the sympathy of trade unionists from the Conservative cause. By the end of 1905 the government was in disarray, being harried by some extraordinarily able politicians from the opposition front bench, and Chamberlain was demanding adoption of his policy of imperial preference. In December, Balfour resigned. The King sent for the Liberal Henry Campbell-Bannerman, who promptly formed a Cabinet of outstanding talent and went to the country to gain a mandate. That mandate was overwhelming: Conservative representation slumped to 156 seats, the Liberals achieving over 200 more seats than their principal rivals. It was – and remains – the Conservative Party's worst defeat since 1832. Balfour was among the electoral casualties.

The eight-year period following the defeat has been characterised as 'one of the least attractive in the history of the party' (Clarke, 1973: 56). The party proved willing to use Conservative peers – in a majority in the Upper House – to obstruct government measures. The rejection of the budget in 1909 precipitated a major constitutional crisis, two general elections and the eventual passing of the Parliament Act of 1911, curtailing the powers of the House of Lords. The Parliament Bill itself split the Conservative Party, divided between the 'hedgers' (prepared to pass the Parliament Bill rather than see the House swamped by new peers to ensure its passage) and 'ditchers' (prepared to fight in the last ditch to oppose the measure). There were sufficient 'hedgers' in the Lords to ensure the passage of the Bill. Balfour's handling of the crisis encouraged dissatisfaction with his leadership. Exasperated by the way things were going, and citing age as a reason, Balfour resigned.

There was no clear successor to 'emerge' in succession to Balfour and the parliamentary party looked as if it would have to ballot in order to choose between the principal contenders, Austen Chamberlain (son of Joseph) and Walter Long, the former a Liberal Unionist, tariff reformer and 'ditcher', the latter a Conservative, free trader and 'hedger'. An election was only avoided when the entry of a third candidate, Andrew Bonar Law, persuaded the two to withdraw in his favour in the interests of party unity. Not for the first time in its history, the party acquired a leader who conformed to no stereotype of a

Conservative leader: Bonar Law, a businessman born in Canada, of Ulster descent and educated in Glasgow, was a Presbyterian who did not mix easily in society. He was a tariff reformer and a 'hedger'. Under his leadership tariff reform remained a potent and divisive issue within the party: there was little public support but the parliamentary party was overwhelmingly for it. However, in view of the government's policy on Ireland it was the Ulster Protestant background that was to prove of more immediate significance.

When, in 1912, the government introduced a Home Rule Bill for Ireland and then reintroduced it in the following session after the House of Lords had rejected it, Bonar Law and other Conservative leaders proved willing to operate on, in some cases beyond, the boundaries of constitutional propriety. Protestants in the counties of Ulster (the nine most northerly counties of Ireland) began to arm themselves to resist domination by the Catholic south. Sir Edward Carson, leader of the Ulster Unionists within the party, announced that the Ulster Unionist Council would set up a provisional government once the Bill was passed. Bonar Law declared: 'I can imagine no length of resistance to which Ulster can go in which I should not be prepared to support them' and even tried to involve the King in the dispute, arguing that the constitution was in suspense and that a dissolution of Parliament was the only way to avoid civil war. The opposition to Home Rule did the party no great electoral damage, but the way Bonar Law and his subordinates conducted themselves on the issue threatened the very integrity of the Conservative Party. Even Lindsay and Harrington (1979: 23), in attempting to justify the party's stance, conceded: 'it was a bizarre situation indeed, when the party of law, order and authority gave its specific support to a group prepared to oppose the law by force.'

Eight years after the disastrous defeat of 1906, the party – despite improved electoral performances in the two elections of 1910 – was still out of office and now playing a perilous constitutional game. It was to be saved from itself, not by its own efforts but by the advent of the First World War.

Return to office 1915–45

War was declared on Germany on 4 August 1914 following the German invasion of Belgium. A little over two years later, the Conservative Party – the official opposition, toying with a policy that would have threatened the maintenance of the King's Government – was the dominant party in government.

Bonar Law and his colleagues were initially prepared to suspend normal party warfare but not enter into a coalition under the leadership of the then Liberal Prime Minister, Herbert Henry Asquith. Various crises in 1915 – a shortage of shells, the resignation of the First Sea Lord and the disastrous Dardanelles campaign – generated popular pressure for a coalition government and both party leaders yielded to that pressure. The Conservatives were

back in office, albeit only as a junior partner; the Liberals retained the principal portfolios and outnumbered Conservative members of the Cabinet by
twelve to eight. The party nonetheless had a foot in the door of government.

The war continued to go badly (both Asquith and Bonar Law lost sons in
the fighting) and at the end of 1916 the Liberal Secretary of State for War,
Lloyd George, and Bonar Law engineered Asquith's resignation. Lloyd
George replaced him and in so doing split the Liberal Party: about half the
parliamentary party stayed with him, the other half supporting Asquith. It was
a split from which the Liberals never recovered. The most senior posts in the
new coalition went to Conservatives. Bonar Law became Chancellor of the
Exchequer. The Asquithian Liberals left the government benches to form the
official opposition. Britain had a Liberal Prime Minister but a predominantly
Conservative government.

With the end of the war approaching in 1918, Lloyd George and Bonar Law
agreed that the next election should be fought as a coalition, Conservatives
and Coalition (essentially Lloyd George) Liberals not contesting seats against
one another. Lloyd George agreed to some concessions, not least on imperial
preference, to make his retention of the premiership agreeable to Conservative MPs, and Bonar Law persuaded the parliamentary party of the need to
maintain national unity once hostilities were at an end. The bulk of Coalition
candidates were Conservatives and in the 'coupon' election, so-called because
coalition candidates received a letter of endorsement (dubbed by Asquith 'a
coupon') from Lloyd George and Bonar Law, held in December, the parties
to the coalition achieved an overwhelming victory; 478 coalition MPs were
returned. Of those, 335 were Conservatives. It was the first election in the
twentieth century in which the party had achieved dominance.

The peacetime coalition lasted four years. Lloyd George, for all his political
flair, was seen increasingly as a liability, especially by Conservative activists.
Conservative MPs were wary of various government policies, not least on the
still divisive issue of Ireland, and of financial and personal scandals that were
engulfing the Prime Minister. In 1921 Bonar Law resigned the leadership of
the Conservative Party on health grounds and the party lost the man who
could have kept Lloyd George in check. The new leader to emerge was
Austen Chamberlain, claiming the inheritance denied him in 1911. Chamberlain lacked Bonar Law's political clout – and his understanding of Lloyd
George – and took a view of the coalition that was increasingly at variance
with opinion within his party. He favoured not only a continuation of the
coalition but a fusion of the Coalition Liberals with the Conservatives. The
Conservative rank-and-file and a growing number of Conservative MPs
favoured an end to the existing arrangement. Some of them, including the
party chairman, made their views public.

To put an end to the growing dissension within the party's ranks Chamberlain summoned a meeting of Conservative MPs at the Carlton Club on 19
October 1922. The parliamentary party was to be given a choice: support the

coalition or look for a new leader. Speeches by Chamberlain and Balfour in favour of maintaining the coalition were overshadowed by a powerful speech by a little-known minister, Stanley Baldwin, arguing that ruin lay ahead if the link with Lloyd George was not broken. When Bonar Law rose and made a similar case, the fate of the coalition was sealed. A motion that the party should fight the next election as an independent party was carried, according to the announcement at the time, by 187 votes to 87. (According to later research, the figures were actually 185 to 88. See Blake, 1970: 204.) Chamberlain promptly resigned the leadership of the party and Lloyd George gave up the premiership. Bonar Law, apparently enjoying better health than in the previous year (in fact, he was dying of cancer of the throat), accepted the King's commission to form a government.

Bonar Law formed the first wholly Conservative government for 20 years. It was not an easy task: most of the party's senior figures had resigned along with Chamberlain. The exception was the Foreign Secretary, Lord Curzon, who had turned against the coalition only a matter of days before the Carlton Club meeting. He retained the Foreign Office. Stanley Baldwin became Chancellor of the Exchequer; Austen Chamberlain's brother, Neville, became Postmaster-General. Winston Churchill dubbed it a government 'of the second eleven', although the accusation was to have little electoral impact. Bonar Law requested a dissolution and in the election – held on 15 November 1922 – led the party to victory: 345 Conservative MPs were returned, compared to 142 Labour Members and 116 Liberals. The Labour Party became the official opposition.

Bonar Law hoped to hold office for no more than a couple of years, giving time for rifts within the party to heal and for him then to retire and hand over the leadership to Austen Chamberlain. Diagnosis of his illness made that impossible. Six months after his election victory his doctor forced his resignation. It was too early for Chamberlain to have been rehabilitated and the choice lay between Curzon and Baldwin. The King summoned the commoner, Baldwin, establishing the precedent for the premier to be drawn from the elected House. The fact that the Labour Party was the opposition appears to have played a part. Had Curzon been summoned to the premiership, the Prime Minister would have sat in a House which contained not one member of the official opposition.

Less than a year after emerging from political obscurity, Stanley Baldwin – a West Midlands industrialist who had entered Parliament relatively late in life – ascended the steps of 10 Downing Street. In political disposition he was essentially a Tory paternalist or 'balancer' (Norton, 1987b). He sought to achieve balance both within the party and within society. He disliked social conflict and disharmony. Upon entering office he saw the principal economic problem facing the nation as that of unemployment.

Action needed to be taken to tackle the problem and the solution was a traditional Tory one: protection. He began advocating protection of the home market. However, he faced a moral dilemma. His predecessor, Bonar Law, had promised no major change in fiscal policy during the lifetime of the existing Parliament. Baldwin resolved the dilemma by requesting a dissolution and, 13 months after the previous election, the country again went to the polls.

In the election the Conservatives lost more than 80 seats, although remaining the largest single party. Baldwin met the new Parliament, was defeated and submitted his seals of office. The Labour leader, Ramsay MacDonald, was called to the palace and formed a minority government with the *de facto* support of the third largest party, the Liberals. Although achieving some policy successes the MacDonald government was short-lived, being broken on the back of the Campbell crisis, the Attorney-General having dropped an action for sedition against the editor of the *Workers' Weekly*: Conservative and Liberal MPs combined to carry a motion establishing a Select Committee of Inquiry. MacDonald treated the motion as one of confidence and requested a dissolution.

The general election of 1924 produced a stunning Conservative victory: 419 Conservatives were returned, the first time in history that the party in its own right had achieved the return of more than 400 Members. The success was partly at the expense of the Labour Party but more especially at the expense of the Liberals, whose parliamentary strength slumped from 159 to 40. Among ex-Liberals now in the Conservative ranks was Winston Churchill. The motivation for his defection was similar to that of many Liberals: the Conservative Party was seen as the principal and most effective vehicle for countering the growing socialist challenge posed by the Labour Party. The election of 1922 had established the Labour Party as a party of government. Any pretensions that the Liberals retained to being such a party were killed decisively by the election of 1924.

Baldwin resumed the premiership and served in office for a full Parliament: there were to be no more rash and precipitate appeals to the electorate. Continuing economic problems appear to have harmed the party when the country went again to the polls in 1929: Labour made considerable gains at Conservative expense and emerged as the largest single party. MacDonald again formed a minority government. That government was brought down by internal dissension in 1931, the Cabinet splitting on the austerity measures deemed necessary by MacDonald if foreign loans were to be raised. MacDonald formed a 'National' government, bringing Conservatives and Liberals into his Cabinet while most Labour members trooped out of it. MacDonald assumed the mantle of a latter-day Lloyd George, leading a nominally national government with the bulk of its parliamentary support being provided by the Conservative Party. It was this National government which then sought a mandate in October 1931; 554 National government MPs were elected, of whom 473 were Conservatives. (Of the remainder 13 were National Labour and 68 Liberal.) Labour was reduced to 52 seats.

MacDonald remained as Prime Minister until June 1935 when he stepped down, allowing Baldwin to resume the mantle. Five months later a general election confirmed the Conservatives' hold on power. In the election 429 National government members were returned, all but 41 being Conservatives. (Only 8 National Labour MPs and 33 National Liberals were elected.) Labour strength increased to 154 and 21 Liberals – who had split from the National Liberals in 1932 – were also returned.

For 15 years, from his summons to the Palace in 1922 to his retirement in 1937, Stanley Baldwin dominated British politics. Those years were marked by continuing economic problems, two major crises – the General Strike of 1926 and the abdication crisis of 1936 – and, towards the end, the problem of Germany.

Within the party Baldwin had at times to fight to maintain the leadership, not least in 1931 under attack from the press barons Lords Rothermere and Beaverbrook, and faced serious dissension on Empire Free Trade and India. It is a tribute to his political skills and tenacity that he survived as leader for as long as he did, retiring at a time of his own volition. However, he did have one advantage denied, for example, to Balfour: for most of his leadership, he was in office.

On the negative side of Baldwin's leadership were the failure to deal decisively with the nation's problems and the need for rapid rearmament in the face of German adventurism. Unemployment remained high and was marked in certain areas of the country and among certain sections of the population. The picture left by history is one of poverty, means tests and a Conservative Party containing wealthy men who did too well out of the First World War.

In foreign policy German rearmament was recognised as a problem but domestic indicators – by-election successes of candidates favouring disarmament among them – suggested little popular support for a rapid build-up of British weaponry and in 1935 Baldwin promised 'there will be no great armaments'. In the wake of the 1935 election the government suffered two hard knocks to its reputation when it failed to support oil sanctions against Italy following its invasion of Abyssinia and in the fiasco of the Hoare–Laval Pact, which it repudiated when its unpopularity became apparent. The general impression left by history is of Baldwin handing over to his successor, Neville Chamberlain, a country unprepared for war.

Negative features have obscured the positive features of the Baldwin era. The government was far more active in both domestic and foreign policy than generally portrayed. Domestically, various measures of social reform were introduced, particularly during Neville Chamberlain's tenure as Minister of Health. He proposed to the Cabinet 25 measures of social reform and achieved the enactment of 21 of them. These included improvement in unemployment insurance, the extension of old age pensions and legislation on housing and public health. Much of this legislation 'has an important place in the development of the Welfare State' (Macleod, 1961: 123). Bellairs (1977) lists more than 50 measures of social and industrial reform introduced during the period of Baldwin's leadership. Economically, various attempts were made to protect industry – or at least particular industries – through the introduction of import duties; goods from the dominions or colonies, with certain exceptions, were exempt from the duties, while a 50 per cent duty was levied on manufactured goods that were flooding the British market. Direct subsidies were provided for agriculture and reductions in the rate of interest helped to encourage a house-building boom and greater consumer spending. The government variously intervened to assist particular industries and, indeed, particular regions: with the 1934 Special Areas (Development and Improvement) Act, it introduced a measure of regional planning. The extent to which these measures contributed to a significant decline in unemployment – from three million in 1933 to less than two million by 1935 – is a matter of considerable debate. They nonetheless constituted a serious attempt to deal with the problem and several, particularly in the field of social welfare, were of more than temporary significance.

In foreign policy the government pursued a policy of dominion status for India – a liberal policy for the period and one vigorously opposed by a substantial section of the parliamentary party – and did at least pursue a policy of moderate rearmament. Indeed, were it not for the policies pursued during this period, not least by Lord Swinton as Air Minister, Britain may not have been in a position to achieve the successes in the air and at sea that it did during the Second World War. It was Swinton who was responsible for the production of both the Spitfire and Hurricane aircraft. With the benefit of hindsight the preparations made for war were not as extensive as they could or should have been, but in the context of the time – and the prevailing political mood – the government was not as tardy as critics have subsequently accused it of being.

During Baldwin's period as leader various reforms were also made to party organisation, both within and outside Parliament. Outside Parliament, the two periods of opposition encouraged an improvement in party machinery, the most significant coming in the 1929–31 period. In 1929 the Conservative Research Department, independent of Central Office, was created (Ramsden, 1980) and in 1931 the position of Principal Agent was abolished in favour of the position of Director-General. Within Parliament, the parliamentary party developed its own structure. Some Conservative MPs newly returned in 1922, led by Gervais Rentoul, formed in 1923 the Conservative Private Members (1922) Committee, which began meeting weekly while the House was in session (Chapter 8). Its meetings began to be attended by a whip and membership was expanded to senior Members who had expressed an interest in joining. Membership was opened subsequently to all Conservative Private Members. The '1922' also began hearing reports from party committees which developed during the decade and which became especially active during the 1930s (see Chapter 8). Baldwin himself also formalised the position of the front bench, with the Shadow Cabinet being styled the Consultative Committee and meeting on a regular basis with a secretariat to service it. What, in 1922, was a parliamentary party with minimal formal structure (other than that provided by the whips) was, by the time of Baldwin's retirement, a party with a highly developed infrastructure.

Baldwin retired in 1937 and was succeeded by his heir apparent, Neville Chamberlain. Chamberlain had proved a competent administrator, a first-rate Minister of Health and a dedicated party man, serving for a period as Party Chairman and also as Chairman of the Research Department (although his loyalty was notably to the party rather than to the leader, as he adopted an ambiguous position during the leadership crisis of 1930–1). However, he proved the wrong man for the wrong time. He was, according to Harold Macmillan (1975: 132), 'full of energy and. . . quite sure of himself. . . at all times he was a difficult man to argue with. Thus in debate he was seldom conciliatory and generally unyielding. He knew he was right on every question.' Had he had to cope with purely domestic problems these characteristics may not have proved fatal. However, faced with a foreign situation – with which he had no previous ministerial familiarity – his belief in his own rightness proved disastrous. Believing he could handle Hitler in Germany he pursued a policy of appeasement, returning from Munich in 1938 with a signed agreement that was popular but ultimately worthless. Anti-appeasers in the Conservative ranks grew in number, centred on the figures of Sir Anthony Eden, who had resigned as Foreign Secretary earlier in the year, and Churchill. They were to prove justified by events. In September 1939, Chamberlain found himself in the unenviable position of having to declare that a state of war existed with Germany and trying to transform himself into a wartime leader. It was a role for which he was ill-suited. The Labour Party refused to enter into government with him and Conservative dissension reached a peak in 1940 with the failure of the Norwegian campaign. At the end of the debate on the campaign's failure, 41 Conservatives voted against the government and a further 60 abstained from voting. The government's majority fell from 200 to 80. Chamberlain at first failed to recognise the significance of the vote but then succumbed to the message that the House of Commons had sent him. He submitted his resignation as premier (although not, significantly, as party leader) and was succeeded, more by popular pressure than by the willing agreement of the parliamentary party, by Churchill. Chamberlain carried the title of party leader for a few months before ill health forced him to relinquish that in Churchill's favour.

Churchill formed a coalition government and partisan conflict ceased. Party organisation during the war years was minimal. The Research Department was closed. Within the House party labels counted for little and, consequently, the government was sensitive to any shifts in parliamentary opinion; it needed to carry a united House (see Eaves, 1958). Churchill weathered some significant criticisms during the early years of the war. When hostilities began to turn in the Allies' favour the government could begin to look to the aftermath of war. The Beveridge Report on Social Insurance and Allied Services was published as early as 1942 and a White Paper on Full Employment in 1944, accepting the maintenance of a high and stable level of employment after the war; 1944 also witnessed the passage of the Butler Education Act that was to form the basis of Britain's education system for more than a generation. The Beveridge Report and the White Paper on Full Employment were not, however, to be implemented by a Churchill-led government.

Once victory over Germany had been achieved and with Labour unwilling to continue the coalition beyond the autumn of 1945, Churchill requested a dissolution. The coalition came to an end and a caretaker Conservative government was formed to continue administration until the election held in July 1945. Churchill had proved to be a brilliant wartime leader and expected to be returned to office, but what counted for more was the popular memory of the 1930s – the period of poverty and means testing – and the fact that Labour, a partner in the wartime government, could not be dismissed as a radical socialist party incapable of assuming the reins of office.

The election results were a shattering blow to Churchill and to the Conservative Party: 393 Labour MPs were elected. Conservative strength was reduced to 213, the party's worst result since 1906. The party was returned to a political wilderness it had not experienced for a generation.

Years of recovery 1945–51

For the Conservative Party in the 1940s, 1945 was undoubtedly the *annus horrendus*. The defeat in the July general election was as resounding as it was unexpected. On 21 August Churchill attended a meeting of the 1922 Committee and, according to one of those present, 'seemed totally unprepared, indifferent and deaf, and failed to stir the crowded audience. I came away fearing that the Tory Party was definitely dead' ('Chips' Channon MP; see James, 1967: 412). Speculation about Churchill's leadership began to be heard within the party; some MPs were reported to favour Harold Macmillan as his successor (Nicolson, 1972: 32), others Quintin Hogg (*Sunday Pictorial* 25 November 1945). Party morale was further weakened in December on the issue of the American loan. Based on negotiations with the American Treasury by J. M. Keynes, the loan allowed the British government to borrow $3,750 million, repayable in 50 annual instalments with an interest rate of 2 per cent per annum; Britain was also held to the convertibility of sterling and given only 12 months in which to achieve this. Churchill, keen to support Anglo-American co-operation – and leader of the wartime government that had begun the negotiations – instinctively supported the loan; he was supported by other members of the front bench. A large section of the parliamentary party took a contrary view. They disliked the harshness of the terms and saw the whole exercise as an attempt to liberalise world trade – and hence, in Max Aitken's words, 'to "ditch" Empire preference' (*HC Deb.* 417, c. 684) – and prise open the markets of the world for the benefit of the United States. From the front bench Oliver Stanley advised the party to abstain. Seventy-four Conservative MPs defied the whips to vote against the Loan; eight entered the government lobby to support it (Norton 1975: 2–4). The party was not to split so decisively in the Commons' division lobbies for another 30 years. Churchill was dismayed by the result and very briefly contemplated resigning (Lord Boothby to author, 1973). The party ended the year demoralised and fissured.

The lessons of 1945 were not lost on party leaders. Pressure for Churchill to retire did not disappear but was confined largely to private meetings. There was also the recognition that Churchill remained an electoral asset (Macmillan, 1969: 287). Although Churchill himself preferred treading the world stage to the floor of the House of Commons and party management, other senior figures recognised the need for change within the party. This took place at two levels: those of organisation and policy.

The organisational changes were extensive and were the product of several party managers, most notably Ralph Assheton and Lord Woolton as Party Chairmen, R. A. Butler as Chairman of Research Department and David Maxwell-Fyfe as Chairman of a National Union committee set up to consider party finances and structure. Assheton and Woolton not only resuscitated the party but effectively galvanised it. A Young Conservative movement was established, replacing the pre-war Junior Imperial League: within four years it was able to claim a membership in excess of 150,000. To promote political education within the party a Conservative Political Centre (CPC) was created. A central feature of the CPC was that of the 'two-way movement of ideas', which it has retained to the present day: discussion topics and questions were circulated to CPC branches, the responses from the branches being collated and circulated for the information of party leaders. In 1948 a Conservative college was opened in Swinton, North Yorkshire, with a small staff of tutors to provide training and short courses for party workers. The Research Department was brought back to life and strengthened. As chairman Butler recruited able young men, many of whom were later to serve as MPs and Cabinet ministers; most notable among these were Reginald Maudling, Enoch Powell and Iain Macleod. The department provided the essential research base for the review and generation of party policy. It also worked closely with the CPC, providing the briefs for its two-way programme (Ramsden, 1980: 106–7).

Woolton organised both a fund-raising and a membership drive, bringing money into the party as well as members. By the end of 1948 the party was claiming a membership of 2,250,000, more than a million members more than it had had the previous year. The Maxwell-Fyfe Committee in 1948 recommended that constituency associations should assume responsibility for candidates' election expenses – candidates themselves being limited to

Beidrog

contributions of no more than £25 a year (£50 in the case of MPs) – and should receive no financial assistance from central funds unless they could show that they had made every effort to raise the money themselves. The recommendations were accepted, providing the opportunity for men (and women) of limited means to enter Parliament and, as importantly, forcing constituency associations to be efficient. They could no longer rely upon the beneficence of rich candidates. Ability came to replace wealth as a primary criterion of candidate selection.

The parliamentary party also witnessed some changes. Party committees were reorganised and expanded, with the officers being brought together with front benchers in a Business Committee. In the 1950–1 Parliament Churchill initiated the practice of appointing committee chairmen, usually the front bencher responsible for the area covered by a committee, a practice maintained in subsequent periods of opposition. The committees, as a result of these changes, became closer to policy makers within the party (Norton, 1979: 40). Each committee was serviced by a member of the party's parliamentary secretariat and, after 1948, when the secretariat was merged with the Research Department, by a member of the Research Department.

These organisational changes provided a necessary backdrop to the policy review undertaken by the party. Strengthening party organisation was a necessary but not sufficient condition for electoral success. The party had to establish its appeal to the electorate of post-war Britain: that necessitated a statement of what the party stood for and where it was going.

Pressure for the party to offer a clear delineation of what it stood for was notable among party activists. The party conference in 1946 carried by a large majority a motion that the party should 'without further delay, prepare and issue a statement, in a concise form easily understood by the electorate, setting forth the policy for which the Conservative Party stands, and simultaneously a statement giving a fuller detail of the principles and programmes of the party' (Craig, 1982: 20). Some leading figures in the party also favoured such a move. Churchill himself showed little inclination to indulge in detailed policy making but did respond to pressure within the party, establishing towards the end of 1946 a committee to define 'Conservative attitudes towards industry'.

Chaired by Butler, the committee combined four front benchers (indeed, four of the party's most outstanding figures: Harold Macmillan, Oliver Stanley, Oliver Lyttleton and Sir David Maxwell-Fyfe) and four back-benchers and was serviced by three members of the Research Department, including Reginald Maudling. Drawing on work already undertaken by the Research Department, as well as on its own research (committee members visiting several industrial cities as well as holding discussions with industrialists), the committee moved quickly to produce its report, entitled – significantly – *The Industrial Charter*. The document was a blend of Tory and neo-liberal strands within Conservative thinking (see Chapter 5), maintaining continuity with past policies while introducing innovative proposals clearly influenced by wartime experience. The neo-liberal strand was reflected in the assertion of the need to free industry from 'unnecessary controls and restrictions', to abolish restrictive practices such as the closed shop, to return road haulage to private ownership and to finance tax reductions through cuts in public expenditure, thus encouraging investment and, consequently, output. The Tory strand was to the fore in the advocacy of a degree of voluntary co-operation between government and industry, the two working together to agree a 'national budget'; in the acceptance of full employment and the status as bodies in the public sector of the Bank of England, the railways and the coal industry; and in the proposal for a Workers' Charter, establishing in essence good practice guidelines on issues such as job security and status.

The Charter was accepted by Churchill and 'welcomed' by the 1947 party conference. Within three months two-and-a-half million copies had been sold. 'Whether many of the recipients read much of the Charter's lucid, but earnest prose is not vitally important. Its symbolism was clear to party members and to the public' (Beer, 1969: 316). The party was signalling its adaptation to the changed conditions, but an adaptation drawn from long-established traditions within the party. To Butler it was a new Tamworth Manifesto (Ramsden, 1980: 112). Subsequent policy documents were also issued for agriculture, Wales and imperial policy. In 1949 the various strands of policy delineated by the party were drawn together – and, to some extent, modified, greater emphasis being given to free enterprise, less to state intervention – and published as a single document. Entitled *The Right Road for Britain*, the document had gone through several drafts before being agreed by the Shadow Cabinet (Ramsden, 1980: 135–40). It constituted the first full-length policy document issued by the party since the war. It was supplemented, in some cases supplanted, the following year by the party's election manifesto, which was somewhat more cautious in the specific promises that it made. There was an emphasis upon reducing taxes (through cutting down on government expenditure), the decentralisation of power and on property-owning democracy. The commitment to full employment and to a Workers' Charter was maintained. There was a pledge 'to maintain and improve the Health Service' but 'we shall bring nationalisation to a full stop here and now'; the Iron and Steel Act would be repealed, supplementing the commitment to return road haulage to free enterprise (Craig, 1970: 126). The 8,000-word document was a mixture of vision, practicalities and principles, the emphasis being more on general goals than on the specific means of realising them.

By 1950 the party had done all that it might realistically be expected to do in order to establish itself as a serious contender for office, but one further condition had to be met in order to return to power. The party in office had to falter. The Labour government was a reforming government but in many respects it reformed too quickly; by 1950 it had virtually worn itself out. Internal divisions were becoming marked. In the general election of February 1950 Labour lost more than 70 seats; Conservative representation rose to 298 seats, only 17 seats fewer than the number of seats held by Labour. With 12 seats going to other parties, the government's hold on power was precarious and after 20 months Prime Minister Clement Attlee sought a fresh mandate. That mandate was denied him. Although Labour received more votes nationally than the Conservative Party – 13,948,605 votes to 13,717,538 – the distribution of Conservative support resulted in the return of 321 Conservative MPs, 26 more than the number of Labour Members. The party was back in office and Winston Churchill once more in Downing Street, although this time as a peacetime premier.

In government: Churchill to Douglas-Home

The return of a Conservative government in 1951 ushered in the longest continuous period in office enjoyed by a single party since the beginning of the nineteenth century. Returned in October 1951 the party won two succeeding elections – in 1955 and 1959 – before being narrowly defeated in the election of October 1964: a total of 13 years in office.

In terms of the measures pursued by government the period was not unimpressive. The most notable success was in the housing sector. A pledge to build 300,000 new houses a year was achieved by Harold Macmillan as Housing Minister in 1953; the proportion of families owning their own homes rose from about 30 per cent in 1951 to 47 per cent in 1964. In an improving economic climate rationing was abolished and income tax was reduced on five separate occasions; as Chancellor of the Exchequer, Butler also achieved a reduction in government expenditure as a proportion of national income (from 29 per cent in 1951 to 26 per cent in 1955). In a period of increasing prosperity the government was able to maintain its dual commitment to reduce taxation while at the same time maintaining – indeed, increasing – spending on the National Health Service. The commitment to full employment was also maintained. For most of the 1950s economic indicators were favourable: capital investment increased, the balance of trade turned in Britain's favour and the economy witnessed significant growth. Consequently, the government was able to boast an increase in the standard of living of 50 per cent during its period of office.

In legislation, a host of minor measures were enacted as well as some major reforms. The latter came especially during the Parliament of 1959–64 and included the reform of local government in London, the restriction of Commonwealth immigration (the Commonwealth Immigrants Act of 1962, a measure generating much interparty conflict) and the abolition of resale price maintenance (the Resale Prices Act of 1964, a measure notable for the degree of intraparty dissension it provoked). Other measures reorganised the electricity industry, established the Atomic Energy Authority, reformed the law on restrictive practices (creating a Restrictive Practices Division of the High Court), introduced commercial television, reformed the law on mental health and young persons, facilitated house purchase, reorganised the police force and provided for the separation of young offenders (in Borstals) from hardened criminals in prison. In line with the party's commitment the road haulage industry was denationalised, as was the iron and steel industry.

Taken together the policies pursued by government – and the measures it enacted – provided a creditable record and in large part are responsible for the electoral success of the party. However, the party suffered from what can best be described as a problem of direction, or rather lack of it. There are two related elements that contributed to this lack of direction: faltering leadership and an unsure response to crises.

As a wartime leader Churchill had displayed a feel for office; he imparted a clear sense of direction to government. As a peacetime leader he was unsure of himself. When he returned to office in 1951 he was already 76 years old and he confided to Oliver Lyttleton that he had little idea how to deal with the 'almost irretrievable' financial problems faced by the nation. 'In the worst of the war I could always see how to do it. Today's problems are elusive and intangible' (Lyttleton, 1962: 343). His health deteriorated and he held on to office longer than his colleagues thought desirable. He had able lieutenants who could carry on while he presided over rather than led government, but the delay in giving up the seals of office had an effect on his heir apparent. Sir Anthony Eden had held the position as Churchill's successor since the party returned to office but the waiting period, until 1955, took its toll on his already nervous state.

Eden's tenure of the premiership was short, destroyed by the Suez crisis. President Nasser of Egypt in 1956 nationalised the Suez canal and Britain took military action, in collusion with France and Israel, to seize the canal zone. The action, although near to completion, was ended as a result of intense pressure from the United States. The episode destroyed Eden's standing and his health. However, Suez was the culmination of poor leadership by Eden rather than an isolated instance of it. Once in office he proved a tense and meddlesome leader. According to Reginald Bevins, Eden 'ought never to have been Prime Minister. His performance prior to Suez had been feeble. He forever temporised and chopped and changed his mind' (Bevins, 1965: 37). The same qualities were apparent during the Suez crisis (Churchill, 1959: 306). His tenure of office lasted 20 months.

There were two contenders for the leadership in January 1957: R. A. Butler and Harold Macmillan. Acting on the advice of senior figures within the party (principally Churchill and Lord Salisbury, the latter having sounded out the Cabinet and the chairman of the 1922 Committee), the Queen sent for Macmillan. Macmillan turned around the fortunes of the party. He had a feel for office, at least during the first three years that he occupied the premiership. Abroad, he restored the 'special relationship' with the United States, establishing friendly relations with President Eisenhower and, more especially, his successor John Kennedy, to whom he was distantly related by marriage. Various Commonwealth countries achieved independence and Macmillan quickly established an international reputation with a tour of the Commonwealth. At home he proved an effective performer, both in Cabinet – where his chairmanship was described by Charles Hill as 'superb' – and on the public platform. Domestically, he favoured an expansionist economic policy. Treasury ministers under the Chancellor, Peter Thorneycroft, favoured a more deflationary approach. When they failed to get their way, they resigned: Macmillan dismissed the resignations as 'a little local difficulty'. Thorneycroft's successor, Derick Heathcoat Amory, was more amenable to Macmillan's approach and in 1959 introduced a highly expansionary budget. The effect of Macmillan's leadership was to restore morale within the party – aided by a highly visible and effective party chairman in Lord Hailsham – and to earn the sobriquet 'Supermac'. The party entered the 1959 election campaign ahead of the Labour Party in the polls and achieved a result that exceeded expectations: the party's parliamentary majority increased to 100. Macmillan was at the height of his power.

Thereafter it was essentially downhill. The party's 1959 manifesto had offered no clear direction and Macmillan was to reap the effects of his expansionary tendency: 1960 was the turning point in the nation's economic fortunes, Macmillan failing to heed Heathcoat Amory's warnings of trouble ahead (Brittan, 1964: 204–5). When faced with an economic downturn the response of the new Chancellor, Selwyn Lloyd, was to produce a 'stop–go' policy, using the brake and the accelerator; one aspect of the brake – wage restraint – proved especially unpopular. To economic problems were added a series of 'local difficulties', Macmillan increasingly appearing to be out of touch with events. In 1962 he attempted to restore the fortunes of the government by bringing in new blood. He dismissed seven Cabinet ministers. The action, and the speed with which it was executed, had the opposite effect to that which was intended. It suggested he was losing control. The Profumo affair in 1963 – when War Minister John Profumo was forced to resign after lying to the House about his relationship with a prostitute – suggested he was out of touch and, in terms of understanding people, out of his depth. His major policy initiative to restore both Britain's economic strength and her place on the world stage – an application to join the European Economic Community (EEC) – was destroyed by the veto imposed on British membership by the French President, Charles de Gaulle, who saw Britain as still too closely tied to the United States. Membership of the EEC was, in any event, unpopular with a significant proportion of the parliamentary party. By 1963 the government was in trouble. In October, Macmillan was taken ill with prostatitis. From his hospital bed, believing he was more gravely ill than in fact he was (see Chapter 9), he submitted his resignation as premier.

Macmillan's resignation did not so much solve a problem for the party as create one. No obvious successor had emerged and, as Macmillan's resignation was announced at the party's conference in Blackpool, there ensued what was virtually a public fight for the leadership. Butler was assumed by many to be the front runner, although Macmillan favoured Quintin Hogg. Macmillan apparently changed his mind and, following soundings within the parliamentary party and Cabinet (soundings that were to be questioned by some of those involved), advised the Queen to send for the Foreign Secretary, Lord Home. Butler agreed to serve under Home, as did other ministers, with two exceptions (Iain Macleod and Enoch Powell). Consequently, Home was able to form a government; in order to comply with constitutional convention, he renounced his peerage and – as Sir Alec Douglas-Home – entered the House of Commons following a by-election in Kinross and West Perthshire.

The new Prime Minister faced an uphill struggle. He had become leader in circumstances that were contentious, the party was doing badly in the country and a general election could not be long delayed. He did not prove an effective performer either in the Commons or on the public platform and faced a young, polished Leader of the Opposition in Harold Wilson. Nor did his background prove an asset; he appeared too much a continuation of the grouse moor image of Conservative leaders. The electoral portents were grave. In the election of October 1964 Labour achieved an overall majority, although only of four seats. The Conservative Party thus fared badly, but arguably not as badly as it might have done. Douglas-Home had persevered with his emphasis on Britain's need for an independent nuclear deterrent and his character had proved a plus as well as a minus: he was patently honest, a gentleman and prepared to listen. Nonetheless, however small Labour's majority, it was a majority. The Conservatives were back in opposition.

The Conservative Party's long tenure of office has since received a bad press. Given the problems faced in the years from 1961 to 1964 and the tribulations of leadership and crisis management, this is not altogether surprising. The picture has been supplemented by subsequent accusations, including from within the party itself, that the party was part of a social democratic consensus, with general agreement between the parties not only on the rules of the political game but also on the substance of economic management. The party, rather than carving out a distinctive stance of its own, was simply adopting a responsive stance to the approach of socialism or social democracy, in effect implementing policies that slowed rather than reversed that advance.

The picture thus painted is open to challenge, both in terms of what the government achieved and the nature of the Conservative Party. The party offered a distinctly Conservative policy, drawing – as already outlined – on different strands within the party. In the 1950s the emphasis was as much on neo-liberal values as on Tory ones, the emphasis shifting only under Macmillan's leadership in the direction of a Tory corporatist approach with the creation of the National Economic Development Council (NEDC) and long-term planning. In so far as there was movement towards the other party, that was far more apparent in the case of the Labour Party than the Conservative

Party. The Labour Party in the 1950s and early 1960s had to contend with a bitter internal struggle as to how to accommodate itself to the conditions of relative prosperity under a Conservative government. The extent to which the Conservatives were setting the political agenda was reflected in the Labour manifesto of 1959 and the promise of the Labour leader, Hugh Gaitskell, that there would be no increase in the standard rate of income tax, improving social services being financed by 'planned expansion' and dealing with tax dodgers.

The Conservative government provided for Britain's transition from austerity to relative economic prosperity. The party demonstrated its capacity to remain together in the face of Suez and the underlying trauma of the loss of Empire. Indeed, the period is remarkable for the capacity of the party – given the buffeting it faced and the problems of leadership – to rally to ensure that the Queen's government was carried on.

Whatever the record, however, in 1964 the party entered a period of uncertainty. It was out of office, led by an aristocrat whose leadership came in for increasing criticism within the party. In July 1965 Douglas-Home decided it was not worth continuing and announced his retirement. The party in opposition was faced with contending candidates for the succession, none of whom came from a grand background. The party was in the wilderness and about to be led by a new type of leader.

CHAPTER 3

History of the party III
Heath, Thatcher and Major

Philip Norton

For the first 65 years of this century, the Conservative Party was led by men drawn from a social elite. Most came from grand, or very grand, backgrounds. Of those to have held the office of Prime Minister, three – the inter-war premiers – were rich businessmen (Bonar Law, Baldwin and Chamberlain) but the others were drawn from 'established' families. One was a marquess (Salisbury), one an earl (Home), one a baronet (Eden) and the rest were drawn from or related to aristocratic families – Balfour (nephew of Salisbury), Churchill (of the ducal Marlborough family) and Macmillan (married into the ducal Devonshire family). Since 1965, the party has been led by individuals drawn from very different social circles, each being distinct in background. Edward Heath was the first leader to be drawn from a modest lower middle class background. Margaret Thatcher was the first woman to lead the party. John Major had the most unusual social background since Disraeli. Margaret Thatcher was also to achieve another distinction. She became the longest continuously serving Prime Minister in the era of mass politics.

In the 30 years following Sir Alec Douglas-Home's resignation the Conservative Party was to move from an apparently vulnerable position – in the 15 years from 1964 to 1979, it was in office for only four of them – to one of apparent dominance. After 1979 it achieved a continuous spell in office that exceeded its 13-year spell from 1951 to 1964, achieving four consecutive election victories, two of them with three-figure majorities. The continuity in office, and the parliamentary majorities, nonetheless masked some notable periods of vulnerability. There was no certainty that the party would end the century in the dominant position that it entered it.

Edward Heath to Margaret Thatcher

The six years from 1964 to 1970 were uncertain ones for the Conservative Party. Sir Alec Douglas-Home resigned the leadership in July 1965 and bequeathed to the party a new method of choosing the leader: that of election by the parliamentary party. Three contenders threw their hats into the ring: Edward Heath, Reginald Maudling and Enoch Powell. Heath achieved a largely unexpected victory, polling 150 votes to Maudling's 133 and Powell's 15. The first Conservative leader to be elected, Heath was also the first since Austen Chamberlain to attain the post while the party was in opposition.

Heath came from a modest social background and was chosen principally because he was judged an effective match for Harold Wilson (Norton and Aughey, 1981: 144). He appeared classless and technocratic, with a problem-solving approach to politics. His appeal was not so much to the deferential working class voter but to the young executive, looking for a modern, business-like approach to the affairs of government.

Heath had little time to establish himself as leader and to restore the morale and electoral appeal of the Conservative Party. Within nine months of his becoming leader he was leading the party in an election campaign. Wilson went to the country in March 1966 to seek a working parliamentary majority. There was little Heath could do to prevent a Labour victory. Conservative strength in the House of Commons dropped from 304 to 253. The Labour government was returned with an overall majority of 98.

Consigned to the opposition benches for at least four or five years, Heath set in motion a series of policy committees to formulate recommendations on a wide range of issues. In many respects reflecting Heath's problem-solving approach, the recommendations were too specific. The party failed to generate a clear political profile of itself. Heath was a fervent advocate of membership of the EEC – he had conducted negotiations when Macmillan had first applied – and clearly favoured greater managerial efficiency as a means of dealing with the nation's economic sluggishness, but there was no overall statement of policy to distinguish clearly the Conservative Party from its opponents. To many within the party the leadership pursued a stance within the House of Commons that was ineffective (Heath was out-performed by Wilson) and adopted positions that were largely indistinct from those adopted by the government. During the Parliament, the parliamentary party split on a number of issues, notably on Rhodesia, immigration and race relations, and Heath's authority was challenged by Enoch Powell. Powell's dire warnings, in a speech in Birmingham in 1968, about the effects of immigration – and the language in which they were couched ('As I look ahead I am filled with foreboding. I seem to see the "River Tiber foaming with much blood"') – provoked Heath to dismiss him from the Shadow Cabinet. Powell then took the opportunity to use the back-benches, and more especially the public platform, to articulate an alternative form of Conservatism to that being developed by Heath. The intellectual level and consistency of his arguments were usually lost on his audiences, but they understood the populist conclusions that flowed from them. His message and his style of oratory roused audiences. Heath's message and manner failed – even if the message was persuasive – to rouse listeners. Significantly, when party managers at the party conference sought on one occasion to upstage Powell as he was beginning a speech, they brought onto the platform someone who was guaranteed to receive a standing ovation: not the current party leader but the former leader, Sir Alec Douglas-Home.

Harold Wilson recommended a dissolution in 1970, with polling to taking place on 18 June. During the campaign, Labour, despite four years of bitter internal conflicts, ran ahead of the Conservatives in the opinion polls. Specu-lation was heard within the party, and at all levels, about Heath's likely successor in the event of electoral defeat; even many close to him now as-sumed him to be a 'born loser' (Roth, 1972: 209). Powell believed that the mantle was likely to pass to him.

When the results began to come through on election night it was clear that either the opinion polls had got it wrong or that there had been a massive shift in voter intentions in the day or so before 18 June. The Conservatives won 330 seats, giving them an overall majority of 30 seats. Heath became the country's 'least expected Prime Minister since Clement Attlee' (Laing, 1972: 1). Heath entered Downing Street not only enjoying the powers of Prime Minister but the authority that flowed from the perception within the party that he had won the election largely single-handedly. He appointed a personally loyal Cabinet and adopted a largely autocratic approach to leadership. Heath was now very clearly, and very firmly, in control. Powell was left to snipe from the back-benches.

The path that Heath had selected for the party was signalled primarily in 1970 following a meeting in January of the Shadow Cabinet at the Selsdon Park Hotel in Croydon – the term 'Selsdon Man' being coined by Harold Wilson to describe the product of what emerged – and in the party's June election manifesto. Although initially misdiagnosed as a neo-liberal, Heath was a corporate Whig (see Chapter 5). The emphasis was on achieving effic-iency. That efficiency was to be achieved through allowing market forces to operate. Impediments such as restrictive practices, income policies and gov-ernment aid to ailing industries were to be swept aside. Membership of the EEC would force British industry to be competitive or go to the wall.

Once in office the task was to get on and implement what Heath declared to be a long-term and history-changing programme. Membership of the EEC was negotiated successfully: Britain became a member on 1 January 1973. Any form of central planning was eschewed. Interventionist agencies created by the Wilson Government, such as the Industrial Reorganisation Corporation and the Prices and Incomes Board, were abolished. At the party conference in October 1970 Trade and Industry Secretary John Davies reiterated that there would be no state help for 'lame duck' industries. Taxes were reduced. Trade unions were reformed and a framework for industrial relations created by the Industrial Relations Act of 1971. The need for greater efficiency was also applied to public bodies. Central government was restructured as was, more radically, the National Health Service and local government.

Having implemented the Selsdon prospectus Heath found that it failed to produce the desired results. Indeed, things started to go wrong within months of taking office. To combat inflation, excessive wage demands in the public sector were resisted. This led to various industrial disputes, not all of which the government won; local authority manual workers, for example, achieved a settlement well in excess of the rate of inflation. In February 1971 the Cabinet decided to nationalise parts of the Rolls-Royce company which had gone into liquidation. The trade unions refused to co-operate with the Industrial Relations Court created by the 1971 Act; their opposition to the Act, generating in the process a number of serious conflicts, largely nullified its intended effect. Industry failed to respond to the new environment created by the government. 'Mr Heath took it hard that the massive reductions in taxation rates had not produced an upturn in orders for plant and machinery. There was a growing feeling that the boardrooms were letting the Government down' (Bruce-Gardyne, 1974: 80). Unemployment also continued to rise; by October 1971, 900,000 people were out of work.

The rise in unemployment and the failure of the private sector to grasp the opportunities on offer – there was a slump in manufacturing investment – provoked a major policy shift. Various pump-priming exercises were undertaken in 1971. Early in 1972, with the unemployment total reaching one-and-a-half million, the government went even further: it abandoned its 'lame ducks' policy. The U-turn on industry involved the creation of an Industrial Development Executive and the provision, through the executive, of regional development grants, grants that need not be confined to assisted areas. The link with employment was made explicit.

A continuing high rate of inflation also provoked intervention. During the summer of 1972 Heath attempted to negotiate a voluntary policy of wage and price restraint with the Trades Union Congress (TUC) and the Confederation of British Industry (CBI). The negotiations collapsed and in November the government introduced a statutory policy commencing with a 90-day freeze on pay and prices. This constituted the U-turn on the economy. What until only months before the Prime Minister had been vehemently opposing was now part of government policy. 'Selsdon Man' was dead.

The new strategy, combating unemployment through reflation while tackling inflation through a pay and prices policy, failed at two levels: the economic and the political. The economic failure was in large part the product of international forces. The rise in oil prices – and consequent energy crisis – and a world recession killed off the chances for expansion. Domestically, the National Union of Miners (NUM) – which had a major success against the government in forcing significant pay rises in 1972 – sought a pay rise that breached the limits of the pay policy. In support of the claim the union, in November 1973, imposed an overtime ban. The following month, with the energy crisis beginning to bite, Heath announced a three-day working week for industry. Attempts by Heath to negotiate a settlement with the NUM failed and on 5 February 1974 the union called a national strike to start on 10 February. For Heath the way out of the impasse was to request a dissolution. On 7 February he announced a general election for 28 February on the issue of 'who governs?'

Politically Heath failed because he failed to carry the party with him. Conservative MPs continued in most cases to vote for government measures but there was little or no enthusiasm, and in many cases little understanding of the government's case. The Prime Minister made little or no attempt to explain to back-benchers why he was pursuing a new direction. MPs were only informed after the event. The announcement in November 1973 of a £300 million trade deficit for the previous month and the imposition of a credit squeeze took them completely by surprise. When back-benchers demurred they were cold-shouldered. Contact between the Prime Minister and his back-benchers was formal and rare. Dissension within the party reached unprecedented levels, with Enoch Powell in the van: during the Parliament he voted against the government 113 times. By the end of the Parliament Conservative MPs were in a state of uncertainty about policy and hostile in terms of Heath's style of government (Norton, 1978). So long as he continued to occupy Downing Street, Heath was able to command the support of his parliamentary party. Without the trappings of office, he was vulnerable.

In the election of February 1974, issues other than that of 'who governs?' crowded the campaign. The Heath government had witnessed serious industrial disputes, major strikes and (consequent) states of emergency and the three-day working week. The campaign did not go well, littered with damaging pronouncements from the Director-General of the CBI, the Pay Board and Enoch Powell, Powell advising voters to vote Labour. When the election results came in the Conservative Party had lost its overall majority. After an unsuccessful attempt to reach some accommodation with the Liberal Party, Heath resigned. Harold Wilson formed his second government.

Returned to opposition, Heath found himself in an increasingly weak position. To the disquiet and dissatisfaction carried over from the last Parliament was added now the resentment at having lost a general election. This was compounded by Heath's approach in opposition – attempting to win the argument but not to force a division – which proved increasingly unpopular; the chairman of the 1922 Committee conveyed back-bench dissatisfaction to the leader (*The Times* 10 May, 14 June 1974). Heath also set up a number of study groups to review policy; a number of MPs objected to their exclusion (*Daily Telegraph* 25 June 1974). In October, Wilson went to the country to try to transform his government from minority to majority status. He succeeded, albeit by the narrowest of margins: an overall majority of three. To Conservatives, however, the most important point was that they had lost.

In the wake of the election defeat pressure for Heath to resign grew. ' We paid the price of Mr Heath's leadership with the loss of the October election' complained one member (quoted in Norton, 1980: 450). Heath was encouraged to offer himself for re-election, even though no formal procedure for such a move existed. Within the 1922 Committee the proposal for the leadership to be subject to regular election – transforming it from freehold to leasehold – gained in popularity and Heath eventually succumbed to the pressure and agreed to a review of the existing arrangements. A committee under Lord Home (as Sir Alec Douglas had again become) was appointed. It recommended an annual ballot with a balloting procedure similar to the existing one. The recommendation was accepted by the 1922 Committee and by Heath in January 1975, with a first ballot scheduled for 4 February.

One expected contender for the leadership, Sir Keith Joseph, effectively talked himself out of the race. He made a speech which appeared to suggest that women drawn from 'socio-economic classes 4 and 5' should not have children because they were least suited to raise them. The controversy generated by the speech made Joseph realise that he was not a viable contender. His place was taken by Margaret Thatcher, who had served as Heath's Education Secretary and been one of the few around the Cabinet table to voice occasional dissent. After a short and hectic contest, which Heath expected and was expected to win, the first ballot resulted in Mrs Thatcher receiving 130 votes to Heath's 119. (A third contender, Hugh Fraser, got 16 votes.) Heath withdrew from the contest. In the second ballot, in which four new challengers took part, Mrs Thatcher achieved an overall majority with seven votes to spare. The Conservative Party had a new leader.

To the party, Mrs Thatcher offered a new direction both in terms of substance and style. A deliberate attempt was made to avoid the characteristics of Heath's leadership style (see Rutherford, 1984). The new leader proved, as one MP put it, 'easy to see'. She injected a more aggressive element in being willing to take on her opponents. She also began to set the tone for the party in terms of what it stood for. Not for her the detailed specifics of Heath's style of policy making. It was necessary to occupy the principled high ground before descending to the low ground of policy specifics. What she articulated in the economic sphere was a neo-liberal philosophy, offered not only as a response to the failures of the Heath years but as a response to the problems faced by the Wilson and Callaghan governments. With the exception of 1978 the annual increase in prices exceeded 15 per cent, on two occasions exceeding 20 per cent. The government was seen as enjoying an overly cosy relationship with, and almost subordinate position to, the trade unions. It was internally divided and vulnerable: as a result of by-election losses and defections, it slipped into minority status in the House of Commons in April 1976. Mrs Thatcher was prepared to lead her troops into battle and had a standard under which to fight.

The standard itself was not fully unfurled. Mrs Thatcher was still developing and honing the approach that was later to be characterised as an 'ism' – Thatcherism – although the free market emphasis was clear (see Chapter 12). Within the party this emphasis was reflected in a number of appointments: Sir

Keith Joseph was given overall responsibility for policy co-ordination, Angus Maude was appointed chairman of Research Department and Sir Geoffrey Howe became Shadow Chancellor; but they did not constitute exclusive brethren. Sceptics remained on the front bench. Jim Prior served on the Economic Reconstruction Group that was set up to consider economic policy. Mrs Thatcher even appointed to her Treasury team Peter Tapsell, who had argued for a prices and incomes policy before Heath had taken it on board.

To prepare for the next general election, policy groups – more than 60 were in operation at one point – were established. Membership of the groups was drawn from different strands within the party and, unlike the policy groups under Heath in the 1964–70 period, MPs played a central role (Burch, 1980: 175). Also unlike the Heath groups, they were not tightly controlled. Reports had to follow a prescribed route before being endorsed by the Shadow Cabinet 'but there were more policy groups, running on an initially lighter rein, than before. . . . More backbenchers wanted to be involved in policy work and the Shadow Cabinet was wisely disposed to let a hundred flowers bloom' (Patten, 1980: 19). When general policy documents were drawn up the emphasis was broad, avoiding overly specific or numerous policy commitments. The two main documents issued prior to the 1979 general election manifesto were *The Right Approach*, published in 1976, and *The Right Approach to the Economy*, published the following year. The former drew together the strands of the policy review. It was broad rather than specific – 'a statement of Conservative *aims*' – and both extolled the record of previous Conservative governments and reminded readers that an economic system 'predominantly based on private enterprise . . . does not make us a *laissez-faire* party. We have always conceded that the state should have a role as a trustee of the whole community in any economic system, holding the balance between different interests.' The latter contained a clearer signal of the preference for monetarism – 'strict control by government of the rate of growth of the money supply' – but that was one of nine main features of the approach advocated; the document called for a 'new spirit of cautious realism' and included reference – at Jim Prior's insistence – to government having to come to *some* conclusion about scope for pay increases if large-scale unemployment was to be avoided (Prior, 1986: 109). The two documents provided the basis for the party's election manifesto in 1979.

Margaret Thatcher's tenure as opposition leader was not trouble free. The parliamentary party divided on a number of issues, notably Rhodesian sanctions (116 Conservative MPs voted against renewal in 1978) and, to a lesser but still significant extent, devolution and the European Communities (Norton, 1980). Some of the leader's more ardent supporters complained about the quality of the front bench team. Although she enjoyed the support of the majority of the parliamentary party, the more senior figures in the party were 'Heathmen'; they were too numerous – and experienced – to be dispensed with. The Callaghan government showed a capacity to survive in office, in

1977 avoiding defeat on a confidence motion by negotiating a pact with the Liberals in the House of Commons. For a time Labour clawed back some of its support in the opinion polls. Victory for the Conservatives at any forthcoming election was not certain.

The picture, however, was far from gloomy. Mrs Thatcher gained in confidence during the course of the Parliament. Her style of leadership, assisted by some of her front bench lieutenants, ensured that dissension within the party was less great than it otherwise might have been (Norton, 1980: 450–1); discord and dissension in the House of Commons were major problems instead on the government side of the House. As Prime Minister, James Callaghan began to lose some of his apparent sure-footedness. A Social Contract with the trade unions was succeeded by union opposition to the government's pay policy. In the closing months of 1978 a series of major industrial disputes produced a winter that was dubbed 'The Winter of Discontent'. The following March, the government was defeated on a vote of confidence in the House of Commons by one vote; by then, the Prime Minister appeared to have reached a stage of almost not caring. On 29 March – the day following the defeat – Callaghan went to the palace to request a dissolution. Polling was scheduled for 3 May.

In the election, the Conservative Party polled two million votes more than the Labour Party – 13.6 million to 11.5 million – and achieved an overall majority in the House of Commons of 43 seats. Labour lost in large part because of the reaction to the Winter of Discontent; two elections later, reminders of the occasion remained politically salient. The Conservatives won because of the promise of tax cuts and the need for a stronger policy on law and order. In her first election campaign as leader, Mrs Thatcher had led her party to victory. Britain had its first woman Prime Minister.

The effect of Margaret Thatcher on British politics has been profound. By being Britain's first female premier she was assured a place in the history books. What was not known at the time she entered 10 Downing Street was the fact that she would still be there 11 years later. After two further election victories, in 1983 and 1987, Mrs Thatcher became Britain's longest continuously serving Prime Minister since Lord Liverpool. She was remarkable not only for her length of tenure but also for what she did. As Prime Minister she was an innovator, almost unique among twentieth-century premiers (Norton, 1987b); her beliefs have been accorded the status of a distinct philosophy, 'Thatcherism'; and she, and her beliefs, have been written about and analysed more thoroughly and extensively than any of her predecessors (see Norton, 1987d).

The Thatcher years

The twin pillars of the Thatcher premiership are identified in the title of Andrew Gamble's book, *The Free Economy and the Strong State* (1988).

When Mrs Thatcher entered office the essentials of economic policy were to combat inflation – the number one priority according to the party manifesto – and to rid the individual of the shackles of government. Achieving those goals entailed slowing the growth in the money supply, reducing public expenditure and withdrawing from as many areas of economic activity as possible. State-owned industries were to be run more efficiently or, in some cases (the list being extended significantly in later Parliaments), returned to the private sector. Market forces, as far as possible, were to operate: consumer choice, not government dictate, was to determine economic activity.

In order to achieve such economic freedom government itself had to be strengthened. Strong government was necessary not only in order to fulfil those tasks which government alone can fulfil (defence of the realm, maintenance of the peace) but also in order to create the conditions within which market forces may operate, in order to achieve some degree of autonomy for bodies in society that had previously exerted too much influence (through corporatist forms created by previous governments), and in order to delimit the economic profligacy of subordinate units of government.

The new government moved quickly on a number of fronts. As was subsequently to be recognised by the leadership, it may have moved too quickly. Tax cuts were introduced while at the same time significant pay increases – especially to the police and armed forces – were implemented. Such measures were carried through against a backdrop of global recession and unease within the party. Economically and politically, 1980 and 1981 were difficult years for the government. 1981 witnessed the creation of a new party – the Social Democratic Party (SDP) – and talk within the parliamentary party of a candidate standing against Mrs Thatcher for the party leadership in the autumn. At one point the SDP achieved a plurality of support in the opinion polls and the Conservatives suffered badly in a number of by-elections. For Mrs Thatcher, 1981 was an *annus horrendus*. Thereafter, conditions changed. Indeed, there were four subsequent phases of government.

The first phase may be described as the Falklands phase. The Argentinian invasion of the Falklands Islands in April 1982 was a massive dent to national pride in Britain, and the government's position – when the House of Commons convened specially on the morning of Saturday 3 April – was highly vulnerable. The despatch of a Task Force and the successful completion of the military operation to restore the islands to British control restored popular support for the government and demonstrated the Conservative Party's commitment to a vigorous defence of Britain's interests abroad. Such a stance was also to be demonstrated by Mrs Thatcher in her dealings with other members of the European Community. At the same time, a number of economic indicators started to turn in the government's favour. The party thus had the basis for a successful election campaign. It was aided by the activities of its opponents, the leader of the Labour Party (Michael Foot) and Labour policies constituting electoral negatives for Labour. In the general election of June

1983, the Conservative Party was returned with the largest overall parliamentary majority (144) it had achieved since 1935.

The second phase may be described as the period of deflection, encompassing the miners' strike of 1984–5 and the Westland crisis of 1986. The government response (and that of the police) to a strike by the National Union of Miners – which began in March 1984 and collapsed 11 months later – proved effective but deflected the Prime Minister and the Cabinet from the policies they wished to pursue; there was a recognition within government, following the end of the strike, that the opportunity to pursue a forward-looking and radical programme during that Parliament had been lost. Ministers were further deflected by the Westland Crisis. A dispute between two Cabinet Ministers – Trade and Industry Secretary Leon Brittan and Defence Secretary Michael Heseltine – at the end of 1985 over the approach to be taken in seeking to save the Westland helicopter company mushroomed unexpectedly and rapidly into a constitutional crisis. Mrs Thatcher favoured the position taken by Leon Brittan, but did not have sufficient Cabinet support to be decisive; Michael Heseltine took exception to the way in which he felt he was being outmanoeuvred in Cabinet; a letter from the Solicitor General to Mr Heseltine was (in a manner designed to undermine the Defence Secretary) partially leaked; the government was put on the defensive in the House of Commons. Both principal Ministers resigned, Mr Heseltine because he felt he was being deliberately gagged and Mr Brittan after he lost suppport among Conservative MPs when parentage of the leak of the letter from the Solicitor General was traced to his Department. Accusations as to the Prime Minister's knowledge of the leak of the letter (and allegations of a subsequent attempt to shield her) were pursued by the Opposition and at one point the Prime Minister conceded that there was a real danger that she might cease to be PM. The affair reached a peak in January and early February of 1986 but lingered in parliamentary consciousness until the summer. It also caused a blip in public support for the government – its standing in the opinion polls declining in the first half of the year – not because of the particular approaches involved to Westland but because of perceptions that the government appeared to be drifting, that it was, in short, failing to deploy – and display – its skills of governance.

The third phase may be described as that of the period of Mrs Thatcher's hegemony. Once the Westland crisis had lost the status of a crisis and the Conservative Party had achieved victory in the general election of June 1987, the Prime Minister enjoyed a largely unassailable position within both government and party. She had led the party to three consecutive election victories, the disputes between economic 'wets' and 'dries' within the parliamentary party (which had marked the first few years of her premiership) had lost their saliency and the government was embarked upon a programme of measures to effect radical changes in education, housing and local government finance as well as to return several other public utilities to private ownership. The Prime Minister continued to lead not only in the domestic arena but also on the world stage, achieving the status of the senior figure among Western leaders. By 1989 psephologists were drawing attention to the fact that a significant proportion of the electorate – those in the 18–24-years range – had little recollection of any government other than a Conservative one. Equally pertinent was the fact that those same electors had little recollection of a Prime Minister other than Mrs Thatcher. By pursuing a high profile and active programme, the Prime Minister was working to ensure that longevity in office did not feed perceptions that it was time for change. At the time of the tenth anniversary of Mrs Thatcher's 'kissing hands' on appointment as Prime Minister, there was a clear expectation on the part of the Conservative Party that Mrs Thatcher would lead the party into the next Parliament and possibly beyond.

After ten years in office, the Thatcher government was able to point to a rapid rise in the ownership both of property and of shares: more than one million public sector tenants had bought their homes since 1979 and more than 20 per cent of the population – three times the proportion in 1979 – owned shares. There had been a significant reduction in the state ownership of industries. Trade unions had been reformed. The tax system was reformed and simplified and reductions in the rates of income tax, especially in the 1988 Budget, were introduced. Inflation, relative to the rate in the latter half of the 1970s, had been reduced, reaching a level of less than 4 per cent in early 1988. Unemployment, after reaching a peak in 1984, declined significantly from 13.3 per cent of the economically active population in 1984 to 7 per cent in January 1989. There were significant rises in productivity. Internationally, the government could point to victory in the Falklands conflict, to a willingness to defend British interests in the European Community and to a prominent position in international summitry. Party publications outlining the government's successes were numerous and lengthy. *Nine Years' Work* (Conservative Research Department, 1988) ran to 46 pages.

Against that, critics pointed to the advantage enjoyed by government in terms of an upturn in the world economy, to a failure to pursue a strict monetarist policy, to the maintenance of historically high levels of unemployment, to the unpopularity of the Community Charge being introduced in 1990 (in England and Wales) as a replacement for domestic rates and to perceived attacks – derived from a 'hidden agenda' – on the National Health Service. A number of specific measures failed to achieve an electoral resonance (notably privatisation of the water industry in 1989) and opponents of the government claimed that there was a growing social divide between North and South.

What critics did not dispute was the extent of Mrs Thatcher's impact on British politics: indeed, they appeared largely in awe and envy of it. After ten years in office Mrs Thatcher had changed the agenda of debate in Britain, she had put the Conservative Party on the offensive, she had presided over a government that had conveyed that it had the essential skills of governance and had generally restored a sense of national pride. In much of this she had, like many of her predecessors, been aided considerably by her opponents, especially in the general elections of 1979 (the Winter of Discontent) and 1983 (Michael Foot as Labour leader); party politics and internal disunity had generated negative electoral responses. This confluence ensured that the Conservative Party maintained the position it had occupied for most of the twentieth century – in government.

Yet at the very time that her place in history was assured and she appeared at the height of her powers, the foundations of her power base began to crumble. The period of hegemony was relatively short-lived, giving way to the fourth and final phase of her premiership – that of vulnerability. Economic indicators began to worsen in 1989 and the following year the issues of the Community Charge, universally dubbed the 'poll tax', and Europe undermined her position. She refused to compromise on either issue. The poll tax generated widespread opposition, a significant element of non-payment and demonstrations and some riots in different parts of the country. London saw its worst riot in living memory. The party's divisions on Europe, and Mrs Thatcher's intransigence which exacerbated the divisions, proved politically damaging. In the spring of 1990, the party trailed Labour in the opinion polls by more than 20 points.

Signs of unease in the parliamentary party over Margaret Thatcher's leadership were apparent in 1989. In the autumn a maverick back-bencher, Sir Anthony Meyer, challenged her for the leadership. He stood ostensibly because of Mrs Thatcher's negative stance towards European integration. His challenge was not deemed a serious one, including by himself. He was standing as a stalking horse, in the hope that a heavyweight candidate could be found (Meyer himself favoured Michael Heseltine). No heavyweight candidate was prepared to take the challenge, leaving Meyer to fight a lone battle. Even so, the figures sent a signal to Downing Street. Margaret Thatcher got 314 votes, Meyer got 33, and there were 24 spoilt ballots and 3 absentees. Sixty Conservative MPs – 16 per cent of the parliamentary party – had failed to support the leader. The figures suggested that not only had her Wet and Damp critics (see Norton, 1990a, 1990b) voted against her, but so had a handful of normally loyal Members. Equally worrying for Mrs Thatcher, it became known that a large number of MPs – up to 60, according to one source – had written to her campaign manager, warning him that their support was conditional and that if there was not a change in the Prime Minister's approach, especially on the issue of Europe, their votes may not be forthcoming in the event of another contest (Norton, 1993: 50–1).

Mrs Thatcher's campaign manager, former Defence Secretary George Younger, signalled that the message had been received. However, the following year there was little evidence of a change in the Prime Minister's approach. Despite a bad spring for the party – poll tax riots, poor performance in the opinion polls – it looked in the summer as if Mrs Thatcher would escape a leadership challenge in the autumn. The party conference in October went well, but then came the event that was to lead to the leader's fall. On 1 November the Leader of the House of Commons, Sir Geoffrey Howe, resigned. In his resignation statement on 13 November he made clear he had gone because of Mrs Thatcher's stance on Europe and because of her style of government. He said he had done what he believed was right for his party and for the country. 'The time has come for others to consider their response to the tragic conflict of loyalty with which I have myself wrestled for perhaps too long.' The following day Michael Heseltine announced his candidacy for the party leadership, thus triggering a contested election.

In the first ballot, on 20 November, Margaret Thatcher got 204 votes, Heseltine got 152 votes and there were 16 abstentions. Under the rules, to be declared elected on the first ballot an absolute majority, plus a majority constituting 15 per cent of all Conservative MPs, was needed. Mrs Thatcher was four votes short of the necessary number. A second ballot was necessary. After declaring her intention to enter that second ballot Mrs Thatcher consulted individually the members of her Cabinet and – told by many she would probably lose – she withdrew from the contest (Norton, 1993: 55–7; see Thatcher, 1993: 846–55). Two senior members of her Cabinet, Foreign Secretary Douglas Hurd and Chancellor of the Exchequer John Major, then entered the contest, with Major – helped by a well-run, although hastily put together, campaign – emerging the victor. Major got 185 votes to Heseltine's 131 and Hurd's 56. Although two votes short of the absolute majority necessary to be declared elected on a second ballot, the other two contenders withdrew from the contest and Major was declared elected. On 28 November Major went to Buckingham Palace. The Conservative Party had a new leader and Britain had a new Prime Minister.

The Major premiership

John Major differed from his predecessor in terms of background, beliefs and style. Margaret Thatcher – like Heath before her – had come from a solid, and unexceptionable, lower middle class background and gone on to Oxford University. Major was born to parents who made a career on the music-hall stage, his father subsequently going into business making garden ornaments and then, to meet a debt, having to sell up. Major himself left school at 16 and took a number of jobs – for a period he was unemployed – before taking up employment in a bank. In his political beliefs he was not a Thatcherite but was instead drawn from the ranks of the party faithful (see Norton, 1990a). In his beliefs he was a fiscal conservative and a social liberal, but willing to be persuaded on issues and to subjugate his beliefs to what he saw as the greater good of the party. In essence, he was a pragmatist rather than a Thatcherite. He was, like many of his Tory predecessors, a 'balancer'. He was concerned essentially with the here and now of British politics. In his style he was more a healer than a warrior, preferring to console rather than to confront. Whereas Margaret Thatcher liked challenging people in debate, John Major simply liked meeting them.

His first year of office proved a successful one. Unpopular measures, notably the poll tax, were jettisoned and the stance on European integration softened. The new Prime Minister had a 'good war' during the Gulf War in the spring and showed a much more deft handling of the situation in Russia – telephoning to give his support to President Boris Yeltsin, under threat from military forces – than that of US President George Bush. He also had a successful summit in December 1991 at which the EC heads of government agreed the Maastricht Treaty. Despite trailing in the opinion polls, Major – after delaying an election until the five-year maximum life of the Parliament was almost complete – led his party to a narrow but unexpected victory in a General Election in April 1992. The victory was largely credited to Major, who had outstripped his party in terms of popularity.

However, no sooner had Major led his party to victory than events turned against him. A run on sterling in the summer forced an unwilling government to withdraw from the European exchange rate mechanism. The recession lingered. The Bill to give legal effect to the Maastricht Treaty ran into trouble in the House of Commons. It was delayed following a 'no' vote on the Treaty in a referendum in Denmark. The Danish vote encouraged Conservative MPs opposed to the treaty. When the Bill was again considered by the Commons, the government was defeated on one amendment and it accepted another under threat of defeat. After the Bill's passage, the government – under the provisions of the measure – had to get the approval of the Commons for its policy on the treaty's Social Chapter. It suffered a defeat in its attempt to get that approval and then, in a second vote to get approval, made it a vote of confidence.

The period was not totally bereft of successes. Major was widely praised for his policy on Northern Ireland. In December 1993, he issued – with the Irish premier Albert Reynolds – the Downing Street Declaration, signalling a willingness to allow those groups engaged in armed conflict in the province a place at the negotiating table if they permanently renounced violence. When the Provisional IRA subsequently announced a cease-fire, followed by Protestant paramilitary groups, Major then waited until he was satisfied that the cease-fire was permanent before moving towards talks with the various groups.

The breakthrough in terms of Northern Ireland was substantial. However, although significant it was one success among what appeared a string of failures in other sectors. The government ran into trouble on a range of issues, including its policy of closing most of Britain's remaining coal mines (1992) and – all in 1994 – a proposal from Michael Heseltine to privatise the Post Office, financing of the European Community and the imposition of Value Added Tax (VAT) on domestic fuel. On Post Office privatisation a number of

Conservative MPs – sufficient to rob the government of its majority in the division lobbies – made clear they would not support the policy and it was hastily withdrawn from the Queen's Speech. A Bill to give effect to a Maastricht commitment to increase the EC budget faced serious back-bench opposition. The Prime Minister made passage of the Bill a vote of confidence. The government got the Bill through without defeat, but eight Conservative MPs failed to support the government at second reading stage. The whip was then withdrawn from all eight. (A ninth resigned the whip in protest; see Chapter 8.) Value-added tax (VAT) on domestic fuel also attracted back-bench opposition and at the end of the year the governnment was defeated on the issue, immediately abandoning plans to impose a second-stage increase.

The government's problems during this period were exacerbated by what the media characterised as a 'sleaze' factor. The Prime Minister launched a 'back to basics' campaign at the 1993 party conference that was widely interpreted as signalling a return to moral, or family, values, even though not intended as such. Various sections of the party fought over what the policy meant – the right emphasising the attachment to 'family values' (marriage, fidelity, a heterosexual two-parent family). The resignation of a number of ministers because of financial or sexual scandal effectively killed the campaign as a positive means of attracting support, attracting instead press ridicule and undermining popular confidence in the government. It was not helped by press claims about MPs accepting money for tabling parliamentary questions and press investigations into links between Conservative MPs and outside interests, leading the Prime Minister to establish the Committee on Standards in Public Life, chaired by a judge, Lord Nolan.

The Prime Minister was criticised by some of his own back-benchers for failing to give a decisive lead on issues. That criticism became more pronounced as the party slipped further behind Labour in the opinion polls. By the beginning of 1995 Labour led the Conservatives by more than 30 points in the opinion polls. Conservative Party membership declined, it had financial difficulties and party morale sagged. For the Conservatives, it was a dire political situation. Back-bench criticism of the Prime Minister increased. The whipless MPs attracted considerable publicity, before having the whip restored in the April. Criticism of the Prime Minister by some MPs became more public and more vitriolic. Talk of a challenge to his leadership in the autumn became more pronounced. In June, Major had a difficult meeting with the 'Fresh Start' group of Conservative Euro-sceptics, facing criticism and heckling. Deciding that things could not go on as they were he announced his resignation as party leader in order to force an immediate leadership contest. His decision proved popular with constituency parties and he was expected to win by a large margin. However, a member of his Cabinet (Welsh Secretary John Redwood) resigned to contest the election. Against a heavy-weight contender the outcome was considered less certain. In the event, Major was re-elected. Of the 329 Conservative MPs eligible to vote, 218 voted for Major and 89 voted for Redwood. A further 12 spoilt their ballot papers and 8 abstained. (Two failed to vote at all.) Major cleared both hurdles required for election on the first ballot. However, the fact that more than 100 MPs had failed to support the incumbent meant that he could not claim the decisive victory he had been seeking. He had himself reportedly taken a figure of 100 failing to support him as a yardstick by which to gauge whether he should stay or go and, according to one report, briefly considered resigning. He was persuaded to stay and to claim a good victory. The result was a disappointment for his critics, who had expected him to get a much lower vote, some predicting that he would not clear the hurdles necessary to win on the first ballot. The party's right, supporting Redwood, failed to poll its full strength.

The Prime Minister's supporters were able to put a positive gloss on the election outcome and the party received a boost – albeit not sustained to any great extent, and not enough to come close to Labour's support – in the opinion polls. In the immediate aftermath of the contest the Prime Minister undertook a ministerial reshuffle, making a Cabinet heavyweight, Michael Heseltine, Deputy Prime Minister.

Conservative MPs generally welcomed the outcome of the contest, believed to have settled the leadership question until after the next general election, but remained beset by fears about the party's standing in the polls and its capacity to win the next election. Some on the right disliked the prominence accorded to Heseltine and the perceived marginalisation of right-wing members of the Cabinet.

For John Major, each year from 1992 onwards appeared to be an *annus horrendus*. What had been his strength in the short term proved to be a weakness in the long term. His pragmatism meant that he was able to get rid of unpopular policies when he took over the leadership, but it also meant that he lacked any future goal – any obvious sense of clear direction – that could be used to rally popular support. He was derided for being too responsive, for being driven by the in-tray and for being too accident-prone. Various Ministers resigned as a consequence of scandal; others were dismissed – such as Chancellor Norman Lamont in 1993 – and subsequently proved a thorn in the government's side. The Prime Minister stood accused of lacking the skills of governance and a sense of purpose..It proved a combination that appeared near-fatal. The danger from the point of view of the Conservative Party was that it could prove politically fatal for the party as well as for the leader. Although some in the party thought a period of opposition would allow the party to recharge its intellectual batteries, others recognised that recharging the batteries would prove useless if the party was not given a chance again to be in control of the vehicle of government. There was the prospect of the party moving from being the 'in' party to being the 'out' party. It was a prospect that was uncongenial to a party that prided itself on its skills of governance. There was the danger of the Conservative Century coming to an end.

CHAPTER 4

Philosophy
The principles of Conservatism

Philip Norton

There is no single corpus of Conservative dogma, no particular text which Conservatives can hold aloft as representing the basis of their beliefs. There has been an absence of what Gillian Peele has called 'magisterial theorists' to whom Conservatives can turn for inspiration (Peele, 1976: 13). This in itself says something about the nature of British Conservatism.

To be a Conservative is to hold a particular view of human nature and society, but it is a view that is generally antithetical to the generation of grand theories, of abstract visions of a society yet to exist. Exponents of Conservatism are notable for the extent to which they eschew such terms as ideology – some even avoiding reference to principles – preferring instead to refer to 'attitudes' (Banks, 1929) or 'dispositions' (Oakeshott, 1962: 168). The distinction is an important one, for to have a particular disposition is to have a feeling about the way things should be: the implication is that it is inherent and natural. Conservatives feel comfortable with such natural dispositions and as such feel little need to articulate them; they are personal and they are part of the way of the world.

A further discouragement to the articulation of philosophy or one's guiding principles has been the long periods which the Conservative Party has spent in office. 'Political parties seldom philosophise when in office' (Blake, 1976: 1). A combination of electoral success and an unwillingness to engage in expounding a well-honed philosophy has led many observers to assume that there is little more to the party than a desire to be in government. 'Of all the features of the Conservative Party, the intense concern with winning elections and holding office is its most notable', wrote Richard Rose (1965: 143); party principles, he added, 'are extremely vague'. Consequently, attempts to locate and delineate the body of principles that constitute Conservatism in Britain have been relatively rare. Conservatives see little need for such an exercise. Critics believe there is nothing to explore.

However, the Conservative Party does not operate in some unprincipled vacuum. Policies are not spun out of thin air. Even the Oakeshottian

68

perception that the purpose of government is to keep 'the ship of state afloat' involves a certain view of the necessity to maintain the ship as well as the inferred need for a view as to how the ship may be maintained. Conservative pragmatism, as Lord Coleraine noted, 'even when it seems to be second nature, is not simply instinctive. It is based on a certain reading of history, a certain interpretation of experience. Even the most hidebound of Conservatives is more rational and less intuitive in his political attitudes than he, or anyone else, supposes' (Coleraine 1970: 20).

What, then, are the basic beliefs of Conservatives in Britain? There is no definitive list. The Conservative Party, as we noted in Chapter 1, inherited the basic beliefs of its Tory predecessor. Other tenets were acquired at different times in its history. It has variously drawn inspiration from particular events in history, from its leaders, from the writings of various men of affairs and from those who have joined the party at different stages in its development. (As the experience of Disraeli reveals, these categories are not mutually exclusive.) These tenets have come together, in effect coalesced, to form British Conservatism.

Basic dispositions

At the heart of British Conservatism are two basic dispositions. One is a scepticism as to the power of man's reason. Individual reason is seen as imperfect and limited. Man is a mix of emotion, instinct and habit as well as thought. The imperfections of man prevent the bringing about of Utopia. Present society is the product of impersonal forces, of the accumulated wisdom of generations. No individual or group of individuals could ever achieve such a result, nor improve significantly upon it. There is thus a wariness toward, and distrust of, abstract ideas untested by experience. From this flows both an anti-intellectual streak – few Conservative thinkers, as Tibor Szamuely observed, would have dreamt of describing themselves as intellectuals (Szamuely, 1968: 7) – and a scepticism towards what government may achieve. The capacity of government to change man's nature is limited and no one individual or collection of individuals has the capacity to foresee fully the consequences of the actions of government. Efforts to remedy existing evils may result in even greater ones. 'By bitter experience Conservatives know that there is almost no limit to the misery of degradation to which bad governments may sink and depress their victims. But while others extol the virtues of the particular brand of Utopia they propose to create, the Conservative disbelieves them all and, despite all temptations, offers in their place no Utopia at all but something quite modestly better than those present' (Hogg, 1947; see also Schuettinger, 1969). Learning – and the practice of government – cannot be divorced from an appreciation of experience, that is, history. For those keen to identify from *a priori* reasoning what *should* be, the Conservative tempers the debate by asking what *can* be.

The second disposition is, in large measure, a corollary of the first. This comprises a concern for, and in essence an adherence to, society as it currently exists. There is an appreciation of both the complexity and the conveniences of society as currently constituted, as well as of the forces that brought it about. For the Conservative the present is not necessarily the ideal, but it is the real. 'It is also a measure of how things are, the conveniences, but also the inconveniences, of a style of living' (Norton and Aughey, 1981: 19). There is an attachment to those institutions which form and help shape society, institutions which exist, which are real and which – absent of any clear evidence to the contrary – are deemed to fulfil some purpose. The effects of their removal are likely to prove unknowable, but rather like chopping off a part of a human body the presumption is that the surgery would be painful with consequences for the rest of the body politic. If surgery is necessary it should be minor, designed to strengthen – not weaken – the product of generations of accumulated wisdom. Even then, many Conservatives prefer the natural solution of self-healing to the surgical knife of government.

These basic dispositions were neatly captured by the fifteenth Earl of Derby:

> A Conservative policy, as it seems to me, tells its own story – to distrust loud professions and large promises; to place no confidence in theories for the regeneration of of mankind, however brilliant and ingenious; to believe only in that improvement which is steady and gradual and accomplished step by step; to compare our actual condition, not with the ideal world which thinkers have sketched out, but with the condition of other countries at the present day, and with our own country at other times; to hold fast what we have till we are quite sure that we have got hold of something better instead. (quoted in Feuchtwanger, 1968: 29)

For the Conservative, then, the real and knowable are to be preferred over the abstract and the unknowable. Hence, whenever established norms and established institutions – be it the Crown or the police force – are under attack, the Conservative disposition is to spring to their defence. In English history this disposition is long-standing and its exposition can be traced back to Richard Hooker in the sixteenth century (Hearnshaw, 1933; Kirk, 1953). Conservatism then – in the words of F. C. J. Hearnshaw – became 'a continuing spirit', finding its later and most articulate expression in the eighteenth-century writings of Edmund Burke. The basic dispositions – the 'continuing spirit' of Conservatism – thus predate the emergence in the 1830s of the Conservative Party and they underpin the basic tenets of party thought.

Basic tenets

The basic tenets of Conservative thought can be identified as eight in number. Five of these were inherited from Toryism and the remaining three adopted in the latter half of the nineteenth century. Collectively, they constitute the corpus of British Conservatism in the twentieth century.

The organic nature of society

A basic tenet of Conservative belief is the organic nature of society. Society is seen as a historical product, a thing of slow, natural growth. To the Conservative, wrote Hearnshaw, 'the great community to which he belongs . . . is a living entity, albeit of a psychological rather than a physical type; a spiritual organism to which every individual in the community belongs' (1933).

Right is a function of time rather than of present rationality. 'Life', as David Clarke expressed it, 'is a process and progress is made by each generation adding its contribution without destroying what has gone before' (Clarke, 1973: 6). To the Conservative this is both a description and a normative observation. To try to work against the accumulated wisdom of generations is the ultimate conceit and bound to fail. As Aubrey Jones recorded, 'there is more than an even chance that the generations of the past, swaying now to this now to that side of the see-saw, will in the end have struck the true balance of authority and power, and that it is this that is handed down to us. The balance, after all, cannot be attained in a generation; there is no mechanical secret which will give it; it is the product of time and of nothing but time' (Jones, 1946: 160–1). Rash reform offers the prospect of injustice and failure. The Conservative eschews such reform, accepting both the organic nature of society and, concomitantly, the imperfections of man. This necessarily delimits the ambitions of government. In the words of the 1979 Conservative manifesto, 'we want to work *with the grain* of human nature'; to do otherwise is to court disaster.

The analogy with an organism has, as Lincoln Allison has noted, both negative and positive connotations. Negatively, by stressing the complex interrelationships between the parts of the organism, it emphasises the difficulties attached to achieving change. On the positive side it stresses that the individual is part of an entity with a character of its own beyond the complete control of conscious plans. 'His incorporation into this larger entity gives his life meaning, place and purpose. It makes him belong' (Allison, 1984: 16–17).

This incorporation extends to classes as well as individuals and also to the different institutions of society. They have grown over time and provide the linkages that hold the polity together. They have a purpose that transcends their individual existence. 'The stability of state and society', recorded Philip Buck (1975: 26), 'is based upon [the] accumulation of rules and precedents, built up through centuries of experience. The balanced elements of the British constitution – monarchy, parliament, Cabinet, courts and the rule of law – have been created by a long process of historical growth. Similarly, the classes of society, their relation to each other, and their place in the unity of the community as a whole have been gradually developed.'

Acceptance of change

Given that society is viewed as evolutionary and not static, a necessary consequence is an acceptance of change. However, that same perception dictates a particular kind of change. Change that is wholesale and threatens the existing fabric of society is anathema to the Conservative. So too is change for change's sake. The purpose of change must be to improve that which exists, to correct proven and palpable ills, doing so in order to preserve – not destroy – the existing social fabric. 'Change should come in small gradations; by way of evolution not revolution; by adaptation and not destruction' (Gash, 1977: 27).

The Conservative attitude to change is most pithily summed up in Burke's aphorism: 'a state without the means of some change is without the means of its conservation' (see Hill, 1975: 285). Indeed, it was Burke – in responding to the French revolution – who provided the most cogent articulation of the belief in an evolutionary rather than a static society. Change was natural, intrinsic to any living body; but changes that were born not of the wisdom of past generations but of abstract notions offered a path to anarchy and destruction. The Terror in France appeared to justify all that Burke had written in his *Reflections on the Revolution in France* in 1790. Political life was being forced to conform to abstract rights and powers – a fault perpetrated by Royalists as well as Jacobins. France paid the price. Burke was writing in order to ensure that Britain did not. His work found a resonance. Within six years his tract had sold 300,000 copies.

In France the revolution had killed the body politic. In Britain its preservation required adaptations, born of an appreciation of what had gone before, change derived from experience and not from abstract reasoning. Hence, change in order to conserve, not to destroy (see Extract 4.1). Burke – a Whig –

Extract 4.1

Edmund Burke argued cogently that some change may be necessary, but that change should be carried through in order to preserve and not to destroy:

Our people will find employment enough for a truly patriotic, free, and independent spirit, in guarding what they possess, from violation. I would not exclude alteration either [of the Constitution]; but even when I changed, it should be to preserve. I should be led to my remedy by a great grievance. In what I did, I should follow the examples of our ancestors. I would make the reparation as nearly as possible in the style of the building. A politic caution, a guarded circumspection, a moral rather than a complexional timidity were among the ruling principles of our forefathers in their most dedicated conduct.

(Burke, *Reflections on the Revolution in France*, in O'Brien, 1969 [first pub. 1790]: 375–6)

Extract 4.2

The Conservative is wary of change but will accept it if the need is proven:

We have in view, not Man, but Englishmen; not ideal politics, but the British Constitution; not Political Economy, but the actual course of our trade. Through this great forest of fact, this tangle of old and new, these secular oaks, sturdy shrubs, beautiful parasitic creepers, we move with a prudent diffidence, following the old tracks, endeavouring to keep them open, but hesitating to cut new routes till we are clear as to the goal for which we are asked to sacrifice our finest timber. Fundamental changes we regard as exceptional and pathological. Yet, being bound by no theories, when we are convinced of their necessity, we inaugurate them boldly and carry them through to the end.

('Reuben Mendoza, A Conservative', in Dickinson, 1955
[first pub. 1905]: 44–5)

provided the reasoning for this disposition; Sir Robert Peel was the first Conservative to apply it.

In the Tamworth manifesto, as we have seen, Peel made clear that he was not a defender 'of abuses or the enemy of judicious reforms', therein embodying the essence of the Conservative approach to change. Proven and gross abuses, if allowed to fester, constitute a greater threat to society than do attempts to remedy them; but reforms need to be judicious, born of reflection and an understanding of the environment in which they are to take place. Abuses must be proven abuses. Where proven, Conservatives are not afraid to take action. Indeed, unencumbered by great theories, they can move quickly (see Extract 4.2); but such moves are rare and must be the product of clear need and some deliberation. Conservatives are wary of calls for reform born of transient fashions, for which the evidence is insubstantial. Conservative leaders, as we have seen, have been willing to entertain constitutional changes when the need has been clear, but when it is not, the reaction is instinctively cautious and – in the case of blueprints for a new constitution – hostile.

Law, order and authority ③

It is a Conservative axiom that there must be order and discipline in society, and that this should flow from a deep respect for the institutions of state and society. 'Order rests on the exercise of authority, on its embodiment in the institutions of society and on the acceptance of those institutions as legitimate' (Clarke, 1973: 11). The role of institutions is functional and symbolic: they represent continuity with the past and they embody the unity of society and the norms of conduct of that society. Institutions are thus central to the maintenance of order, but their authority derives from not being all-powerful:

they are subject to the rule of law, which regulates definitively the relations between citizens. The rule of law applies equally to the governors and the governed. Equality under the law is what Conservatives believe to be vital, not economic or social equality. When injustice arises the cause usually 'is not so much the content of the law as a failure to apply it impartially' (Patterson, 1973: 16). A stable social order is thus dependent upon the maintenance of the rule of law.

Order, thus defined, is a condition of freedom. It is an order born of relationships and structures that allow individuals to go about their affairs without undue interference from others. Society is diverse. There are natural inequalities. Men and women have different abilities, pleasures and interests. To try to make them equal by dictation from above is to try to impose a universal order that is impossible and a denial of the freedom through order shown by Conservatives. To the Conservative, order – born of adherence to the rule of law – provides a basic framework within which citizens can interact, pursue their own pleasures, achieve their own goals and ambitions, without direction from above. In essence, a society characterised by Oakeshott as 'societas' – entailing a tolerance of diversity in social life and a natural harmony born of the 'conversation of mankind' – as opposed to a Utopian 'universitas', seeking some centrally imposed future goal to which all must strive.

The rule of law, then, is central to Conservative thought, providing a bulwark against arbitrary government. Law itself is a reflection of the values of society and hence derived from something more substantial than the transient whims of governments, and its universal and impartial application ensures that society is not dependent upon the arbitrary will of the powerful. The rule of law holds institutions to their responsibilities and is a prerequisite of a stable community. 'Knowledge of the legal limits of individual activity – which only derive from actual experience of how people must compromise to live in harmony – is essential to freedom. The rule of law provides that essential breathing space of predictability and security of redress which is at the heart of liberty' (Norton and Aughey, 1981: 27).

Property ownership

'The possession of property by the individual', declared Quintin Hogg in *The Case for Conservatism* in 1947 – echoing Burke more than 150 years previously – 'is the essential condition of liberty.' To the Conservative the ownership of property, in whatever form, assumes an almost mystical quality. It is deemed essential to human freedom and social stability.

Property is seen as an extension of personality. 'No man is fully free', declared Hogg, 'unless possessing some rights of property in something, since property is the means whereby he develops his personality by impressing it upon his external surrounds without dependence on the will of others' (Hogg, 1947: 99). Property is a joy, something to be developed in one's own image. It ensures a sense of belonging and, concomitantly, imparts duties as well as rights. 'The right to the enjoyment of property carries the corresponding duty not to use it in ways that infringe the enjoyment and dignity of others. While this applies most obviously to the use of land, it must guide also the owners of industry in relation both to their environment and to their employees' (Clarke, 1973: 13). It also provides the means of protecting one's family, contributing towards both a stable environment and provision for the future, as well as a vital stimulus. 'Property', declared Clinton Rossiter, 'provides the main incentive for productive work. Human nature being what it is and always will be, the desire to acquire and hold property is essential to progress' (quoted in Harbour, 1982: 150–1).

The ownership of property also contributes to stability. It imparts a sense of responsibility and a desire to protect one's possessions; part of that responsibility resides in recognising the desire of others to protect *their* possessions. It also imparts a necessary bulwark against the over-mighty state. To vest all property in the state would be to leave the citizen naked in confronting tyranny. The private ownership of property helps diffuse economic power and ensures the independence of the owner. Such independence, as Rossiter noted, can never be achieved by one who has to rely on others for shelter and material comforts. 'Property gives him a place on which to stand and make choices; it grants him a sphere in which he may ignore the state' (quoted in Harbour, 1982: 150).

That ownership will be unevenly spread – necessarily so, since enforced equality would negate the benefits derived from ownership (most notably the stimulus to productive endeavours) and vest too much distributive power in the hands of the state. Property, to the Conservative, is not to be seen in quantitative terms of equal distribution but in qualitative terms. Man's needs will differ; so too will his abilities to realise them. What is important is the quest for, and achievement of, property, even though the size and nature of that property will vary, perhaps enormously. 'An Englishman's home is his castle' may not be true in a physical sense (except for a few), but to the Conservative it is true in a vital, psychological sense. Without such castles, the state is free to plunder.

Strong but limited government

Conservatives accord a role to government, but for particular purposes. They are, as we have seen, wary of government, especially government bent on the realisation of abstract designs. Unfettered government is a threat to liberty. Consequently limited government should be realised through a series of checks and balances, both formal checks and balances within the nation's constitution and informally through checks and balances throughout society, through the maintenance of multiple and complex small battalions, such as civic societies, cricket clubs, Women's Institutes and charitable bodies. A plural society is a *sine qua non* of limited government.

Although limited, there must nevertheless be government. Government is necessary in order to fulfil those enduring tasks which government alone may fulfil: essentially defence of the realm abroad and maintenance of the Queen's Peace at home. It is also necessary in order to intervene to prevent or check abuse when there is a demonstrable need to do so. Conservatives have never rejected strong government, as long as the use of power has been justified by the special circumstances of the case. It may be necessary in order to repel enemies, as in wartime. It may be necessary – as perceived by the government of Margaret Thatcher – in order to create the conditions in which the free interplay of market forces may be achieved (see Gamble, 1988; Norton, 1987d). However, even strong government is, and must be, accountable. Government must be permitted to govern – indeed, some degree of autonomy is essential if it is to govern free of vested interests – but it must be answerable, and in Britain it is, as it has been for several centuries, answerable to the political community through the medium of Parliament (see Norton, 1987a). Parliament is an essential body in ensuring both the effectiveness of government, constituting, as it has done for most of its history, a policy influencing rather than a policy making assembly (Norton, 1987c) and the maintenance of consent, citizens recognising as legitimate the process through which public policy is determined and authorised. The political culture of England has historically favoured, and indeed produced, such a relationship between government and Parliament, and Conservatives are instinctively sceptical of grand schemes of reform designed to upset the subtle and delicate relationship borne of history and confirmed by the Glorious Revolution of 1688. Unlike the United States, history has ensured that Britain has not required a written constitution, bestowing it instead with a part-written but uncodified constitution that permits evolutionary adaptability while maintaining the essential checks and balances necessary to a free society. Conservatives are content to stand on what Burke described as 'the firm ground of the British constitution'.

'One Nation' at home

There are two aspects to the Conservative perception of 'One Nation'. One is the 'oneness' of the nation in terms of avoiding sectional preferences. The other is the scope of the 'nation'. The first entails policies designed to achieve some degree of social harmony. The other entails a commitment to the Union.

The concept of 'One Nation', though not the term itself, was added to the lexicon of Conservative thought by Disraeli. The Conservative Party was, as he recognised, 'national or it is nothing'. His contribution was to give it that national appeal, extending its appeal beyond the landed classes and emphasising that which united rather than divided the nation.

The essence of 'One Nation' in domestic affairs was encapsulated in his speech at Crystal Palace in 1872, committing the party to the maintenance of institutions 'and the improvement of the conditions of the people'. That improvement took place through a diverse range of measures of social reform, none unduly radical but significant in combination (see Chapter 1). The measures themselves were not the product of a clearly developed programme and Disraeli himself had little interest in applying himself to particular proposals. His Home Secretary, Richard Cross, found him 'above or below mere questions of detail' (Southgate, 1977: 186), but what he did was to carve out for the party an appeal beyond the boundaries of landed interests, articulating a commitment that not only demonstrated the soundness of the party to all classes but also providing inspiration to future generations of Conservatives. Measures of prudent social reform have been a feature of successive Conservative governments (Bellairs, 1977), Neville Chamberlain in particular carving out a substantial programme while Minister of Health in the 1920s (see Chapter 2). It was in introducing the Widows' and Orphans' and Old Age Pensions Act 1925 that Chamberlain expressed the essential purpose of such reforms. 'Our policy', he declared, 'is to use the great resources of the state, not for the distribution of an indiscriminate largesse, but to help those who have the will and desire to raise themselves to higher and better things' (quoted in Bellairs, 1977: 31).

Conservatives, then, acknowledge a role for the state in social provision, but a role that is not unbounded. By providing a safety net for those that are most in need helps provide a basis for returning to self-dependence and contributes to social stability; but the role of the state must necessarily be limited. 'Conservatives will wish to look to social improvement, but will not hesitate to point to the limits of its effectiveness' (Jones, 1946: 166). Total provision by the state is to create the over-mighty state and to kill the stimulus to individual endeavour. Preferable to state provision is help by those individuals who take seriously their responsibilities as citizens and property-owners. 'For it is far better that a man should look for help to an employer to whom he stands in a personal relationship rather than to an impersonal state' (Jones, 1946: 166). The state, in short, is not the only, or even necessarily the most significant, contributor to the realisation of 'One Nation'.

The other aspect of 'One Nation' is a commitment to the Union (see Chapter 15). The United Kingdom has been formed through a series of incorporating unions. The Kingdom has generated a Britishness that transcends national identities. Conservatives cherish diversity and have avoided the imposition of any cultural or social uniformity within the Kingdom, arguing instead that the strength of the Kingdom derives from that very diversity. The loyalty within the Kingdom is to the constitutional processes that serve to provide balance and fairness, militating against national and regional conflicts. The unifying elements are Parliament, the Crown and a balanced constitution. In essence, as Arthur Aughey shows in Chapter 15, a very English idea – the commitment to parliamentary institutions – enveloped the other parts of the Union to generate a sense of Britishness and a constitutional patriotism. As Quintin Hogg noted:

> Free parliaments were in part the result of successful rebellion against the traditional kings. But Conservatives also rejoice in the fact that the course which events took in England enabled the British peoples to combine with the principle of reasonable discussion by representatives in Parliament the *mystique* and prestige of a traditional monarchy, symbolising the unity of the nation above party strife and the respect and majesty of the law and lawful authority over individual opinion. (Hogg, 1947: 34)

Disraeli brought the two strands together, with the social dimension providing an integrative element in the Union without threatening the distinctiveness of the different parts. The Conservative 'One Nation' provided a safety net and not an identikit citizen dependent on the state.

'One Nation' abroad

Conservatives place special stress on the need to defend and promote Britain's interests abroad. The party, they believe, embodies the traditions of the nation and has a unique perception of British interests in foreign affairs. They have little interest in moral crusades or the advocacy of universal brotherhood. Conservative statesmanship entails defending or advancing the real interests of Britain in the world, informed by a respect for other countries. 'The function of an enlightened foreign policy', declared Lord Hugh Cecil (1912: 211), 'is to uphold national greatness with due regard to the place of other nations in the world.' National strength is important; a nation can only have self-respect if it is strong and respected internationally, and if it has the power to influence world affairs.

Disraeli, as we have seen (Chapter 1), played the imperial card, associating the party with the defence of the Empire. Empire was the projection of British greatness on a world scale. It provided a source of inspiration – appealing to the patriotism that transcended all classes – and an opportunity for Britain to exert a Christian, civilising influence over a quarter of the globe. Its death knell was to be sounded less than a century later. The Second World War left Britain unable to maintain its economic commitment to its far-flung territories while at the same time transferring leadership of the Western world to a nation espousing the cause of anti-colonialism. Coming to terms with the change was a difficult one for the party. Not until the 1970s did it find a substitute for Empire as a vehicle for exerting its influence on the world stage: the European Community. To Edward Heath, the Prime Minister responsible for British entry, membership of the Community would 'give Britain back her place in the world ' (Laing, 1972: 248).

The projection of British influence on an international, if possible global, basis remains central to Conservative thinking, a strong defence providing the basis for confidence and for uniting the nation. The Conservative appeal to patriotism has often been the ace in the party's electoral pack.

Wealth creation

Conservatives have always accepted the importance of creating wealth. Burke had been influenced by liberal economic theory and wrote, in *Thoughts and Details on Scarcity*, that 'the laws of commerce' were 'the terms of nature and consequently the laws of God'. The acceptance of the imperatives of capital accumulation was to be subsequently secularised and given greater emphasis as a consequence of the late nineteenth-century haemorrhage of Liberal support to the Conservative Party.

Central to wealth creation is the belief in the superiority of market forces over government intervention. Government intervention, it is argued, can only lead to inefficiency, monopoly and a decline in the ability of the nation to compete internationally. Allowing the free interplay of market forces is both a guarantee of individual freedom and an essential dynamic of national prosperity. Market forces allow flexibility in responding to changing resources and consumer demands. Generating wealth produces employment and often necessitates pouring resources into local areas, imparting a dynamic that centrally provided funds (and direction) can never achieve. Such wealth generation entails, indeed is a product of, inequalities in wealth. Such inequalities encourage those with limited wealth to emulate and surpass those who have generated greater wealth. Imposed equality kills individual initiative and the stimulus to produce more. Government activity is thus necessarily limited:

> Conservative wisdom is to allow intervention in this natural order of work and remuneration only in order to strengthen its generation of wealth, to prevent abuse and to achieve a satisfactory balance between the human elements in production. The role of the state is to conserve the natural order based upon the realities of capitalist production, and that of course means protecting the inequalities in the possession of private wealth. (Norton and Aughey, 1981: 33)

The purpose of government is to maintain the social disciplines of capitalism, not to run the economy.

Principles into practice

The Conservative Party in the twentieth century can thus boast significant and recognisable tenets. They provide a corpus of thought that establishes the party as a more thoughtful and complex entity than critics have often made it out to be. To be a Conservative means something other than simply a desire to win elections and to preserve the existing order of things.

How, then, are the tenets of Conservative thought translated into practice? What does Conservatism mean in hard policy terms? In translating thought into public policy, there are obvious problems.

One is that the basic tenets of Conservative thought do not themselves lead unambiguously to specific measures of public policy. What *precisely* is needed in order to achieve the domestic goal of 'One Nation'? The concept is one that has meant something to succeeding generations of Conservatives, but – as already noted – it was not well defined by its progenitor. It was the child of romanticism and political ingenuity (see O'Sullivan, 1976: 99–103); and at what point is strong government necessary?

In terms of political measures it is much easier for Conservatives to say what they are against than it is to say what they are for. If there is an attack on the property rights of citizens, if there is a challenge to the rule of law or if there is an attempt to abolish a central, functioning institution of the British polity, then Conservatives know where they stand. Such certainty in reacting to attacks has served to emphasise the Conservative attachment to continuity, suggesting at times – in popular perception – an indifference to the need for change, and over time suggesting a party that responds but never leads. Recent critics within the party itself – such as Sir Keith (later Lord) Joseph in the 1970s – have argued that such a response has served to favour the party's opponents, the party moving to conserve that which its opponents have variously introduced – what Sir Keith termed as 'the ratchet effect of Socialism'. Such a reactive stance, it is argued, has also left the party looking shapeless, its stance on political issues being determined by whatever its opponents seek to promote.

Could not the problem be resolved by the basic tenets of Conservative thought being subject to greater analysis and philosophical definition? Perhaps even by the generation of an over-arching theory? Basically, no. For to engage in such an exercise would be to deny the very thing which is being investigated. Conservative scepticism does not permit such grand exercises. There is no shining vision of society which politicians can or should pursue. Conservative statesmen, in grappling with the issues of the day, are informed by their basic tenets of belief, not dictated by some abstract theory divorced from the harsh realities of life.

Even if such an exercise were to be found palatable it would face another inherent difficulty: the basic tenets of Conservative thought are not necessarily compatible with one another. Indeed, within the tenets we have identified three separate but interrelated tensions may be discerned. One is between continuity and change. Conservatives are concerned with the here and now, with the maintenance of institutions and with the preservation of order; there is a natural tendency to protect and preserve, to nurture the existing society. However, they also recognise the need for some change, for occasional intervention by government, for some dislocation in order to create wealth. Burke, as we have noted, recognised that some change was necessary in order to conserve, but the enduring conundrum for Conservatives is determining the point at which change is necessary. If change is not necessary then it is necessary not to change. The need for change must be clear but there are no hard rules, no prescriptive criteria, that determine at what point the need for change has been proven. The different emphases within Conservative thought ensure that at times some Conservatives are disposed towards accepting the need for change while others harbour no such disposition.

The second tension may be subsumed within that of continuity and change but has a distinct character of its own, and that is the tension between the free market emphasis of wealth creation and the willingness to contemplate government intervention. The emphasis on the organic nature of society, on the need to maintain social order and to achieve a harmony between the different elements of society – in other words, 'One Nation' – dispose the Conservative towards accepting government intervention in order to achieve social harmony. Conservative governments have variously proved willing to engage in such intervention. However, the Conservative is also sceptical of government, recognising its limitations and its potential for evil. The emphasis on the need to achieve wealth creation leads to the preference for government to withdraw from the marketplace. Such a withdrawal, it is argued, is in the long-term interests of the nation, albeit at the potential short-term expense of social disharmony. For most Conservatives the quest has been to find a balance between the two emphases. For some, the two are mutually exclusive.

The third tension is essentially a corollary of the second and that is the tension between the individual and society. To the Conservative, society is organic and something beyond the control of conscious plans. It is greater than the collection of individuals that inhabit it. Nonetheless there is a recognition, indeed a vital recognition, that society is comprised of individuals and that those individuals are different, necessarily so. However, the problem arises that there is, in a part of the free market thinking acquired in the late nineteenth century, a particular emphasis on the individual to the extent that the role of society is diminished or denied altogether. The emphasis on the autonomous individual – what Allison (1984: 12) has termed the extreme form of 'marketism' – is rare within the Conservative Party but it informs part of a particular strand of thought within the party. It was less rare in the 1980s, with some vocal adherents both inside and outside the party. Its advocacy has generated a dialogue and tensions within Conservative discourse.

That such tensions exist few Conservatives would deny. Their recognition of them derives not from philosophical reflection (except for a very few) but rather, as we shall see (Chapter 5), from observation and a knowledge of the party's history. As we have seen in earlier chapters the party has variously split, the attempt to achieve a balance between continuity and change not achieving immediate success. The divisions within the party have on occasion been severe and, as we have seen, near-disastrous. Yet, while regretting the political effect of splits, the party also recognises the value of such tensions. They are sometimes creative tensions. For the party, the task is one of achieving balance. The basic scepticism of Conservatism ensures that no one view of society is accepted unquestioningly as being the 'right' one. Conservatives must temper one emphasis against another, applying whichever appears relevant to the circumstances of the case. By such a process the most appropriate policy is likely to emerge. What Aubrey Jones (1946: 160) perceived in the nature of society – 'there is more than an even chance that the generations of the past, swaying now to this now to that side of the see-saw, will in the end have struck the true balance of authority and power' – is seen also as a feature of the living entity of the Conservative Party. Although generating tensions such a process also permits flexibility, the party responding as seems appropriate to the particular problem being confronted, rather than applying mechanically policy derived from a philosophic straitjacket. This flexibility has formed an important part – but only a part – of the party's genius to win elections.

CHAPTER 5

Philosophy and faction

Arthur Aughey

The events of recent years, recounted in Chapter 3, have made Lord Kilmuir's view, so long cited as a truism, that the Conservative Party's secret weapon is loyalty, appear rather ridiculous. The bitter divisions on European policy have suggested either of two things. First, that Kilmuir's view belongs to a previous age when the party understood the meaning of trust, authority and honour and what is more acted on that understanding. Secondly, that it was never true, that Conservative divisions were formerly concealed from the public and that what has changed is that the media are more adept at revealing and reporting them. This chapter examines this question in terms of a number of oppositions – unity and division, party and principle, nature and history, people and measures. It identifies a number of strands of Conservative thought and concludes by considering the current acrimony over Europe in terms of the history of that issue within the party.

Unity and division

In October 1993 John Major reminded his party conference how Conservatives are expected to behave. 'We have our agreements in public', he told representatives, 'and our disagreements in private.' What Major asserted is a concise exposition of the 'traditional family model' of the Conservative Party (see Chapter 9). It was a model recognised by Maurice Edelman in his novel *The Minister*. He has the Tory Stour-Benson tell the Labour MP Yates; 'We believe in keeping our differences within the family' (Edelman, 1964: 47). This understanding of the party has been exceptionally influential with journalists, academics and even with politicians of all parties. The reason for this influence is simple. The model or analogy renders accurately an ideal of Conservative political culture and, more importantly, the key wisdom of Conservative practice.

The cultural ideal of Conservative politics is one of loyalty and harmony. It is of course a myth, albeit a venerable myth. If the Conservative Party understands itself to be a family then it has never been a particularly happy family.

Bulpitt, for instance, notes that while there 'are aspects of the family in the Party's make-up . . . it was never a family in which the members had, or wanted, much to do with each other' (Bulpitt, 1991: 9). Yet, as Coleridge once argued, a political ideal 'has real existence, and does not the less exist in reality, because it both is, and exists as, an idea' (Coleridge, 1972 [first pub. 1830]: 9). The assumption that the unity of the party and the continuity of its purpose are the common objectives of all members and the further expectation that everyone will act according to those objectives is the cultural context in which disputes within the party have been conducted. This culture is not the product of personal affection. Calculation of political interest is the main consideration. Nevertheless, the injunction against 'letting the side down' has often as much force as that against 'shaming the family'. The 'rally round' syndrome exerts a powerful institutional force. As Julian Critchley once observed, Conservatives 'have never believed it necessary to love one another, in order to dislike the other side' (1973: 402). Whether individuals or groups within the party like one another or not it is felt that they ought to pull together against the 'enemy'. This was an appeal which was made frequently by John Major's team in the leadership election of July 1995.

Critchley went on to identify the key wisdom of Conservative practice which is also the wisdom which helps to foster that aspect of party culture we have just discussed. Conservatives, he asserted, 'have always known that the object of political activity is power, and that sustained and obvious disunity would oblige us to relinquish it'. This practical wisdom has traditionally acted as a limit to division. It has been a factor of cohesion and a focus for action. Of course, it is not a wisdom which is the exclusive property of the Conservative Party. Labour leaders are also concerned to maintain the unity of their party and for precisely the same reason. What experience has shown hitherto is that the Conservative Party simply has been more effective in sustaining cohesion and more successful in containing divisions than its opponents. Culturally and organisationally the party has tried to innoculate itself against the virus of faction-fighting and ideological splitting. One important factor in this experience is the organisation of the Conservative Party itself which, unlike the Labour Party, stresses the authority of leadership rather than the democracy of opinion. Conscious of sounding rather smug, William Deedes noted how difficult it was sometimes for a Conservative to keep and to convey a sense of proportion when writing of divisions within the party. 'It would be boastful and misleading to claim that the differences between us, which tend to be miscellaneous, are of the scale and grandeur of those which so exercise the Labour Party' (Deedes, 1973: 391).

That was in 1973. Deedes' proposition that the differences between Conservatives were only miscellaneous and not concerted repeated the conventional wisdom, established in the 1960s by Richard Rose, that the Conservative Party was a party of 'tendencies' – fluctuating alignments on specific issues – and not of 'factions' – stable, self-conscious, programmatic groups (Rose,

1964: 33–46). That is a proposition which is difficult to accept uncritically today. Indeed, the historian John Barnes has called it 'erroneous' and argued that 'factionalism has been endemic in the party' (Barnes, 1994: 342–3). It might be more balanced to say that all generalisations about political institutions are contingent. Circumstances rule and circumstances change. The times can call forth factions within the party sufficient to contradict both its cultural ideal of general loyalty and its practical wisdom of public unity. Barnes, however, is correct to argue that no satisfactory account of the Conservative Party can ignore the part played in its history by factions. On the other hand, as he himself intimates, the existence of Conservative factionalism makes the party's historic achievement of containing the effects of division (electoral defeat) and of promoting the cause of unity (electoral success) that much more striking.

Party and principle

In this debate about the claims of unity and the tendency towards division Conservatives provide a distinct example of that permanent tension in political life between political ideas and political practice. In a recent study, Conservative members were asked whether their party should stick by its principles, even if that meant losing an election. Eighty-one per cent said it should. As the researchers concluded:

This suggests that down at the grass roots there exists a party which is keen to retain its ideological distinctiveness, and is unwilling to make electoral compromises. But the precise nature of these principles is not easy to ascertain, since the Conservative party is often reticent about defining them. (Whiteley *et al.*, 1994: 52–3)

That is a judicious and balanced assessment, and it reveals that Conservatives today are still struggling with a question which is as old as the party itself and to which there *can* be no satisfactory answer. The question is: what is the relationship between political principle and party interest? The answers are usually contradictory.

For instance, the Benjamin Disraeli who once sought through his character Coningsby a virtuous response to the request: 'Before I support Conservative principles, I merely wish to be informed what those principles aim to conserve' was the same Benjamin Disraeli who later famously advised Edward Bulwer-Lytton: 'Damn your principles! Stick to your party.' Equally, the Enoch Powell who told South Kensington Young Conservatives in 1976 that all his life he understood a party to be 'a body of persons who hold, advocate, and desire to bring into effect certain political principles and policies' (Berkeley, 1978: 94) is the same Enoch Powell who had written in 1968 that Conservative principles were merely an abstraction from 'the way in which the Conservative Party views society and life and acts in politics in the history of this country' (Powell, 1968: 8). In both these examples it is suggested that, on the one hand, principles define what the party should do. On the other hand it is proposed that principles are only shorthand for what the party, or rather its leadership, actually does.

There is much room here for discord and disaffection. There is sufficient evidence of this discord and disaffection in the last two decades. Some may believe that the practice of the Conservative Party has become destructive of Conservative principle. Sir Keith (later Lord) Joseph once confessed that he had only become a real Conservative after 1974 despite having been an MP since 1956 and a Cabinet minister in the Heath Government from 1970–4. Until that time he had accepted the pragmatic drift of the party as it sought to occupy a notional 'middle ground' of British politics, a middle ground constantly shifting towards the left. Sir Keith's enunciation of true Conservatism helped create the conditions in which Mrs Thatcher became leader. She set about the task of trying to put those principles into practice (Letwin, 1992: 17–49).

Equally, there are those who believe that an obsession with Conservative principles may represent a real threat to the integrity and purpose of the Conservative Party. Sir Ian (later Lord) Gilmour found it difficult to accept the intellectual hubris of those, like Sir Keith and Mrs Thatcher, who were arguing 'that the whole Tory Party has been marching in the wrong direction for thirty years'. He went on:

> For another, there is some incongruity in a party which gives intellectual
> speculation a lower place in politics than do its opponents and which believes
> politics grow out of the needs, fears, hopes and wishes of the people and out of
> the demands of the time, coming to the conclusion that it has been intellectually in
> error since 1945. (Gilmour, 1977: 12)

The likelihood is that it is the 'principled' critic who is intellectually in error. It is a Conservative rule of thumb – a traditional Burkean assumption – that the individual is foolish but the species (or the party) is wise. The historical irony in Gilmour's case is that in a later book, *Dancing with Dogma*, he himself was to argue that while he had remained true to traditional Tory principles the party had deviated in a false 'Thatcherite' direction for more than 15 years (1992: 3). In this engagement of charge and counter-charge the cynic might have some sympathy with the view that 'politicians do not pick up ideas because they like them, but because they need them'; that is, principles are useful to them in order to advance their own agendas (Bulpitt, 1991: 27).

Arguments within Conservatism will always be conducted in these large and general terms, between critics who believe that the party has taken leave of its principles and those who believe that critics of the party have taken leave of their senses. The insults exchanged between the leadership and the nine 'whipless' rebels in the winter of 1994 and the spring of 1995 (see Chapter 8) were couched in such language of betrayal and madness. While arguments like these can split the party and severely damage its credibility, the instinct of members and the culture of the organisation operate against such an outcome. As the excellent study by Whiteley *et al.* (1994) would seem to show, Conservatives in the constituencies are less than willing to make absolute distinctions between principle and party. Their 'idea' of party is neither one of organisation nor one of principle but both.

In this broader view our Disraelian or Powellite 'contradictions' are more apparent than real. If there were a practical consensus it would be this. Of course the party must have its principles but those principles will be damned if the party does not stick together. Of course the party exists to implement certain principles but these principles do not matter a damn without the Conservative Party to implement them. Such a common-sense approach can never resolve the dilemma but it does help to temper it. For instance, while he acknowledged that the party was not immune from quite antagonistic and bitter exchanges between members, John Biffen also noted the importance of that cultural restraint we mentioned above. 'The Tory approach to politics is such that compromise is considered, if not virtuous, at least good form' (Biffen, 1961: 259). This convention of 'good form' has been a valuable custom. Rather like the Church of England with which it has been compared, the Conservative Party has sought to contain 'conscience' within the breadth of its institution. It is suspicious of the demands of principled political puritanism although it may respect the puritans themselves. (Problems of discipline within the Conservative Party today may not be unrelated to problems of authority within the Church of England.) Indeed, what is interesting about the findings of Whiteley *et al.* is that the Thatcherite community of saints remains as much a minority confession in the constituencies as it is at Westminster (Whiteley *et al.*, 1994: ch. 6; see also Norton, 1990a). Such findings, however, invite the question: what is the ideological character of the Conservative Party and how does this character reveal itself in the forms of philosophy and faction?

Nature and history

The philosopher Michael Oakeshott proposed that we do not have a nature, we have a history. Such an anti-essentialist view is particularly appropriate to our understanding of the character of the Conservative Party. Acute observers of the party both from within and from without have identified in its contemporary form the features of its own history. For instance, Angus Maude described what he called the 'palaeontology' of Conservatism, namely that the Conservative Party:

> still contains within itself perfectly preserved and visible like the contents of archaeological strata, specimens from all its historical stages and acquisitions from the Liberals. It still comprehends virtually the entire 'landed interest' and the

Anglican believers in church and state. It preserves in vestiges of their former splendour the last territorial magnates of Grand Whiggery. It can show here and there a romantic of Disraeli's 'Young England' period and quite a number of reforming Tory Democrats of the era of Lord Randolph Churchill. It contains all types of businessmen acquired from the Liberals, including a few who still believe in competition and laissez-faire . . . (*Spectator* 15 March 1963)

As Maude concluded, the Conservative Party 'can digest almost anything and turn it to some account'. For Gilmour, the party was more like an archaeological site on which successive civilisations have left layers of remains, 'each layer being different from the others but having common characteristics imposed upon it by the geography and topography of the site' (Gilmour, 1977: 144).

A perceptive and critical outsider employed a less flattering analogy although he made substantially the same point. Conservative rhetoric, it was proposed, 'often embodies the driftwood of a rich and complex history. Few Conservatives probably know the ships from which the driftwood came, the incidents in which the slogans were important. . . . The rhetoric encouraged the loyalty of the old, and was an induction rite for the new' (Harris, 1972: 14). To take this analogy further one could suggest that the historical driftwood of ideas, for all its different shapes, has contributed significantly to the political buoyancy of the party this century. The character of the party is thus a product of a varied political inheritance.

Biffen captured this in a striking phrase when he wrote that the 'Tory Party is a coalition of interests in continual debate' (1961: 259). Debate and the intensity of that debate will change according to the issue. As the issues change over time so also will change the configuration of interests within the party and therefore the character of the coalition. We explore in Chapters 13 and 15, for instance, the declining salience of the imperial and Ulster Unionist interests but also the way in which those interests may linger and still influence the politics of the party. Of course, the membership of the party will also change and this will have a vital effect on both image and policy. As Andrew Adonis has argued, 'if much in "conservatism" is constant, the Tories' perception of their ability to marry it with politically marketable programmes has changed over the century' (Adonis, 1994: 151). He went on to observe that while it is difficult to identify a single Conservative generational attitude to specific issues, social change can have 'a dramatic impact on the style and approach of the party'. In particular, the politics of Thatcherism was in large part due to a Conservative elite 'more assured in its rapport with the electorate, and more confident of its ability to sustain its support, than any in the party's modern history' (Adonis, 1994: 162–3).

Since the party has no single nature but only a complex history of personalities and interests, students of Conservatism have tried in a variety of ways to capture the component parts of that coalition of interests and to define as exactly as possible what it is that they contribute to the continuing debate. Because it is a human institution and not an ideological absolute there has been large scope for the free play of the intellectual imagination; and because it is a human institution there is usually enough personal and historical evidence to substantiate some of the claims made on behalf of these analyses. The problem is not whether these definitions are valid or not, intelligible or not. Questions do arise, however, about their comprehensiveness and the extent to which they can convey not only the controversies of the moment but also their historical lineage. It will suffice to mention three examples of these attempts to characterise the diversity of views within the party.

Robert Behrens made a distinction according to dispositions toward change, between those who are diehard and those who are ditchers (Behrens, 1980). W. H. Greenleaf divided the party into the philosophical categories of paternalists and libertarians (Greenleaf, 1983). In a lighter vein, Hugh Montgomery-Massingberd differentiated between the classes, between 'heavy swells', 'landed gents' and the *omnium gatherum* 'group threes' (*Daily Telegraph* 5 January 1991). Such generalisations are as much art as they are science and the art lies in a sense of proportion.

Strands of Conservative thought

Attempts to categorise strands of Conservatism have often suffered from a lack of such proportion, mainly by their too intimate association with practical politics. Too often the categorisation has had to do with attempts to distinguish 'good' Conservatives from 'bad' Conservatives and to attach these distinctions to policy issues of the moment. This has been activity found not only on the Left of British politics but also on the Right (see, e.g., Russel, 1978 and Gilmour, 1992). The author of this chapter and the editor of this book together tried to state a more neutral and less engaged categorisation of Conservative styles (Norton and Aughey, 1981: ch. 2). Our approach distilled and adapted from many Conservative sources, both historical and contemporary, four strands of 'Toryism'. Toryism we defined as that disposition which is concerned with the conditions of a just political order that can answer the needs of the nation. These strands were Pessimistic Toryism, Paternalistic Toryism, Progressive Toryism and Combative Toryism. Their concerns have provided much of the impassioned rhetoric of Conservative politics.

These political concerns, we argued, have been also bound up with theories of economic policy. Abridging from a rather complex web of propositions about political economy, two reasonably consistent traditions of economic argument were identified. We termed these the Whig strands after the somewhat different distinction made by Lord Coleraine (see Coleraine, 1970). These strands were 'corporate Whiggery', which emphasises the role that governments should play in ensuring the dynamic equilibrium of modern capitalism, and 'neo-Liberalism', which emphasises the virtues of free markets and limited government regulation.

Pessimistic Toryism is often wistfully nostalgic, tending to subscribe to the myth of a golden age when society and political life were more virtuous and from which present standards have drastically fallen. Generally, however penetrating its criticisms of present conditions, the pessimistic strand of thought lacks any clearly defined alternative to what exists. It would hold with Lord Eldon's position on the 1832 Reform Act that the best way forward is backwards. It would not be surprised when Conservative leaders fail to act on such wisdom. The recent, fatally botched proposal, to get 'back to basics' (Chapter 3) confirmed that pessimism. Against fashion, as Lord Salisbury once said, it is almost impossible to argue.

The *paternalistic* strand in Conservatism is a modern expression of a tradition of *noblesse oblige*. It never questions the assumption that there is a natural aristocracy in society and that such social distinctions are essential to order and happiness in the state. It accepts, however, that privilege entails obligation and that as a matter of prudence as well as duty the governors have a responsibility for the welfare of the people. It is the voice of One Nation Toryism (see Chapter 4). This paternalistic strand of Conservatism Samuel Beer believed was crucial to the party's rapid adaptation to the demands of welfare state politics after 1945 (Beer, 1965). Its spirit was expressed recently by the late Lord Stockton (formerly Harold Macmillan) who thought that privatisation meant 'selling off the family silver'.

Progressive Toryism is concerned to make Conservative politics relevant to contemporary demands and yet to retain enough of its principles and traditions to ensure a sense of continuity with the past. It has been concerned to relieve the party of unnecessary encumbrances and lumber inherited from specific commitments and interests of the past. It treads a very narrow line between principle and opportunism. For most of the post-war era its adherents were defined by a common belief that the state had an important role in ensuring a fair distribution of wealth and in promoting the economic strength of the nation. The 'wets', as advocates of this strand of thought became known in the 1980s, suffered a series of major defeats under Mrs Thatcher and their progressivism came to look rather *passé*. Yet its concern to make sure that the Conservative Party does not become narrowly based on the interests of the well-to-do was echoed in John Major's commitment to a 'classless' Britain.

Combative Toryism has tended towards populism and believes that Conservative values really are the people's values. It has little time for paternalism or progressivism if that is taken to mean making concessions to the philosophies of other parties. It has enough confidence to believe that it is not only possible to defend what one has but even to recover what has been conceded in moments of fahionable delusion. Combative Tories tend to see themselves as the true radicals in British politics. The conviction of combative Toryism, which is in conformity with its basic populism, is Powell's view that 'salvation lies within the group of people themselves; that, by their unhampered pursuit of their own insights, we shall forge ahead in the future just as we advanced in the past' (quoted in Utley, 1968: 95). A vital moral element in Thatcherism was this celebration of the 'vigorous virtues' of the British people (Letwin, 1992).

Corporate Whiggery views society as a partnership of economic interests between capital, labour and the state. It is the task of the state to ensure planned stability and an expansive equilibrium in the economy. Such an approach is deemed essential because of the interdependence of politics and economics and by the necessity of international competition. The state must intervene to co-ordinate economic activity and to ensure protection of the national interest in a hostile trading world. Michael Heseltine's promise as President of the Board of Trade to intervene before breakfast, lunch and dinner if it were for the good of Britain was a contemporary restatement of the corporate Whig's key principle.

Neo-Liberalism asserts that the state should play only a very limited role in the economic affairs of the nation. It does not deny that intervention may be valuable in specific instances; but it is predisposed towards limiting such intervention because it believes market forces to be superior to political direction. Economic prosperity is not in the gift of politicians, nor is it to be found in cosy deals between the state and vested economic interests. It is only to be found in the decisions of those in business who respond accurately and intelligently to market signals. As Mrs Thatcher was fond of saying, 'you can't buck the market'.

The character of the Conservative Party at any one time in recent history has reflected the association and interplay of these strands. They are an ambiguous inheritance. They represent *either* the positive resources upon which a leader can draw *or* the negative tensions within the party which a leader must manage and control. These Tory and Whiggish categories were intended to give an insight into the history of the Conservative Party and not simply to provide a description of its contemporary status. They have been found to be reasonably accurate abridgements of Conservative attitudes in more recent scientific surveys of party opinion, even though these studies have modified the definitions (see, e.g., Crewe and Searing, 1988 and Whiteley *et al.*, 1994; for the modifications of the latter, see Chapter 7).

People and measures

Some of these historic ideas and interests sit uneasily one with another. Some are entirely contradictory. This is the common ground upon which factions and tendencies, groups and clubs, will take root. The task of Conservative leadership is therefore to provide coherent and cohesive leadership to an institution which embraces a diversity of interests, attitudes and prejudices. This is never an easy task as divisions over India, Suez, Northern Ireland and Europe (for example) have shown. Sometimes – over the Corn Laws, over

Tariff Reform and, again, possibly over European Union – it has proved an impossible task. The distinction between party and principle is one way in which such arguments may be understood. Another is to understand them as the sometimes tense association of distinctive strands of thought. A final way, with an equally long tradition in Conservative politics, is to consider them in terms of the distinction between people and measures. This helps us to get to grips with the politics of faction within the party and their consequences for party unity.

Disraeli's youthful criticism that the party leadership consisted of Tory men and Whig measures has been a *leitmotif* of Conservative argument for a century and a half. As we have seen, it was the criticism which Sir Keith Joseph and others made of the party in the mid-1970s. Those within the party who disagree with the authoritative trends of policy have a number of options of which the most critical would be three. First, they can try to build support within the party for their point of view and exert sufficient influence to change the men or women and therefore to change the measures. This is what Mrs Thatcher and her supporters were successful in doing in 1975 and what her opponents succeeded in doing in 1990. It is what Enoch Powell failed to do in the late 1960s and what, in different circumstances, John Redwood failed to do in 1995.

Secondly, they might accept that while the measures are indeed unacceptable to them, the good of the 'cause' and the continuation of, in particular, a Conservative government require their acquiescence. Here is a different formula of people and measures. Although the measures are offensive to particular interests and to cherished beliefs it is better that Conservatives put them into operation rather than the other side. Perhaps in that way the damage may be limited and the consequences of change made more palatable. With varying degrees of success, many Conservative changes were approached in this manner from the passage of Disraeli's Reform Act of 1867 to the passage of Major's Bill on Maastricht in 1993. In this case the men and women, and the influence they can assert to mitigate the effect of change, are ultimately more important than the measures which must come to pass. It depends on trusting the leader. This was a 'realist' view held with some consistency by Lord Salisbury at the end of the last century.

Thirdly, it may be the case that the importance of the measure and the distaste for those in office is so overwhelming that a split is inevitable. There may come a point in the affairs of the party when those such as Lord George Bentinck would say of Peel's 'betrayal' on the Corn Laws, we can stand anything but being sold and we break on this. There may come a point when ambitious personalities will think the time right to attach themselves to a principle whose time has come, as did Joseph Chamberlain on Tariff Reform. If there are no easy options for party members nor are there easy options for party leaders. What are the general circumstances which may help transform a tendency into a faction? What is it which changes the balanced association and intermingling of strands into a possible or actual split?

A rule of thumb would appear to be this. Whenever a reconsideration of Britain's role in the world is implicated in controversy about the character of the nation itself then the possibility of a dangerous convergence of dissent is immeasurably increased. This rule of thumb is based on what seems to have been common in the experience of major disputes over, for example, the Corn Laws, Tariff Reform, Suez and Europe. Hugh Berrington's study of Conservative revolts in the 1950s entered a suitable caveat about a simplistic division between 'those who combine domestic reform with internationalism being ranged on one side, and those who couple resentment of the Welfare State with a yearning for a 'robust' foreign policy confronting them on the other' (Berrington, 1961: 364). Yet he did note some overlap of domestic and foreign concerns, on Europe especially, which in the pace and stress of events might present difficulties for the party leadership. Norton's work on the party since the 1970s reveals the frequent interlinking of domestic and foreign issues in Conservative dissidence in the House of Commons (see, e.g., Norton 1978 and 1994c). The European issue is the current and most dramatic example of this.

Conclusion: the party and European Union

The issue of European policy, as we observe in Chapter 13, has been the source of much contention and dissent within the modern Conservative Party. As we note there, current arguments are far from novel. As Deedes predicted in 1973, the great political divide in the country would be broadly on this issue:

> how far the people of this cosy island are willing to exert and perhaps inconvenience themselves to close the steadily widening gap between ourselves and our European neighbours and rivals. Do we contract in, or do we contract out – accepting then, as I do not think we would readily do, a standard of living sharply below present levels? For reasons already plainly discernible, that could also be the great divide within the Conservative Party. (Deedes, 1973: 400)

What is novel is the circumstances. What appeared in the 1960s and 1970s to be the potential of a federal Europe now appears in the 1990s to be the real possibility of a federal Europe. Pessimists are appalled by the idea but are sceptical of reversing course now (and it is better that 'our men' do the deal and salvage something). Paternalists are divided on the prospect. Progressives are more sanguine. They would rarely be enthusiastic federalists but have few qualms about the prospect of further European integration. Combative Tories, on the other hand, are overwhelmingly opposed. Corporate Whigs are sympathetic to a European protectionist model. Neo-Liberals are hostile and look to a free market Europe of the nations.

The status of Britain's relationship with the European Union is bound up with a wider debate about the character of Britain itself and the identity of the 'constitutional people' (see Chapter 15). To those opposed to greater powers being ceded to European institutions – groups such as the Bruges Group, European Research Group, Conservative Way Forward, Fresh Start Group and the 92 Group (see Chapter 8) – the defence of representative and responsible government in Britain, based on the principle of parliamentary sovereignty, is what the Conservative Party is all about. Compromise on that is to compromise the party and to betray the people of Britain. To those in favour of further integration – such as the Tory Reform Group and the Conservative Group for Europe – the capacity to secure British interests within the new Europe takes priority over sentimental constitution-worship and a longing for the political certainties of the past. This was a battle fought and won under Ted Heath in 1970–2. The war must not be lost now through a loss of nerve. This, too, would betray the national interest and condemn the country to an uncertain future. Both of these principled positions, of course, are also bound up with the ambitions of personalities.

It may be that it is impossible for these positions to be reconciled. It may be that elements in the party can accept neither the people nor the measures. It may be that the conditions now exist for the Conservative Party to suffer the sort of split it underwent in 1848 and 1906 (Baker *et al.*, 1993b). On the other hand, as Berrington understood in the different circumstances of 1961, the strength of the party lies in the extent of its pragmatic centre. 'Apart from the committed Europeans and the diehard Commonwealthmen, there is a large middle group in a state of genuine indecision, looking hopefully for some reconciliation between the claims of Europe and the claims of the Commonwealth' (Berrington, 1961: 370).

Apart from the few committed Europeans and the larger number of committed Eurosceptics or Eurorealists (and the atrophy of the commitment to the Commonwealth) that remains the case. The hope for reconciliation, however, has a Micawberish quality about it today which it did not have in the past. The culture of fudging compromise which has served the party well hitherto has been and will continue to be severely tested. It is uncertain whether the philosophy of common purpose will overcome the faction of competing principle.

PART 2

Structure, organisation and support

CHAPTER 6

The party in the country I

Development and influence

Philip Tether

Origin and development

Successive extensions of the franchise in the nineteenth century transformed the political landscape. The need to compete for popular support on the basis of coherent programmes which could then be delivered led to significant organisational developments in extra-parliamentary organisation where the party developed structures capable of attracting, servicing and mobilising a mass membership. By about 1875 the tripartite structure, still in place today, had been established. Alongside the parliamentary party, Conservative Central Office (CCO), founded by Disraeli in 1870, was providing professional support with the National Union of Conservative and Constitutional Associations (the 'National Union') at the apex of a growing number of Conservative associations in the constituencies.

The main features of the institutional developments surrounding the emergence of the party's voluntary wing have been noted in Chapter 1 – the rise of Operative Societies post-1832, the growth of Working Men's Associations after 1867, and so on – but it is worth looking at these in a little more detail since they raise organisational and social issues that have helped shape the composition, organisation and role of the party's voluntary wing for more than century.

The spur to organisation and recruitment after 1832 was the complex registration procedures introduced by the Reform Act of that year. The extension of the franchise meant that it was necessary, for the first time, for constituencies to maintain an electoral register. In county seats the maintenance of the register was entrusted to the Overseer of the Poor, in borough seats responsibility was vested either in the Overseer or Town Clerk. In no seat was there an automatic right to be on the register. Voters who believed they qualified had to make a formal application for inclusion and an annual list of existing voters and claimants was exhibited which could be challenged in peripatetic Revising Barristers' Courts.

These courts rapidly became the focus of intense partisan activity as the rival political parties struggled to get sympathisers on to the register and to deny the claims of opponents. The parties were represented in court by paid agents, often solicitors, from whom the modern-day agent is descended. Interestingly, the Conservative Party appears to have been the first to recognise both the challenge and the opportunity offered by the new system of registration. Urged on by Sir Robert Peel to 'register, register, register' (Gash, 1977: 70), Conservative Associations spread rapidly. In county and borough the new bodies:

> brought in regular subscriptions, appointed permanent secretaries and treasurers, attended to the business of registration, employed solicitors, often made themselves responsible for seeking out and recommending candidates and almost always held periodic dinners where MPs, candidates, local landowners and civic dignitaries could meet, speechify and demonstrate the Party's strength. (Gash, 1977: 68)

However, it is important to note that these first Conservative Associations 'were not elected by the whole body of members [but] were self-elected and self-perpetuating' (Bulmer-Thomas, 1953: 18). In short, they were oligarchic groupings of notables without an extended membership or internal representative arrangements. The party's Liverpool Registration Association established in 1832 was reorganised on representative lines in 1848 but it was the exception that proves the rule.

Alongside these groupings of notables could be found, in West Yorkshire, Lancashire and Cheshire, the Operative Societies; bodies of working men organised and funded by middle class patrons in those places where the vagaries of the franchise made such support important. The first Society was apparently established in Leeds in March 1835, although one contemporary observer suggested that 'the flame . . . first broke out in Manchester' (Warrington Operatives Conservative Association, 1836: 12). Regardless of which was the first such organisation, others followed with remarkable rapidity for in '1836 Operative Societies in a hundred centres were holding their first anniversary' (Hill, 1929: 54). The Societies depended for their existence on the patronage provided by gentlemen of a parent Association. The meeting to set up the Bolton Operatives Conservative Association was attended by 50 gentlemen and operatives and 'a subscription paper handed around the room raised £43 15 shillings in a few minutes' (*The Bolton Chronicle* 7 November 1835). At its first annual dinner (roast beef and plum pudding served up by Mr Adams of The Golden Lion Inn between 5 p.m. and midnight) it was observed that the top table contained a number of gentlemen 'who have always distinguished themselves in the "right cause" and who have ever evinced a warm and affectionate zeal to promote the true interests of the people' (Bolton Operatives Conservative Association, 1836: 3).

The Operative Society movement is notable for two important reasons. In the first place it provides the first glimpse in British electoral history of the

Conservative working class supporter, the famous 'angel in marble' described by Disraeli. In modern parlance Peel had succeeded in mobilising some of the C1s and C2s. The Operative Societies were built on a procrustean bed of working class Conservatism at least partly fuelled by a yearning for a better past. The industrial revolution had 'left in its train a great body of people who saw only its evil side . . . the Tory whose little world of rank and station was being overturned in the march of progress, and the Radical whom the march of progress had rendered desperately hungry, together looked to the past, to a half-legendary paradise when there was no machinery, no Political Economy' (Hill, 1929: 31). These inchoate feelings came to the surface of politics in Yorkshire in the shape of Oastler's brand of Tory Radicalism and in Lancashire where they were overlaid by a fervent anti-Catholicism (see Sykes, 1982).

However, it is a mistake to see the Operative Societies simply as curious manifestations of bewildered nostalgia. They provided specific practical benefits for their members since 'many were clearly continuations of earlier societies; and even in their new form must often have retained something of the convivial character of the old pre-reform benevolent and entertainment clubs catering for the poorer classes of electors' (Gash, 1977: 67). They performed a valuable electoral function since in a number of northern towns 'the working class vote was then of major importance' (Greenwood, 1974: 6). Indeed, a number of Bolton spinners were housed in 'ten pound houses' by their employers to ensure they had a vote. Even without a vote, members were valuable both as campaigners and to demonstrate the party's strength and appeal. Opposition claims that not all were genuine operatives but clerks, book-keepers, tradesmen and so on were probably true but this is not the important point. What matters is that the newly named Conservatives were broadening their appeal and creating electoral machinery in the new industrial areas.

Secondly, the Societies are interesting in that they constituted a separate, parallel but subordinate structure for working class supporters. Greenwood (1974) has noted that this solution to the problem of accommodating working class support reappeared (as we shall see in Chapter 7) later in the nineteenth century and again in the twentieth century with the creation of a separate organisational structure for Conservative Trade Unionists.

Most Conservative organisations, both middle and working class, withered on the vine following the split over the Corn Laws in 1846 and Palmerston's ensuing dominance kept the Conservatives on the political sidelines for a generation. However, the pattern of organisation established after 1832 re-emerged in the years around the Reform Act of 1867. In the run-up to reform Working Men's Conservative Associations, reincarnations of the Operative Societies, sprang up in Lancashire and the West Riding. Their impact on the broader development of the party should not be underestimated. The National Union was created in 1867 with the aim of 'bringing together in some federal or confederal form existing Associations as well as encouraging the creation of new ones' (Norton and Aughey, 1981: 203) but it should be emphasised that the infant Union was founded by 'a group of young Conservatives in London who were in the habit of assisting the party managers' (Hanham, 1959: 106) with the principal aim of encouraging the spread of Conservative Working Men's Associations during the reform agitation of 1866–7. Hence its original title, 'The National Union of Conservative and Constitutional Working Men's Associations'.

Like the Operative Societies before them, the Working Men's Associations met in public houses, school rooms and church halls. Again, like the Operative Societies they relied heavily on middle class patrons who provided substantial support which often came to include club premises where party literature and newspapers were provided and where lectures and social events could be held. Considerable emphasis was put on providing recreational facilities as a means of attracting working men. The Operative Societies had been frequently charged with being excuses for drinking clubs and so it was with the Working Men's Associations. When this charge was levelled at the organisation in Salford it was rebutted by the claim that their political opponents were too busy dismantling the institutions of the country to know how to enjoy themselves (Garrard, 1988: 148). Many did indeed seek simply to 'provide club facilities or something very like club facilities for the ordinary working man anxious to enjoy a pint of beer after work' (Hanham, 1959: 109). Nevertheless the electoral significance of Working Men's Conservative Associations can perhaps be gauged from the fact that the Conservatives increased their representation in Lancashire and Cheshire from 18 out of 38 seats in 1865 (48 per cent) to 31 out of 46 seats in 1868 (68 per cent) (Blake, 1970: 112). Moreover, their educational function should not be underestimated. They sought to provide political education through extensive if earnest lecture programmes and the provision of party literature and newspapers. In fact, these organisations should be seen as part of the wider movement in the nineteenth century to provide educational-cum-social facilities for the working class which led to the establishment of the Working Men's Club and Institute Union (CIU) in 1862 by the Reverend Solly, a Unitarian Minister (Tether, 1988: 37).

By 1874 about 150 Conservative Working Men's Associations had been established but, despite their success, the principle of separate class-based structures for the party's working class supporters failed to gain Disraeli's entire approval. As he explained in a speech to working men in Glasgow in 1873, 'I have never been myself at all favourable to a system which would induce Conservatives who are working men to form Societies confined to their class. In the Church and polling booth all are equal' (McKenzie, 1955: 148). John Gorst, Disraeli's Principal Agent from 1869 to 1974, was a Lancashire man born in Preston in 1835 and he fully shared Disraeli's view that the working man could become a major electoral asset. However, he also agreed with him that separate local structures were unhelpful and he sought to promote the development of associations open to both working and middle class members but he was not successful in this aim. Working men were reluctant to participate in socially comprehensive local organisations along-side middle class supporters and, after reaching a peak in the mid-1870s, Working Men's Associations decayed into Working Men's Conservative Clubs (see Tether, 1988) effectively leaving local political activism and the party's mass wing to the middle class. When Gorst was given the task of overhauling the infant National Union 'the expression "Working Men's" was dropped as being unsuitable to a party which sought to minimise class conflict' (Blake, 1966: 536). The current distribution of Conservative clubs still reflects the rapid spread of Working Men's Conservative Associations in Lancashire and the West Riding in the late 1860s and early 1870s. About a third of all Conservative clubs are to be found in these areas. Many still retain 'Working Men's' in their title. The Conservative club movement retains a distinct organisational identity with the Association of Conservative Clubs (ACC) housed in Central Office.

Other developments shaping the emergence of the modern Conservative Association also occurred at this time. The reforms wrought by the Reform Act of 1867 demanded changes in the oligarchic nature of the Working Men's Associations' parent bodies. The direction and government of associations by 'self-elected and self-perpetuating' cliques and groups was no longer adequate as an organisational principle or acceptable to an expanding membership. The Radicals in Birmingham sought to increase the ability of their local machinery to capitalise on the post-1867 expansion of the electorate and, more speci-fically, to ensure that the two votes of each supporter were judiciously distributed among the three Liberal candidates in the city. Their Birmingham organisation, which introduced the concept of the 'caucus' to British political language, was guided by a central body largely made up of elected members from the wards. Sometimes copying the Birmingham example, sometimes developing and refining their own rules and practices, local Liberal organis-ations rapidly developed powerful pyramidal electoral machines based on branches in municipal wards and polling districts each of which sent elected representatives to a central Executive Committee. This kind of organisation 'provided a framework within which all sections of the Party could work together and within which all the local leaders, whig, moderate or radical could be found a place' (Hanham, 1959: 125). The Birmingham Radicals were instrumental in forming the National Liberal Federation in 1877 in an effort to promote their organisational model and obtain a leading hold on Radical opinion throughout the country.

The success of the Liberals' representative model had a considerable im-pact on the Conservatives. Following their shock general election defeat in 1880, Disraeli conceded that the party had neglected its mass organisation after its 1874 victory. He admitted to the Queen that 'the Conservatives have been too confident and that they had not had that same organisation or worked as hard as the Liberals had . . . the Liberals had worked on that American system called caucus, guided by the great Radical Mr Chamberlain' (Hanham, 1959: 144). The Conservatives were not slow to emulate their rivals and they soon built up Associations of a similar type which were 'quite as representative and popular as those on the Liberal side, although usually less pretentious' (Hanham, 1959: 145).

The importance of possessing vigorous and effective organisations in the constituencies was cemented by the Corrupt Practices Acts of 1854 and 1883, the introduction of secret voting in the Ballot Act of 1870 and the Reform Act of 1884 which effectively completed the extension of the franchise to the adult male population. Older and more personal ways of winning friends and influencing people were now completely redundant. Thus, by the late 1880s the modern Conservative Association had emerged through and alongside changes in the electoral system. It was determinedly middle class in character. The working class Conservative was, and has continued to be, vital to the party but as a voter, not as an activist and organiser. It was internally differentiated into branches and organised on the representative principle with a central, elected governing body.

Affiliated to the National Union and serviced by Central Office the party in the country had, by the end of the nineteenth century, taken on its modern-day form. However, we turn now to an important issue which remained to be settled and which may be returning to vex the party again in the last decade of the twentieth century. That is the place of the voluntary organisation within the wider party.

Influence in the party

The representative structures developed in the 1880s not only helped to create more efficient electoral machinery but they were necessary if a newer kind of middle class member was not to be alienated by the oligarchic 'Old Identity'. The 'new members' were increasing and they understood their importance to the party. In the larger boroughs 'the Conservative share of the polls since 1868 had gone up from 37.5 per cent to 44.3 per cent in twelve years' (Blake, 1970: 152). Suburban 'villa conservatism' had begun its long historical march. With working class supporters sidelined into clubs and spurred on by the Liberal's striking organisational successes, these representatives of suburban Conservatism created associations which were more middle class in composition and less pliable *vis-à-vis* the leadership than the traditional oligarchic structures. In particular, the representatives of the urban middle class resented being dominated by the recently established National Union which like the older associations themselves was 'largely cooptative and unrepresentative' (Hanham, 1959: 151). Their grievances were exploited by Lord Randolph Churchill and other members of the so-called 'Fourth Party' in their dispute with Disraeli's successor, Lord Salisbury, over 'Tory Democracy' which was famously, if vaguely, described by Churchill as 'a democracy which votes for the Tory party' (Lindsay and Harrington, 1979: 14). Churchill's romantic if ill-defined radicalism sought to forge a Tory–working class alliance, and was essentially a reworking of the party's 'Young England' movement of the middle decades of the nineteenth century when Disraeli, Lord John Manners and others 'reacting against free trade and industrialism, created the image of a feudal paradise governed by high-minded paternal aristocrats devoted to the well-being of the common people' (Lindsay and Harrington, 1979: 4).

Churchill's espousal of 'Tory Democracy' was opportunistic and, in the end, doomed to failure, broken on the rocks of Salisbury's cool scepticism and Churchill's precipitate resignation from the Exchequer over the Army estimates. However, it was important *vis-à-vis* the party's burgeoning mass wing. Churchill, on behalf of the National Union, claimed a greater role for that body in the counsels of the party via a more representative structure and a greater role in policy-making. In modern parlance he was seeking to create a power base as a springboard for 'Tory Democracy'. These demands exploited the grievances of the representatives of 'villa Conservatism' concerning their place and status in the wider party. The eventual settlement of the dispute between the 'Fourth Party' and Lord Salisbury gave the representatives of middle class urban Conservatism what they *really* sought: 'recognition and a voice in organisational matters' (Blake, 1970: 125). The stalking-horse of Churchillian ambition did not seek to be the 'tail that wagged the dog'; the caucus feared by the leadership. Rather, the party in the country wanted to be recognised as both important and competent within its own sphere and for that importance and competence to be institutionalised through a more representative National Union structure. In the event, the 1884 conference in Sheffield found a compromise acceptable to the leadership and the party in the country (although of course not Churchill). The main focus of discontent had been the Central Committee, a small group controlling party funds and organisation. This body was under the direction of the leadership but in 1884 the Central Council, the National Union's governing body, agreed to a solution which, although questions of policy and finance were left to the Committee, stressed the importance of constituency organisation and the need for a more representative Central Council.

Now, as then, Associations are mindful of their importance and resentful of anything that can be construed as 'interference' by the party's bureaucracy in the shape of Central Office, especially where candidate selection is concerned. Traditionally, however, the party in the country does not have, nor has it sought, any direct involvement in policy making. Attempts to describe the exact relationship of the leader to the rest of the party, parliamentary and voluntary, range from 'monarchical' through 'Hobbesian' to 'familial' (see Chapter 9) but the practical consequences of that relationship are not in doubt. The leader is expected to lead and the rest of the party to follow, at least while the leader is successful. All its parts are to be subordinated to this end. The role the party in the country is expected to play within the wider party is made clear in party literature directed to, or about, Associations which 'tends to emphasise the organisational functions' (Norton and Aughey, 1981: 214).

The annual conference has been seen as providing proof positive of the voluntary wing's subservient role in relation to policy making, being variously described as a 'public relations exercise' (Ingle, 1989: 62) and a 'great rally or jamboree' (Byrd, 1987: 218). Ever since McKenzie's (1955) seminal study of British political parties, received wisdom has run along these lines allowing the Conservatives' voluntary wing generally, and the annual conference in particular, little influence within the party except in certain unusual and atypical situations, such as when divisions in the parliamentary party have led to the membership being courted. Lord Randolph Churchill attempted to do just this, as did the anti-appeasers in the 1930s. The anti-federalists in the European debate in the 1990s have also sought to win support among constituency activists. Conference can be difficult and fractious when its collective nerve is touched over issues such as immigration, Northern Ireland or Europe but this in itself is nothing new and was ever thus, as Balfour's struggles with conference over tariff reform and Baldwin's with his India policy illustrate. However, so it is said, the platform can generally stage-manage affairs to its satisfaction by manipulating the deference of representatives and the careful selection of motions for debate, only two of which are selected by a ballot of conference representatives for discussion. Just occasionally the platform fails in this exercise in subtle control, as in 1950, when representatives forced it to accept a housing target of 300,000 new buildings. However, this is seen as an aberration, the exception that proves the rule, significant only in so far as it suggests that the Conservatives' annual conference could have real power if it chose to stand up and be counted.

Much of this analysis is fuelled by a comparison, explicit or implicit, with Labour's conference. The Labour Party, unlike the Conservative Party, does have a formal constitution specifying the powers of its parts and their relationships. As befits a party that grew up from the grass roots to become a parliamentary force, considerable emphasis is put on intraparty democracy and its constitution confers on its annual conference supreme policy making powers. However, it has long been recognised that, in reality, the actual power of Labour conferences to determine policy is more circumscribed than the theory suggests (see McKenzie, 1955). Moreover, under Kinnock, Smith and Blair the party has become much more conscious of the importance of managing and presenting conference in a way which enhances the party's image. Nevertheless, although intraparty politics and the policy making process inside the Labour Party certainly cannot be reduced to 'members make policy', its mass organisation and other extra-parliamentary institutions (such as the trade unions) do have a formal place in the scheme of things, they do exercise their powers and they do play a significant part in the party's making of policy (see Minkin, 1978, 1992). Comparisons are invidious and the Conservative conference, with its strictly controlled agenda and ballots which, neither theoretically nor practically, bind the leadership, appears deferential and supine.

There is much to give credence to this view. The National Union was described by an early President as a 'handmaid to the party' (Ostrogorski, 1902: 251), a phrase redolent of decorous servitude. Balfour also reached below stairs for appropriate language when he famously remarked that he would rather take advice from his valet than from conference. In 1911, on Balfour's resignation, 'the general view was that a meeting of all Unionist MPs should be summoned to elect a leader, and that this should be done as soon as possible, to avoid the leadership being decided by constituency representatives at the party conference, due to convene shortly' (Bogdanor, 1994: 72). The election procedure introduced in 1965, and revised since, does allow for the views of other sections of the party (peers, the voluntary wing and MEPs) to be canvassed before the parliamentary party votes but MPs can and do ignore their views. This happened in 1975 when the party in the country was predominantly pro-Heath and again in 1990 when it was overwhelmingly for Mrs Thatcher. Following the re-election of John Major as leader of the party in July 1995 Sir Norman Fowler, a former Party Chairman, suggested that the party needed to examine whether annual elections should be allowed when the leader is Prime Minister and also whether the party in the country should be formally included in the electoral process, possibly in some sort of electoral college akin to Labour's. Had the Conservative Party had such a system, Mrs Thatcher probably would not have lost the leadership. Neither would she have won it.

While a patriotic duty to work and campaign for the party is accepted by all voluntary workers, it is said that few appear interested in any involvement in policy making (Ingle, 1989: 66; McKenzie, 1955: 244; Gamble, 1979: 40). As a result the party's voluntary wing is undistracted by the issue of internal democracy, which can only get in the way of the leader leading. Bogdanor (1994) argues that in the Conservative Party, leaders are seen as more significant than policies. In the Labour Party electoral failure is interpreted as an indictment of policies while in the Conservative Party the blame lies with the leader. A successful one must be supported and sustained by all while the unsuccessful must, as Sir Winston Churchill crisply observed, be pole-axed (Chapter 9). In other words, the Conservative Party has two secret weapons. One is loyalty, the other is disloyalty. This attitude toward leadership springs from the party's general endorsement of hierarchy and is both a blessing and a curse for a leader since it gives 'leaders more freedom to act during a more precarious tenure' (Williams, 1982: 55).

This analysis of the Conservative Party's power structure and culture has shaped perceptions of the National Union as a subordinate organ in the

Conservative body politic with control from above and deference from below leading to its emasculation. However, it is possible to reach other conclusions about the role of the National Union in general and conference in particular without rejecting the undoubted importance of leadership, loyalty and electoral success. Indeed, there is another analysis which reaffirms them.

The National Union's functions may, as the Maxwell-Fyfe committee on party organisation observed in 1948, be indeed 'primarily deliberative and advisory' but it is important to remember that an 'absence of formal policy making powers does not mean that an advisory role is tantamount to no role at all' (Norton and Aughey, 1981: 206). First, it should be noted that the leadership and senior politicians need the support and approval of conference. Prior to Edward Heath, party leaders descended on the annual conference after it had completed its business to 'rally the troops'. Now they attend for the duration. On 10 May 1995, the Chancellor Kenneth Clarke used the Scottish Conservative annual conference in Glasgow to mount a defence of his handling of the economy in the wake of disastrous local election results. It was observed that 'Mr Clarke will be aware that the Scottish conference proved to be the swan song for his predecessor Norman Lamont, who was sacked a fortnight after he addressed the same Tory gathering in Edinburgh in 1993' (*Daily Telegraph* 10 May 1995). In the event, Mr Clarke was not well received.

It is clear that conference can be a testing ground for leading personalities and their records and policies. However, it has recently been persuasively argued by Kelly (1989) that it also allows for a genuine two-way exchange of opinions and views and that it has more influence on the development of party policy than has been recognised. Kelly points out that academic attention has focused on the annual conference, whereas this is only the apex of what he calls the 'conference system'. This is a series of conferences representing different groupings within the party such as women, trade unionists, Conservative students, the Young Conservatives (YCs) and local government councillors, which are held at different levels in the party's national structure. These groupings and the organisation of the party in the country are discussed in the next chapter.

The total number of participants in a year at all conferences at all levels of the party is of the order of 20,000 activists of one sort or another. It is here, in this 'conference system' that, according to Kelly, opinions and views constantly circulate between the leadership and party members with the latter making a real contribution to the development and evolution of policy. Formal machinery is employed circumspectly. Views are expressed and representatives trust the leadership to take note of them. Pursuing the matter to a hostile vote would undermine the mutual trust upon which effective influence depends. It would also advertise divisions which never do anyone any good. Informal contacts are more important than formal mechanisms but either way the platform, MPs, Central Office, are able to gauge the mood and atmosphere of each conference and to take the messages conveyed into account. The annual conference can thus afford to be a relaxed and generally celebratory gathering – most of the hard work has been done elsewhere. However, if the leadership fails to read mood and atmosphere aright, to absorb important messages or to anticipate reactions correctly, then trouble can surface at the annual conference. If it does, commentators who have failed to appreciate the extent of the 'conference system' or its *modus operandi* claim that it is becoming more assertive and, therefore, more interesting and significant.

This revisionist analysis does suggest that a more subtle approach to the question of the influence and role of the party in the country is required. It is difficult to believe that the entire 'conference system' is simply acclamatory or an exercise in public relations, especially when most of it is hidden. Moreover, many members do believe they are helping to shape policy. A recent study of the politics of Conservative Party membership found that many activists feel they make a difference and that consequently, 'it would be quite wrong to argue that in general they feel powerless and unable to influence the party leadership and Conservative party politics' (Whiteley *et al.*, 1994: 38). Indeed, given the psychological properties generally associated with activists and 'joiners' it would be odd to find such people meekly accepting a walk-on role. In this connection it should be remembered that the 'conference system' is populated not only by activists but activists involved with groupings and interests such as 'women', 'trade unionists' or 'local government'. The possessors of specific concerns and specialist expertise are even more likely to feel they have something to contribute. A majority of the CTU representatives interviewed by Kelly believed that the conference existed mainly so that 'sensible' trade unionists could tell the government 'what was really going on in the workplace' while another claimed that credit for trade union legislation since 1980 belonged to the CTU (Kelly, 1989: 175). A very full analysis of Conservative annual conferences this century provides so many examples of its importance to the leadership and its influence upon aspects of policy that it is difficult to sustain the view that it is of little or no importance (see Kelly, 1994). Taken in isolation, these examples can be explained as exceptions that prove the rule. Cumulatively, they must put 'the rule' in doubt.

This analysis is also given credence by the conduct of local Conservative Associations, an area of the party to which few academic commentators have had access. Anyone attending meetings at constituency level will have been struck by the lack of importance attached to formal 'constitutionalism' – arguments over rule interpretation, points of order, votes and so on – and the considerable authority and influence wielded by the Associations' leadership. At the same time there is a lively sense of fairness. People must be heard and others must be prepared to listen and, sometimes, be persuaded. Views evolve within a directed, if informal, democracy.

The key to this analysis of the role and influence of the party in the country generally and the 'conference system' in particular is not so much deference but conditional trust. The leadership maintains the trust of the party in the country by recognising its importance and respecting its views. If it leads sensitively and successfully it is given plenty of leeway. However, failure, especially sustained failure (which includes a failure to listen), can lead to dissatisfaction and an important question in this review of the voluntary wing's place in the wider party is – will the party's current problems give rise to demands for more overt and formalised intra-party democracy? The deep concerns of the membership with the disastrous local government election results in May 1995, policies on Europe and Northern Ireland, pit closures, Post Office and railway privatisation, taxation, sleaze and scandals (see Chapter 3) or a major general election defeat could spark demands for reforms which ensure that the views of the membership are voiced more clearly and unambiguously.

An agenda for change is already in place. In the late 1960s a group of Greater London YCs published a pamphlet, *Set the Party Free*, which demanded a greater role for Conference, less Central Office control of the National Union and more focus on political activities and issues at all levels of the voluntary wing. The ensuing Chelmer Report's recommendations were effectively ignored (see Seyd, 1975). The only recommendation which had any impact at all was the proposal that 'at each level of the National Union Constitution, there should be one body which will commit itself principally to political matters' (National Union of Conservative and Unionist Associations, 1972: 3). This led to the establishment of Political Committees in some Associations (Tether, 1990: 153) although not at any other level of the National Union. Despite the failure of this initiative, demands for greater intraparty democracy were subsequently resurrected by the Charter Movement, a campaigning group drawn largely from the party's Kent- and Surrey-based membership. It established a Party Reform Steering Committee in 1992 to promote two particular reforms. These are that one-half of the members of the National Union's Executive Committee be directly elected and that the National Union take over responsibility for party finances from Central Office.

The proposal that the National Union take over responsibility for party finances is an expression of frustration at what some activists allege to be a lack of accountability surrounding party funding and expenditure. In this connection it is important to note that the party's acknowledged deficit was £19 million in March 1993 (Fowler and Conservative Central Office, 1993: 21). By 1995 it was still running at £15 million. As Justin Fisher discusses in Chapter 10, the deficit is proving difficult to shift. Local parties give financial support to Central Office through the 'quota system' introduced by the Maxwell-Fyfe Committee in 1948. Under this scheme, associations are assessed according to electoral performance. The more votes a local party achieves in parliamentary elections, the higher its quota. The scheme is, however, strictly voluntary and by no means all associations pay the quota in full or even in part. In 1993–4 associations 'gave only £745,000 . . . 5 per cent of the £14.1 million raised by the national party' (*The Times* 11 October 1994). Problems with their own finances and deepening doubts about financial management at the centre are to blame for this decline in associations' contributions. The party in the country is, however, providing loans to help Central Office service its debts. According to Central Office's accounts these amounted to £3.6 million on deposit in March 1994.

The reformers are contesting the influence of Central Office over the affairs of the National Union. The representative organ of the National Union is its Central Council whose annual meeting constitutes the voluntary wing's annual general meeting but with over 300 members it is too large to meet regularly. Consequently day to day business is handled by a National Union Executive Committee (NUEC) and a General Purposes Committee (GPC). The responsibilities of the NUEC include considering 'aspects of the policy of the party as may be selected from time to time' (National Union of Conservative and Unionist Associations, 1994: 15) and dealing with such things as rule changes and disputes. The GPC is responsible for the co-ordination of National Union activities including the agenda for Central Council and the Annual Conference.

Central Office, with substantial *ex officio* membership of both the NUEC and the GPC, is said to exercise a decisive controlling influence. For instance, Central Office membership of the NUEC includes *inter alia* the Chairman, Deputy Chairman and Vice-Chairmen of the Party Organisation, Party Treasurers, the Chairman of the Conservative Board of Finance, the Director General of the Board of Management (of which more later) and all the Directors of its principal departments. In total, the NUEC has 226 members of whom 30 represent the constituencies while the GPC, with 40 members, has no constituency representatives. Moreover, in neither case are the representatives of the voluntary membership directly elected by the Central Council, as the Party Reform Steering Committee is demanding in respect of the NUEC. Rather, they obtain their places on both committees by virtue of National Union office. Being indirectly, as opposed to directly, elected to high National Union office, representatives are said to lack independence and legitimacy.

There have been changes in response to concerns over party organisation and finances but they have not been in the direction of greater autonomy for the National Union. Indeed, to activists committed to this cause they appear to exacerbate the situation. Two inquiries have recently been held into the role and workings of both Central Office and the National Union and their relationship. The first was headed by Sir Norman Fowler, then Chairman of Party Organisation. The ensuing report announced the creation of a Board of Management to bring together the elected, voluntary and professional parts of the party. Its aim is to 'provide oversight and direction (and to) instil a sense of purpose in all sectors of the Party' (Fowler and Conservative Central Office, 1993: 19). Headed by a Director General with a place on the NUEC, the avowed aim is to bring 'business style' practices into party management. The other inquiry into the National Union endorsed the Board of Management concept. It also increased the level of constituency representation on the NUEC to the 30 places noted earlier in order to 'make the NUEC more representative and bring it closer to our grass roots' (Feldman and Conservative Central Office, 1993: 25).

These changes are viewed with suspicion. For advocates of greater intra-party democracy, the Board of Management is a step in the wrong direction which can only tighten bureaucratic control of the National Union. Only 3 of the Board's 13 members have any link with associations and none are directly elected. Indeed, some suspect that the Management Board has been devised to give the leadership and its bureaucratic servants access to constituency funds and assets which could clear Central Office's deficit several times over (Kelly, 1995a: 13, Kelly, 1995b: 81). An Inland Revenue ruling in 1982 made it clear that Central Office's debts are its own separate responsibility. Centralisation and a fusion of the professional and voluntary elements of the party under the Board of Management could overcome this legal obstacle. The increase in constituency representation on the NUEC is seen as little more than a sop to demands for greater democracy.

Suspicions over the colonisation of the NUEC and the GPC by Central Office and the role of the Board of Management were confirmed for some by the NUEC proposal at the 1994 Central Council (the forum for any rule changes) that the power to amend Associations' 'model rules' should lie exclusively with the NUEC without recourse to the Council. This 'would have given the Board of Management, via its colluding NUEC members, a procedural way to govern local parties on Central Office's behalf' (Kelly, 1995a: 14). The initiative was defeated but by dint of selecting inaccessible venues and debating rule changes on Fridays rather than the better-attended Saturday sessions 'recent Central Councils (or at least the tiny fraction of those entitled to attend them) have compelled local associations to choose only "approved" parliamentary candidates, furnish national officials with details of their accounts . . . and permit the power of expulsion to shift from the NUEC to the smaller and more decisive GPC – Billericay beware' (Kelly, 1995b: 81).

The claims of bureaucratic insensitivity to grass roots dissent have been given even greater credibility by the recent refusal to allow the Party Reform Steering Committee's proposals to be debated at a special Central Council meeting even though the request was supported by 50 constituency Associations as stipulated by the party rule book (Whiteley *et al.*, 1994: 32). The significance and desirability of the changes introduced by the Fowler and Feldman reports can be debated. What cannot be disputed is that discontent exists, as does an agenda for change. At the 1995 Central Council, Associations submitted 21 motions on 'Party Policy, Party Organisation and National Union matters'. This was the largest single category of motions and many were critical (Kelly, 1995b: 81). If electoral recovery continues to elude the party the demands made by what is, admittedly, currently only a small group of organised activists could become more attractive to more members. A more assertive membership, imbued with 1980s doctrines of individualism and consumerism and the equally Thatcherite belief that Conservatives can be 'the new vox populi with a sure feel for the "average" voter' (Kelly, 1995a: 11), may not prove pliable material if the erosion of trust continues.

CHAPTER 7

The party in the country II

Members and organisation

Philip Tether

The membership

Conservative Associations are the building blocks of the party in the country with one Association in each parliamentary constituency. Individuals joining the party become, on payment of a subscription, members of particular Associations. There is no such thing as membership of a national Conservative Party since the party possesses neither organisational unity nor a corporate legal identity.

Who are the members? According to a recent major survey involving a little under 2,500 subscribers spread across 35 constituencies, the typical Conservative member is retired, middle class and white (Whiteley *et al.*, 1994). The average age was found to be 62 years, with one-half of all members aged 66 or over. Two-thirds thought of themselves as belonging to a particular class and, of these, three-quarters described themselves as middle class. Only 8 per cent could be described as traditional working class manual workers.

Given the high average age, only a minority (29 per cent) were still at work and over half of these were part of the salariat. Teachers were the largest single group followed by financial services workers. Marketing and public relations executives and administrative workers in central and local government also formed significant groups. Routine non-manual workers such as clerks, cashiers and typists made up a further 18 per cent. The *petit bourgeoisie* (overwhelmingly proprietors of small businesses) were also solidly represented with 13 per cent of the employed total. The medium household income was found to be in the £15,000–£20,000 range. Almost three-quarters (70 per cent) owned stocks and shares. While participating in the privatisations of the 1980s, 62 per cent had held shares prior to this period. The sample was found to be 99 per cent white and 1 per cent Asian. Efforts to recruit ethnic minorities appear to have failed. Well over three-quarters belonged to

Protestant churches (established and non-conformist). Roman Catholics constituted 10 per cent and Jews 1 per cent.

These findings are perhaps unlikely to cause much surprise. The survey did, however, unearth a number of interesting features of Conservative Party membership which are not so stereotypical. For instance, it was found that 'the typical party member lacks many of the formal educational qualifications which are common among the middle class today: almost one-third (31 per cent) have no educational qualifications at all and only 12 per cent possess a university degree' (Whiteley *et al.*, 1994: 44). This relative lack of formal educational qualifications is directly attributable to the high average age of members. It sets them apart from many of the MPs they are responsible for selecting, among whom private education and university degrees are common (see Chapter 8). Just as the voluntary wing in its age profile and 'middle classness' is unrepresentative of the party's electoral support (it is a truism of the textbooks that the Conservative Party cannot win elections without a substantial raft of working class voters) so the party elite is unrepresentative of its voluntary organisation.

Party members are, of course, right-wing by definition but they are by no means stereotypical 'extremists'. It is frequently assumed that activists in any political party are likely to have particularly firm and uncompromising views both in relation to their own party and the electorate as a whole. This view is misplaced. The United Kingdom's first-past-the-post electoral system forces parties to maximise their appeal. As a result they are 'broad churches' reflecting and promoting a diversity of views. This diversity is found in the membership as well as among elected representatives.

The survey found evidence for three ideological groupings in the party in the country; traditionalists, individualists and progressives. Traditionalists represent the oldest ideological 'tendency' within the party and it is the one most commonly equated with stereotypical Conservatism. Here the emphasis is on the need for strong social and moral discipline, loyalty to established institutions such as the monarchy and a rejection of closer involvement with Europe. Individualists stand four-square on the doctrines of economic liberalism and *laissez-faire* which were grafted onto the body of Conservative beliefs in the late nineteenth and early twentieth century in response to the growing collectivism of the Liberals and the rise of Labour. Individualists defend the rights of private property and emphasise the wealth-creating potential of the free market. Progressives, on the other hand, as the heirs of Disraelian 'One Nation' conservatism, are prepared to accept responsibility for the collective welfare of the people which entails a certain degree of social reform, state intervention and redistribution of resources. The Conservatives' pre-Thatcher commitment to the so-called 'post-war consensus' consisting of the managed economy (with full employment as its goal), the welfare state and substantial public ownership was sustained by this dimension of Conservative thought.

Two things should be noted about this characterisation of members' ideology. First, it is only one of a number of attempts to characterise aspects of, or emphases in, Conservative thought which prides itself on rejecting first principles and is so fluid and imprecise that some commentators claim that it cannot be properly characterised as an ideology (see Chapter 4). As may be discerned from Chapter 5, this particular typology has its roots in Norton and Aughey's (1981) broad division of Conservatives into Whigs whose primary concern is with wealth creation and economic effectiveness and Tories who are more concerned with the maintenance of social, moral and political integrity in a flawed, uncertain and threatening world. Secondly, the most significant variables were found to be income, age and religiosity but these did not create neat exclusive groupings of traditionalists, individualists and progressives. Tendencies were discernible but there was considerable blurring around the ideological edges. Thus, affluent party members tended to be individualistic, anti-progressive (in their rejection of economic interventionism) and anti-traditionalist, preferring free-market solutions to economic problems and individual choice on issues such as abortion and divorce. Elderly Conservatives leant heavily toward traditionalism but were 'qualified individualists' in their support for privatisation. At the same time they were not noticeably anti-progressive, favouring as they did consumer protection and tighter regulations on industry if necessary. Religious conservatives revealed themselves to be more supportive of state intervention and both rather anti-individualistic and anti-traditionalist except where certain moral issues such as abortion are concerned (Whiteley *et al.*, 1994: 148–9). Overall, then, the picture is one of ideological complexity with, surprisingly perhaps, the bias tipped to the centre-left with only 20 per cent of the membership surveyed putting themselves in right-wing categories. The party in the country appears to lean toward liberal Conservatism with strong anti-traditionalist and anti-individualist elements (Whiteley *et al.*, 1994: 141).

Other interesting points to emerge concern the professions and the role of women in local constituency organisation. The survey found that, perhaps contrary to expectations, the traditional professions are not heavily represented and that 'there are, in fact, more nurses than consultants or doctors among the membership' (Whiteley *et al.*, 1994: 46). Similarly, there are very few farmers who are traditionally among the staunchest of supporters. They are, in fact, outnumbered by farm-workers who constitute the largest single group in the traditional manual workers' category.

It is often claimed, not least by the Conservative Party itself, that women are the mainstay of the party's voluntary wing (Conservative Women's Organisation, 1986: 5). Women are indeed important and have been so for a long time. For instance, 'Central Office records show that at a 1904 by-election in Oswestry, no fewer than 26 women's branches turned out to assist the party's candidate' (Conservative Women's Organisation, 1986: 5). However, the survey showed that, at 49 per cent, women are not, at least today, in a numerical majority. However, are women in the Conservative Party, while not numerically preponderant, in a majority among activist members? The distinction between activist and passive members is of vital importance when discussing the mass membership of any party. Many members do nothing beyond paying their annual subscription and, perhaps, occasionally attending social events. Others are more active. They may be prepared to display a poster at election time or give a few hours to distribute leaflets or collect subscriptions. Others will be even more active, sitting on committees, helping to run ward branches and organising vital fund-raising events.

A survey of 20 Conservative Associations found that about 12 per cent of total membership could be counted as activists (Tether, 1990: 165) although this survey did not distinguish between activists on the basis of gender. On the other hand Whiteley *et al.* (1994) put the activist figure much higher, with 60 per cent of members active to some degree. The difference can be explained by the fact that the former study focused on identifying absolutely key activists who held office and/or regularly attended meetings, gave time for electioneering and so forth while the latter distinguished between degrees of activism. One such degree was 'very active' and here the figures are in close agreement with almost exactly 12 per cent of members surveyed giving regular and committed help and support (Whiteley *et al.*, 1994: 106). Interestingly, no appreciable difference in activism between men and women was found in any of the categories of activism. About 12 per cent of male members and 11 per cent of female members were to be found in the crucially important 'very active' category.

Total party membership is difficult to assess since central records are not kept. Membership records are held and serviced by constituency Associations which regard any proposals to monitor membership levels with deep suspicion. Central Office's role is restricted to stimulating and servicing membership campaigns. It has also undertaken direct mail recruitment campaigns using commercially available lists of individuals likely to be sympathetic to an approach from the party, such as the purchasers of shares in privatised enterprises (see Tether, 1991b). In such campaigns, however, names and addresses of recruits are passed to the constituencies for action. The only exception is in the case of overseas electors – British nationals resident overseas to whom the Representation of the People Acts 1985 and 1989 gave the right to vote in parliamentary and European elections. Central Office has encouraged the development of about 50 overseas branches. Most are in Europe but can also be found in places such as Hong Kong, Japan and the United States. Central Office assists overseas voters to register in their UK constituency of last residence and generally maintains and services this special group. In the 1992 general election there were 34,454 registered overseas voters; about 53 per constituency. Thus far, overseas electors appear to have been decisive in only one constituency contest (see Tether, 1994).

At the beginning of the 1950s the party claimed a membership of about 2.75 million (Butler, 1955: 107). This averaged about 4,500 members per constituency. Two decades later, the Committee on Financial Aid to Political Parties estimated average membership of Conservative Associations to be 2,400, which yielded a national figure of 1.5 million (Houghton Committee, 1976: 5). A recent estimate puts the figure at about three-quarters of a million or about 1,100 per constituency (Whiteley *et al.*, 1994: 25). However, averages must be treated with great caution. Numbers vary considerably from seat to seat and can range from a handful of members in safe Labour seats to 3–5,000 in safe Conservative seats (Tether, 1990: 50; *The Times* 10 October 1994).

Clearly, there has been a very substantial decline in membership since the 1950s. This can be explained by the adverse impact of long-term socio-economic trends and shorter-term political and organisational ones. Party identification and loyalty were strong in the 1950s and the two-party system reigned supreme. Political parties and their local organisations were almost the sole focus for those interested in political issues. They also provided an important venue for socialising in a world where leisure opportunities were still comparatively limited.

Greater prosperity has brought with it many competing possibilities and attractions. The impact of these is particularly clear if we look at the situation facing the Conservative Party's youth wing, the Young Conservatives (YCs), once hailed as the largest political youth movement in the free world. In the early 1950s the YCs claimed a national membership of about 150,000. In 1990, the Youth Department at Central Office estimated YC membership to be 6,500 spread over 300 branches (Tether, 1990: 148). More recently it is reported that the YCs are virtually defunct 'with a membership reduced to 5,000 or less' (*The Times* 10 October 1994). The emergence of a youth culture and the opportunities it provides for leisure and pleasure has clearly reduced the appeal of the YC movement for young people, while the expansion of higher education has taken many of them away from home just at the time when they might, once, have become involved with their local Association. This decline is ominous for the party given its ageing membership. With only 5 per cent of its membership below the age of 35 years (of which 1 per cent is aged 25 or less) the party in the country does not have the replacements for its many older members (Whiteley *et al.*, 1994: 43; *The Times* 10 October 1994).

Increased prosperity and leisure opportunities have affected membership; so too has the ever-growing range of cause or promotional groups which have mushroomed since the 1960s. This proliferation is, of course, not unrelated to the increase in prosperity and leisure opportunities noted above. People have more time to become involved with causes and more inclination and knowledge thanks to the post-Robbins expansion of higher education and the influence of the media, particularly television. Such groups provide multifarious opportunities for 'doing politics' outside the formal political system.

The effect has been to increase the opportunities for political participation broadly defined, to the detriment of local party membership.

Shorter-term political factors have also adversely affected membership levels. The party has been in power since 1979 and, even in the normal course of events, it is always more difficult for a party to recruit members when it is in power and its own shortcomings, rather than its opponents', are on display. The Conservatives have, of course, been beset by problems of every kind and the impact on membership levels of the resulting unpopularity has been marked. Whiteley *et al.*'s (1994) survey of 35 Associations yielded a national membership figure of about three-quarters of a million. A larger survey of 250 seats 'suggests that membership fell by 15 per cent between 1992 and 1994 reducing the total to about 540,000' (*The Times* 10 October 1994).

Organisational factors have also played a part in the decline in membership. Mrs Thatcher's electoral strategy was to make a direct populist appeal to the voters and, as a consequence, the very period that produced four general election victories has also seen a serious decline in party organisation. As a result, 'the party now has only one member for every three it had when Margaret Thatcher became party leader 20 years ago' (*The Times* 10 October 1994). It is a curious fact that victorious parties often neglect the organisational base which they assiduously honed in their search for power. Good organisation is apparently necessary to win power but not to keep it. In defeat, parties then have to begin the process of overhauling the machinery to put it in working order once again. The last major overhaul of structure, process and relationships in the Conservative Party was undertaken by the Maxwell-Fyfe Committee set up in 1948 in the wake of the party's crushing defeat at the hands of Attlee's Labour Party. Party chiefs may come, like Disraeli after the election defeat of 1880, to rue their neglect of organisational issues and to call for a grand inquest into what was not wrong before.

Long-term socioeconomic factors are affecting the membership of all parties in Great Britain and indeed across Western Europe. The Conservatives' problem is that the long- and short-term factors adversely affecting membership levels are mutually reinforcing and cumulative. The long-term trends can be bucked in certain circumstances, as the achievement of the Labour Party illustrates. Cashing in on anti-government feeling, it has recruited about 100,000 new members in the last few years. Under Tony Blair, 19,700 young people under the age of 26 (mostly students) have joined the party which now has a Youth Spokesman and a Youth Taskforce to decide on Youth Policy (*Guardian* 19 June 1995). If voters can be convinced that economic recovery has indeed taken root, then the Conservative Party may persuade at least some lapsed members to return to the fold, but, even so, serious erosion of the party's comparative superiority in membership will have been sustained.

Does this matter? One of the justifications for local government is that central government could not sensitively deliver services to all localities. It could not possibly organise such a vast undertaking or respond flexibly to all the variations in demand and local circumstances. The same is true of political parties. Voluntary effort sustains grass roots democracy in Great Britain and all parties' local organisations have vital functions to fulfil. Most obviously they select candidates for local and parliamentary elections (both national and European) and they finance, plan and deliver their candidates' election campaigns. In Conservative Associations the finance is raised by an endless round of social events and fund-raising schemes – fêtes, coffee mornings, race-nights, 'auctions of promises' and so on. Less obviously, but equally important, vigorous local parties are a link between their electorates and the local, national and supranational political systems. The link is two-way. Local organisations are advertisements for their parties. Members are their ambassadors or perhaps more accurately, their advocates, promoting them between as well as at election times. This can be done simply by being members and through canvassing, distributing newsletters, membership recruitment and renewal, writing to the press and responding to political concerns. This last role becomes particularly important when, as with the Conservative Party, a traditionally friendly written media becomes less sympathetic. Members are their party's advocates but they are also a channel for transmitting information from the electorate to the wider party. Last but not least, local parties are a training ground for political leaders, although by reducing the scope and power of local government the Conservative Party has itself helped to erode part of the purpose and attraction of Association membership.

The need for vigorous and active local parties can be cogently argued on both organisational and participatory 'health of democracy' grounds. It can also be argued that they are vital for electoral success. However, the impact of sound and effective organisation on electoral outcomes is difficult to calculate and the dominant orthodoxy has usually had it that these are decided at the national level by national issues, national leaders and the national media. One direct measure of local electoral effectiveness which is acknowledged is the organisation of postal votes. It is recognised that the Conservatives have enjoyed an advantage in this area, with estimates of seats won as a result of better organisation at different general elections ranging from 6 to 17 (see Butler and King, 1966; Butler and Pinto-Duschinsky, 1971). More generally, it has been shown that turn-out in general elections from 1955 to 1979 was higher in the all-important marginal seats than in the safe ones (see Denver and Hands, 1974, 1985). Some of this differential turn-out might be attributable to voters' realisation of the significance of individual votes but the greater proportion is probably due to a naturally greater campaigning effort mobilising the electorate. One study has suggested that exceptionally efficient constituency Labour parties (CLPs) in about 40 marginal seats brought Labour to the verge of a hung parliament in 1992, despite the fact that it polled 7 per cent fewer votes nationally than the Conservatives (Whiteley and Seyd, 1992). This was achieved by localising the case for Labour and by urging tactical voting, strategies at variance with Labour's national organisers. There is a lesson here for any national party seeking to impose control and direction on its local organisations. In other words, local campaigning was found to stimulate the Labour vote.

There is confirmation that the same is true of the Conservative vote with a high correlation between the variables of membership, activism and campaign spending (expressed as a percentage of the maximum allowed) (Whiteley *et al.*, 1994: 197–9). Simulations applied to the 1987 general election indicate that an average increase in constituency spending of 10 per cent would have increased the Conservative vote by 1 per cent. If canvassing had been increased by 10 per cent this would have yielded another, additional 1 per cent and the Conservative Party would have received just over 44 per cent of the poll instead of just over 42 per cent (Whiteley *et al.*, 1994: 213). Put another way it means that if local Conservative Associations' campaigns had been 30 per cent below their actual rates of campaigning in that election and other parties had campaigned at 25 per cent above their actual rates then the party would have lost 47 seats, close to its overall majority (Seyd and Whiteley, 1994: 28). Local parties do appear to make a difference and, if they do, the decay in Conservative membership which is taking place alongside a growth in Labour membership threatens the comparative advantage in local organisation which the party has enjoyed for so long. Ominously, the organisational decline is greatest in those most vital seats – the Labour-held marginals which 'have been nearly abandoned by the Tories' (*The Times* 10 October 1994) where, out of 59 held by Labour with majorities of no more than 10 per cent, only seven Conservative Associations had a full-time, qualified agent in March 1994. Membership in Labour-held marginals averages 500 compared with the 1,000 in Conservative-held marginals. Membership, morale and, hence, electoral effectiveness may improve if the government's fortunes improve. However, the restoration of something like real dominance in membership levels may well hinge on the kind of fundamental re-evaluation of the role, purpose and place of the party's voluntary wing within the wider party discussed in the previous chapter.

Organisation

The model rules for Conservative Associations (including the groups of constituencies which constitute European Constituency Councils) identify 11 organisational 'Objects' (National Union of Conservative and Unionist Associations, 1993: 2). Broadly, these commit local parties to providing an efficient local organisation capable of securing the return of Conservative candidates at local, parliamentary and European elections. To achieve these electoral aims Associations form branches in wards or polling districts (subdivisions of wards). The work of branches is directed by committees, consisting of officers and members elected at the branch's annual general meeting. The officers include a chairman, one or more vice-chairmen, a treasurer and a secretary.

An Association's governing body is its Executive Council. Its officers are elected at an annual general meeting open to all subscribing members. Each branch elects at least two of its members to the Executive Council. The Chairman of the Executive Council is the Chairman of the Association. Since the Executive Council usually only meets several times a year, it appoints a General Purposes/Management Committee to oversee the ongoing business of the Association.

A reduced membership severely affects this kind of labour-intensive organisational structure, resting as it does on a network of ward and polling district branches. In fact polling district branches are now only found in some safe seats, usually in rural areas, and ward branches are often given responsibility for several wards. In some very inhospitable urban environments branch structures can be greatly attenuated or even non-existent. The danger of organisational atrophy of this kind is that decline can be self-perpetuating, with the development of a defensive and inward-looking culture inimical to political initiatives and the encouragement of new members. Conservative Associations tend to have a well-developed social aspect and function which, at its best, promotes cohesion and helps to sustain the primary goal of political activity. However, organisational decline can lead to goal displacement with the pursuit of inward-looking social goals replacing the outward-looking political ones (see Tether, 1990). Social and political goals conflict instead of complementing. This is particularly dangerous and inappropriate at a time when interelection political activities have become more important thanks to the campaigning zeal of local Liberal Democrat and, increasingly, Labour Parties.

Geographical branches provide Associations with their basic framework but to this structure there has been added, over the years, a variety of organisational vehicles to accommodate special interests and concerns. Special provision can be made for women, the YCs and Conservative Trade Unionists (CTUs). In addition, two organs exist to foster political awareness and initiatives at the local level. These are the Conservative Political Centre (CPC) and Political Committees.

Branches can establish separate women's sections but this is uncommon due to the decline in membership. The women's section of each branch, or the whole branch where there is no separate section, can elect representatives to a Women's Constituency Committee with its own officers and representation on the Executive Council. Its purpose is to provide a focus for all women members of an Association in political, social and money-raising matters. In practice, where Women's Constituency Committees exist, they are usually principally concerned with organising social events and, hence, fund-raising. In the preceding section it was noted that, contrary to popular belief, women are not today numerically preponderant in the party, although it should be added that they once were. Between the wars, the Conservative Women's Organisation was very active and important. Women outnumbered men and, indeed, 'in the 1920s some agents and executives became concerned about their control over these huge and semi-autonomous branches and the Women Organiser which the more prosperous employed' (Ball, 1994c: 274). Times have changed. Numbers of women have declined both absolutely and relative to the male membership but they are still disproportionately important to the social cohesion and political success of Associations through their social and fund-raising activities.

At constituency level YC organisation, where it exists, is also based on its own branch or branches culminating in a committee with representation on the Executive Council. The decline in YC membership and its implications for the party has been noted in the previous section. However, this decline has been offset to some extent by the fact that 'those who are left are far more politically minded than their forebears, who were mainly attracted by table tennis and the opportunity to meet 'suitable' members of the opposite sex' (Ball, 1994c: 275). In this connection it should be remembered that it was a group of Greater London Young Conservatives who produced the pamphlet *Set the Party Free* which led to the establishment of the Chelmer Committee, the Charter Movement and the Party Reform Steering Committee discussed in the previous chapter. The impact of the expansion of higher education on YC membership has been compensated for to some extent by the organisation of young people in colleges and universities. The Federation of Conservative Students which had been firmly on the left of the party became the preserve of the radical right in the 1980s and such an embarrassment that it was disbanded by its Central Office organisers. Purged of its undesirable elements, it was re-formed in 1986 as the Conservative Collegiate Forum. With a membership of 'between 6,000 and 10,000 this has become equal in size and weight to the dwindling YCs' (Ball, 1994c: 276). Ideological disputes and a greater assertiveness mean that, in recent years, the Conservative youth movement both inside and outside the constituencies have come to resemble much more nearly their traditionally 'difficult' Labour counterparts.

Conservative Associations make separate organisational provision for both women and young people. Another group for which such provision is made are trade unionists in the shape of the CTU. Attempts to harness trade union support go back to the beginning of the century, but the direct antecedents of the CTU can be traced to constituency Labour Committees promoted by the Lancashire Provincial Council (part of the subnational structure discussed below) after 1919. Under the pressure of Labour advances (whose share of the popular vote increased from 8 per cent in 1910 to 22.2 per cent in 1918), this initiative was rapidly taken up by associations outside Lancashire. The function of Labour Committees was to advise on all aspects of 'Trade Union and Co-operative Society Movements and on any topic of special interest to wage earners' (Conservative and Unionist Central Office, 1933: x).

Revamped in the late 1940s the CTU seeks, today, to encourage trade unionists to support the Conservative Party, explain the party's industrial policies within the union movement and encourage non-socialists to 'contract out' of the political levy (Hart, undated: 4). At constituency level CTU members can be organised in interest groups which elect a CTU Constituency Committee. A CTU Constituency Committee can, if members so wish, operate as an individual committee or it can agree to operate jointly with one or more adjacent CTU Committees to form a CTU Joint Constituency Committee. Whether Committees are based in one constituency or several, the purpose is the same, 'to co-ordinate activities in an area and provide information on employment and industrial matters for the Party locally and nationally' (Conservative Trade Unionists, undated). A CTU Constituency Committee is a committee of the Executive Council established under the model rules. However, interestingly, these do not specifically mention CTU Constituency Committees or make any reference to their constitutional position at the local level. In particular, it is striking that CTU Constituency Committees are not among the bodies and groups which the rules suggest should be represented on Executive Councils. The CTU movement as a whole is only lightly connected to constituency organisation and should perhaps be regarded as a largely free-standing body. In 1986, the CTU claimed 70,000 members (Kelly, 1989: 163) but in the absence of a national registration system this claim must be treated with some caution.

The CPC was established in 1945 but it was essentially a revival, extension and refurbishment of a pre-war institution – the Central Education Department of Central Office. It was the brainchild of R.A. Butler, who was determined that the party should develop the policies and arguments that would enable it to debate effectively and to challenge socialism's intellectual credentials. The CPC then, as now, organised a range of lectures and courses and eventually developed an important publishing facility which provides a ready means for the dissemination of ideas and policy proposals. However, the core of the CPC's activities is the Contact Programme. Under this programme, monthly or sometimes bi-monthly briefs on topics of concern and interest are issued to CPC discussion groups in the constituencies. The recommended size of groups is 8–12 people and considerable emphasis is placed on representativeness, since it is deemed important that groups reflect different shades of opinion within the local party. Topics for discussion are decided by the Director of the CPC in consultation with other senior figures. Main findings from the subsequent reports submitted by CPC groups in the constituencies are collated, summarised and circulated to party leaders and ministers and 'after deliberation, a considered reply is prepared by the Minister and this is then circulated (with the summary) to the discussion groups' (Norton and Aughey, 1981: 218).

The key question in any evaluation of the CPC is does it provide a genuine channel for the articulation of views and ideas from the constituencies or is it, primarily, a means of 'educating' the membership? It would seem that the latter is largely the case. Thus, while the CPC does keep the centre informed of views on the periphery, its main function is to 'inform the rank and file of where the party is going or, indeed, has gone' (Aughey, 1981: 10). CPC groups do act as a sounding board, ensuring that the leadership does not get too far out of step with their followers, but this is a limited role. An increasingly assertive voluntary party may want more influence over the topics selected and a briefing format which is less constraining.

The other political organ is the Political Committee. As noted in the preceding chapter, these committees were the only fruit of the Chelmer Committee set up in the wake of the Greater London YC's demands for party reform, adumbrated in *Set the Party Free*. They are designed to stimulate political activity and it is suggested that they 'should be relatively small . . . and . . . consist of key people appointed by the Chairman and officers of the Association' (National Union of Conservative and Unionist Associations, 1993: 17). It is envisaged that the committees should be responsible for arranging debates and discussion, liaising between Associations and Conservative groups on local authorities and recommending the formation of specialist advisory groups. However, in practice many Political Committees are both rather more and rather less than the formal prescriptions imply. They tend to become groupings of activists which undertake political work of one kind or another themselves, rather than 'stimulating' it in other parts of the organisation. With the reduction in membership and, hence, branches, a Political Committee is often the best and most appropriate vehicle to promote and deliver political initiatives such as leafleting, canvassing, recruiting and renewing membership, compiling and delivering newsletters, identifying and capitalising on issues and so on. Political Committees are, therefore, an important antidote to the tendency toward organisational introversion and that process of goal displacement (where inward-looking social goals replace outward-looking political ones) which can accompany membership decline and a discouraging electoral environment. The centralisation of some Association functions is necessary at a time of depleted membership. Properly conceptualised, the Political Committee could have an important cultural, organisational and electoral role in the local party of the future.

This kind of husbanding, consolidating and focusing of resources is either being recommended or has already occurred in other areas. Full-time qualified and professionally trained agents strengthen Associations' organisation and effectiveness but at the end of 1994 'local associations were employing only 207 qualified agents, the lowest number since immediately after the Second World War' (*The Times* 10 October 1994: 8). Three-quarters were employed in safe Conservative seats where they are least needed with the fewest in Labour marginals. The answer, many believe, 'is for Central Office to abandon its vision of an agent in every constituency and to maximise the efficiency of existing resources by pooling agents and overheads' (*The Times* 11 October 1994). The kind of regrouping that some see as necessary in respect of constituency agents has occurred with the party's subnational structure where Central Office's regional organisation in England and Wales descends to meet the organisation of the National Union ascending from the constituencies. Central Office used to maintain offices in each of the 11 provincial areas of the National Union in England and Wales in which constituencies are grouped on a geographical basis.

Financial problems after the 1992 general election led, on 1 June 1993, to the 10 Area Offices in England being reduced to 6 Regional Offices with the largest – London and Eastern – containing 135 constituencies. Each of these units has a Regional and, in some cases, a Deputy Regional Director. Both officers are experienced agents (Fowler and Conservative Central Office, 1993: 24). Scotland has its own Central Office, under the control of a Director of Organisation, servicing a separate Scottish Conservative and Unionist Association (SCUA). The Scottish constituencies are grouped into five regions. Although it possesses a distinct organisational structure and Scottish Conservatives have their own Annual Conference, the SCUA is represented on the National Union's Central Council (see below) and Scottish constituency organisations are affiliated to the National Union. Thus, 'the organisation of the party in Scotland falls between the national and regional tiers and incorporates features of both' (Ball, 1994b: 205).

This 'slimming down' has broken the obvious link that has existed since the 1930s between Central Office subnational organisational structure and that of the National Union. In the case of the latter, constituencies continue to be grouped in 11 provincial areas since 'voluntary workers will not spend too much time or money in travelling to meetings and are more influenced than professional organisers by personal attachment to the regions generally understood by the public' (Ball, 1994b: 207). This uncoupling of the professional and voluntary wings of the party may create difficulties although an attempt has been made to avoid problems with the appointment of regional Campaign Executives in the new Central Office regions. These are new posts. Campaign Executives are experienced agents with special responsibility for helping marginal seats and assisting Associations without agents to develop their resources so that they can employ one of their own. In regions which contain two areas, regional Campaign Executives will be based in the areas so each one will, it is stressed, continue to have the services of a senior agent (Fowler and Conservative Central Office, 1993: 24).

The provincial areas, supported by Central Office services and resources, constitute an important intermediate and regional level in the organisation of the National Union but it is a level hidden entirely from public view. The governing body in each provincial area is the area council made up of MPs, parliamentary candidates and agents together with officers and representatives from the constituencies. Between meetings of the area councils, business is delegated to area Executive Committees. Each area has a range of Advisory Committees representing the constituency groupings discussed above and other interests within the party. Thus, the *Annual Report of the Yorkshire Area Council* meeting held in April 1995 gives news of the work of Women's,

YC, CTU and CPC Advisory Committees. The *Report* also refers to Education and Local Government Advisory Committees and a body known as the Agriculture Forum (National Union of Conservative and Unionist Associations, Yorkshire Area, 1995).

Education Advisory Committees represent a relatively new element in Conservative organisation and reflect a growing concern over this topic. Some Associations now have Education Committees to bring together members interested in this subject and committees at both area and constituency level liaise with teachers within the CTU who have their own separate organisation within that body. The Local Government Advisory Committee represents the views of Conservative councillors within an area. The Agriculture Forum is an advisory committee representing agricultural and rural interests within the party. In 1994, the Yorkshire Area's Agriculture Forum made representations to ministers on subjects as diverse as 'set aside' land, sheep quotas, the General Agreement on Tariffs and Trade (GATT) and problems associated with the proposed Vale of York National Grid line (National Union of Conservative and Unionist Associations, Yorkshire Area, 1995). All the groupings represented by area Advisory Committees (and sometimes subgroupings such as teachers in the CTU) hold conferences at area and national levels. These constitute the Conservatives' hidden 'conference system' explored by Kelly (1989).

Structures at the top of the National Union necessarily duplicate those found at area level. Area Advisory Committees elect representatives to a string of national equivalents. Members of the provincial area councils elect representatives to the National Union's governing body – the Central Council. The day to day business of this large and unwieldy body is delegated to a National Union Executive Committee (NUEC) and a General Purposes Committee (GPC). The Central Council of the National Union is jealous of constituency autonomy which it seeks to preserve from what it sees as Central Office 'interference'. Thus, in March 1993, rule changes proposed by the Party Chairman, Norman Fowler, were angrily rejected 'precisely because they would have eroded the independence of constituencies, in particular in the sensitive area of finance' (Ball, 1994c: 262). Nevertheless, Central Office has in recent years managed to push a number of contentious reforms with implications for constituency autonomy through Central Council (Kelly, 1995b: 80–1). The claims by advocates of more internal democracy that Central Office has colonised the NUEC and GPC and seeks to manipulate Central Council meetings have been discussed in the previous chapter. The task of Central Office staff in Smith Square and the newly formed Regional Offices in England and Wales is to support and service this complex structure and considerable effort and planning are required to enable all the meetings to take place and the conferences to be held. In addition, Central Office provides Associations with the advice, training and publicity materials without which they would not be able to function. It oversees the training of agents and maintains an official candidates' list. Its contribution is particularly important at election time when it is responsible for every Conservative candidates' bible, *The Campaign Guide*, and co-ordinating national and local campaigning on an hourly basis.

Since 1992, Central Office has consisted of three main sections covering Campaigning, Communications and Research, each under its own Director. The whole is headed by the Chairman of the Party Organisation, appointed by the leader (see Chapter 9). Advocates of more intraparty democracy, perennially suspicious of Central Office, periodically call for the Party Chairman to be elected by the voluntary wing. The weight and status of Chairmen tend to vary with the electoral cycle, with more senior and heavyweight figures being appointed in the run-up to elections. However, party management is not always an attractive option for ambitious and leading politicians with an already heavy ministerial workload and leaders can find it difficult to fill the post with a figure of appropriate calibre. The Party Chairman is assisted by one or two Deputies (the best-known of whom has been the novelist Jeffrey Archer) and a number of Vice-Chairmen to 'provide leadership and co-ordination for specific aspects of the party's work' (Ball, 1994b: 183); they are the bureaucratic and administrative equivalents of Ministers of State.

The professional wing of the Conservative Party functions with relatively few full time salaried employees. In December 1993, thanks to financial stringencies, Central Office staff was reduced by about 60 to 236, with 182 in Smith Square and 54 in the Regions. In 1994–5, the number employed in Central Office was further reduced (to 159). However, as with the Party Chairman, Central Office as a whole moves to the pulse of the electoral cycle and this figure is likely to rise in a pre-election period. At the 1992 general election 'the party's payroll amounted to 342 persons . . . this was a force substantially larger and better equipped than that of any other party' (Ball, 1995: 192).

CHAPTER 8

The party in Parliament

Philip Norton

At the beginning of the twentieth century Conservative MPs were the dominant force in the House of Commons. They had three observable and important characteristics. First, despite their numbers, they lacked any formal organisation of their own. Secondly, they were remarkably cohesive in their voting behaviour. Thirdly, they were drawn largely from professional and business interests.

The effect of the 1867 Reform Act has already been detailed in Chapter 1. A mass electorate necessitated party organisation. Organisation was necessary in order to make contact with electors; but organisation was not a sufficient condition for electoral success. The party had to deliver on its promises. Candidates were selected by their local parties and depended for their election on their party label. The party quickly dominated not only electoral behaviour but also parliamentary politics. MPs were elected on party labels and were expected by those who selected and elected them to support loyally their party. Cohesion rapidly became a feature of voting behaviour in the House of Commons. By the turn of the century, party votes were the norm.

Within the House of Commons the organisation necessary to ensure that cohesion was in place. Whips in the House have their origins in the eighteenth century. Their role and number increased throughout the nineteenth century as public business increased and party became more important. After the 1832 Reform Act, for example, the number of government whips increased from two to five and, on occasion, six (Aspinall, 1926: 396, 398; Aspinall, 1952: iii). Their tasks were essentially those of communication, management and persuasion (Norton, 1994a: 99–100). They kept their party supporters in the House informed of business, usually through the circulation of a weekly document (also known as the whip), and also kept leaders and led informed of the views of the other. It was also their task, if in government, to ensure that sufficient of their supporters were present to carry the day in the event of a vote. The more important the business, the greater the need to ensure a full turnout. The whips adopted the practice of letting MPs know the importance that the party leaders attached to particular items by underlining the items on the written whip. The more important the item, the greater the number of lines. Today (as early in the nineteenth century) a three-line whip signals that the business is deemed the most important and that the Member's attendance is vital. At the turn of the century, the whips were employing four- and five-line whips.

Members usually acted in accordance with the requests made through the whips. They did so because they wanted to. They were elected on a party label and supported the goals of the party. They wanted to support their side against the other side. They often had other activities to pursue outside Parliament. Many had estates to look after or to use for hunting and shooting; an even greater number were likely to be invited to go hunting and shooting on those estates. A number had business interests to pursue. The time they could devote to service in Parliament was limited and they were therefore grateful for the guidance offered by the whips. On those occasions when MPs might not like what the party proposed to do, it was the task of the whips to persuade them to support the leadership. Appeals to party loyalty were usually sufficient. If they failed, the whips could make life unpleasant both within the House and, usually through the Chief Whip, with the local party. Until 1911, the Chief Whip had responsibilities for campaign management and the dispersal of some campaign funds.

It was, in any event, difficult for an individual back-bencher to cause problems. The MP might mix socially with other Members, but he was dependent on the party leadership to give a lead and had little opportunity to discuss matters with other MPs on a regular or structured basis. If MPs were upset by a particular proposal and sought to rally fellow Members against it their attempts at organisation were *ad hoc*, encompassing letters, meetings called by one of their number and delegations to the leader. The organisation of the whips was anything but *ad hoc* and could be deployed immediately to counter any dissension.

The Conservative Party in the House of Commons at the beginning of the twentieth century was thus a very hierarchical and essentially regimented body. Leadership was very much top-down, with meetings of MPs being called only as and when deemed necessary by the leader and for the purpose of letting MPs know what the views of the leader were. MPs were then expected to vote as directed.

The situation in the House of Lords was not substantively different. Peers did not have the same party pressures as MPs – they had no local parties and electors to answer to – and were not as easy to manage as their counterparts in the Commons (see Ridley, 1992: 241). Conservative peers were also more prone to gather together than were Conservative MPs (Norton, 1994a: 135). However, they lacked any formal organisation and would normally support the leader. The 1911 Parliament Act – a measure bitterly opposed by some Conservatives – formally limited the powers of the Upper House and thereafter the House receded in political significance. This was reflected in a low attendance by peers. Although there were more than 700 peers in the 1920s, with almost 500 of them in receipt of the Conservative whip, it was rare for the daily attendance to reach three figures. Between 1919 and 1957 the average number taking part in a vote was around 80; the number voting on an important issue was about 150 (Bromhead, 1957: 32). There were therefore, relative to the Commons, fairly few people to organise.

What the twentieth century has witnessed has been a change in the characteristics of the Conservative Party in Parliament. It has become more organised, especially in the House of Commons. It has also become less cohesive in its voting behaviour and more middle class in its social composition. The development of an internal organisation is a feature of the inter-war years. Although the party in Parliament has split on a number of important issues throughout the century, such as (quite dramatically) free trade in the first two decades and India and rearmament in the 1930s, the decline in cohesion has been a feature especially of the years since 1970. Changes in social composition have also taken place since 1900, but have been most marked since the mid-1970s.

The consequence is that Conservative MPs in the 1990s are notably different from their predecessors at the beginning of the century. The typical Conservative MP in 1900 was a businessman or professional gentleman who devoted only part of his week to the House of Commons and who would vote as requested by the whips. The typical Conservative MP in the 1990s – in so far as there is a typical MP – is a middle-aged, middle class career politician, devoted to a life in politics, using official or unofficial party groupings in the House to acquire information or to influence party leaders, and prepared on occasion to vote against the party line.

Organisation

The 1922 Committee

The absence of any means of discussing matters among themselves caused concern to some newly elected Conservative MPs in 1922. One of their number, Gervais Rentoul (MP for Lowestoft), brought together in 1923 some like-minded MPs to discuss how they might be better informed about parliamentary life. They started to meet regularly and formed a body known as the Conservative Private Members' (1922) Committee (Goodhart, 1973). The committee was addressed by the Chief Whip and by a number of invited guests. Membership of the Committee was offered to new Members of the subsequent Parliament and in 1926 opened up to all Private Members in receipt of the Conservative whip.

The body known popularly as the 1922 Committee was thus born. It was, and remains, an 'unofficial' body, sometimes portrayed as the 'trade union' for Conservative MPs. Despite this status it enjoys formal links with other parts of the party – being represented, for example, on the party's National Union Executive Committee – and since 1965 has had responsibility for organising the election of the party leader.

The practices of the 1922 Committee established in its early years have largely remained in place since (Norton, 1994a: 108–9). Each year it elects officers and an executive committee, meeting once a week, preceded by a meeting of the executive committee. Initially, the Committee invited important outside figures to address it – speakers in the 1930s included the Commissioner of the Salvation Army and the chairman of Lloyds Bank – but that practice has largely disappeared. The principal guest speakers in the 1920s and 1930s were ministers and that remains the case today. (The party leader addresses the Committee each year, shortly before the summer recess.) The Committee meets to hear an announcement about the next week's business in the House and to discuss usually important subjects of a parliamentary or party nature. The topic discussed most often by the Committee since its inception has been that of MPs' pay (Norton, 1994a: 109).

It is common in the press to refer to the Committee as 'the influential 1922 Committee'. It is influential, but very much on a sporadic basis. The regular weekly meetings attract little interest from most Conservative MPs and are often poorly attended. The Committee attracts attention usually only at the beginning of a session when officers are elected, and when a minister, or the party leader, faces calls to resign.

The election of officers at the beginning of each parliamentary session provides an opportunity for different groups within the parliamentary party to push their own candidates. Groups such as the right-wing 92 Group organise slates of candidates. The results are then analysed by the media in terms of what they reveal about the strengths of the left and right within the parliamentary party. Traditionally, the executive of the 1922 Committee has been portrayed as dominated by centre-right MPs. Elections for the chairman and members of the executive are also sometimes seen as ways of sending messages to the leader or to recalcitrant back-benchers. In 1993 the chairman of the 92 Group – Sir George Gardiner – lost his place on the executive, seen widely as a punishment inflicted by MPs loyal to the Prime Minister because of Sir George's failure to support the Prime Minister in votes on the Maastricht Treaty. In 1994 a contest for the chairmanship was seen as a battle between a candidate loyal to the Prime Minister (the incumbent, Sir Marcus Fox) and one who wanted a more critical approach by the Prime Minister to the issue of European integration (Sir Nicholas Bonsor). The incumbent won, reportedly by a narrow margin.

The Committee is also important when a leadership challenge takes place, being responsible for the organisation of the ballot. However, it plays a more direct role if a minister, or the party leader, comes in for attack from parts of the parliamentary party. If a crisis involving a minister (assuming the party is in power) blows up, the matter is likely to be raised at a meeting of the 1922 Committee. The Committee in effect may determine the fate of the minister. A rough reception may influence the minister to resign. In 1982, the Foreign Secretary Lord Carrington was heavily criticised when he faced 'the 1922' following the invasion of the Falklands Islands by Argentinean forces. He was already contemplating resigning and the reaction from MPs at the meeting confirmed him in his intention to go. Leon Brittan, the Trade and Industry Secretary embroiled in the Westland affair, resigned in January 1986, the day after facing a stormy meeting of the Committee. Realising he did not have the support of the parliamentary party he decided to quit. The influence of the 1922 Committee may also be seen in the departure from government of junior health minister Edwina Currie in 1988 (over controversial remarks about salmonella in eggs), National Heritage Secretary David Mellor in 1992 (over a scandal concerning his private life) and Northern Ireland minister Michael Mates in 1993 (over his support for a fugitive businessman). Mr Mellor resigned shortly after receiving a telephone call from the chairman of the Committee. Mr Mates resigned a few hours before the 1922 Committee was to meet to discuss his fate.

The executive also becomes important if criticism of the party leader becomes widespread. In 1974 the executive was instrumental in instigating a review of the rules for electing the leader, resulting in the provision for annual election. Although the leader may now be subject to a formal leadership challenge, the executive of the 1922 may seek to head off such a drastic outcome by conveying back-bench concerns to the leader. In 1990 the chairman, Cranley Onslow, was criticised for failing to express with sufficient vigour to Margaret Thatcher the concerns of back-benchers. In 1995, the 1922 executive presented to Prime Minister John Major some proposals to restore support for the party.

Even with the provision for election, it is claimed that a delegation from the 1922 may visit the Prime Minister to tell him to go, should he lose the confidence of back-benchers. During the leadership contest forced by John Major in July 1995 it was suggested that if the Prime Minister won but only by the narrowest of margins, the officers of the 1922 would tell him his position was untenable. This derived in part from the presumption that a visit from a delegation of the 1922 – dubbed 'the men in grey suits' – was the traditional means of removing a leader. In practice, no leader had ever gone as a result of any such visit; nonetheless, this mythology has helped underpin the influence of the 1922 Committee.

Party committees

The 1922 Committee rarely influences policy. This in large part is because specific policy proposals are not brought before it on a regular basis. Such proposals are discussed instead in party committees.

The 1922 Committee established some committees shortly after it came into being but these were superseded in 1924 by official committees set up by the party leadership. They have remained in place since. Although reports from the committees may be presented to meetings of the 1922 Committee, the committees are independent of the 1922. They are not subordinate to it but rather exist in parallel to it.

The committees established in the 1920s soon became an important part of life in the parliamentary party. The practices they adopted have largely remained in place since. Each committee has officers – elected at the beginning of the session – and meets on a regular basis to discuss topics pertinent to the committee's interests and to listen to guest speakers. Unlike the 1922 Committee, the practice of inviting outside guest speakers has continued and constitutes a central part of the committees' activities. Meetings of each committee are open to all Conservative MPs who wish to attend. There is no fixed membership. Peers also may, and variously do, attend. Conservative peers acquired their own organisation, the equivalent of the 1922 Committee, in the 1920s (Norton, 1994a: 130–44) but have not developed a system of party committees.

Like the 1922 Committee, the election of committee officers now attracts considerable interest, with different groups seeking to get 'their' candidates elected. As Julian Critchley observed in 1973, conflict within the party rarely surfaces at meetings of the 1922 Committee. 'It is more likely to manifest itself in the fight for election to office in the minor, specialist, committees' (Critchley, 1973: 409). The Finance Committee became a battleground in the early 1970s for groups with different approaches to economic policy. Since it was established in the 1975–6 session, the officerships of the European Affairs Committee have been variously fought over by supporters and opponents of greater European integration. Euro-sceptic MPs managed to get their candidates elected in 1990 but then MPs loyal to the Prime Minister ousted them in 1991.

Despite the publicity that attends such elections the committees are not much covered by the media in the period between elections, yet they provide a consistent focus for MPs' activities. There are currently 24 committees covering the principal sectors of public policy (foreign affairs, finance, agriculture and so on) and seven regional committees, drawing together the party's MPs from each particular region. Each seeks to meet on a regular basis, the more important meeting once a week.

The committees provide an opportunity for MPs to acquire information about a particular subject. For those MPs wishing to concentrate in a particular sector of public policy, they provide the means for specialising and for making a name through committee activity. Serving as a committee officer provides some status within the party and gives one some claim to catching the Speaker's eye during an appropriate debate. In a debate on the economy, for instance, the chairman of the Conservative Finance Committee is almost certain to be called to speak if he wishes to do so. For new MPs, serving as a committee officer is a good way of becoming socialised into the parliamentary party and may provide a first step on to the road to recognition as being of ministerial quality.

An important meeting can draw a good attendance. When the Chancellor of the Exchequer addresses the Finance Committee shortly after he has delivered his budget there is normally a three-figure turnout. When the President of the Board of Trade, Michael Heseltine, addressed the Trade and Industry Committee in October 1992 following an announcement about pit closures, more than 150 MPs crowded into the committee room. Such attendances are rare; regular committee meetings rarely draw double figures. Attendance in recent years has declined, largely because of the increasing pressures on MPs' time (Norton, 1994a). The decrease in attendance has led to some committees meeting less regularly than before – fortnightly instead of weekly, for example. This has caused concern among committee officers and has been the subject of discussion in the 1922 Committee.

Despite the decline in attendance the committees remain important features of the Conservative Party in Parliament. They provide a means of essentially private two-way communication between interested back-benchers and the appropriate front bencher. Doubts can be expressed privately before an issue reaches the floor of the House. A whip attends each meeting and any criticisms are reported to the minister and the Chief Whip.

The committees also remain means of communication between MPs and bodies outside the House. Organised interests are keen to offer speakers to address the appropriate committee. A survey of more than 250 organised interests in 1986 found that just over 40 per cent of them – 103 in total – had had some contact with party committees. Of these, most had been invited to attend a committee meeting and almost three-quarters rated their contacts with the committees as useful or very useful (Rush, 1990: 286–7). Although the contact was rated as less important than that with select committees and individual Members (Rush, 1990: 292) it remains a useful way of getting a particular point of view over to a body of interested MPs.

Unofficial groups

The party committees are official party committees. They absorb some of the time of many (not all) Conservative MPs. However, for some of those MPs, as much, if not more, time is devoted to unofficial groups within the parliamentary party.

Unofficial groupings within the party have existed for some time, although usually forming on an *ad hoc* basis to oppose a particular policy. Early examples in this century include the Halsbury Club, formed by MPs and peers opposed to the 1911 Parliament Bill, and a 'Die Hard' Group opposed to Irish Home Rule (Norton, 1979: 33). Since 1945 they have become more numerous and more organised. They are also very varied. They encompass a range of dining groups as well as several groups organised to promote a particular strand of Conservative thought or to promote (or oppose) a particular policy.

The dining groups within the parliamentary party are numerous. Each comprises a number of Conservative MPs drawn together, on a self-selecting basis, to dine regularly and discuss matters of common interest. Some are composed of MPs who are politically like-minded and meet to discuss strategy for achieving their particular views. The 1979 Parliament was notable for two of the dining groups set up by newly-elected members (Oakley, 1980: 44–5). One was the 'Blue Chip' group which brought together some of the more intellectual of the new intake, including William Waldegrave, Chris Patten and John Patten. The group had a reputation for being somewhat 'wet' politically and in 1981 published a pamphlet calling for more government aid to industry. The other group was the 'Guy Fawkes' group, which first met on 5 November and which was seen at the time as bringing together some other MPs who were on the party's left, such as Stephen Dorrell, David Mellor and Robin Squire. (The group also included John Major.) The dining groups are popular with MPs, not least because they provide a socially congenial, and private, environment for discussion and one confined to those MPs who tend to get on with one another. Unlike party committee meetings, they are not open to any MP who feels like attending.

The groups formed on a more political, organised and open basis (that is, open to those MPs sharing their aims) are varied in aims, size and longevity. The groups representing the right of the party are more numerous. They include the 92 Group, named after the address (92 Cheyne Walk) of one of their original number (Sir Patrick Wall) and which in the Parliament elected in 1992 has about 100 MPs, although the degree of commitment to a right-wing agenda among this number varies considerably. The numbers involved, however, make it an important group. During the 1995 leadership election contest, both candidates – John Major and John Redwood – addressed a meeting of the group.

There is a smaller group of Thatcherite MPs forming the 'No Turning Back' Group, active since the 1980s and committed to maintaining a Thatcherite agenda. Some MPs are also members of groups which are not confined to a parliamentary membership, such as Conservative Way Forward, formed after Margaret Thatcher ceased to be party leader in order to promote the policies for which she stood (this group claims about 80–100 MPs as members, overlapping considerably with the 92 Group), the Selsdon Group, committed to a neo-liberal economic policy and the Monday Club (much more prominent in the 1970s), committed to the policies of the traditional Tory right. On the left of the party about 40 MPs are members of the Tory Reform Group, which is not confined to a parliamentary membership but which has senior ministers as its vice-presidents. Some on the left also operate through dining groups – a well-known early example, predating the ones already mentioned, was 'Nick's Diner', set up by Nicholas Scott in the

1970s – and through short-lived groups, such as Centre Forward set up by Francis Pym in the latter half of the 1980s.

The issue of European integration has split the party since it first was mooted and has led to some degree of organisation among MPs opposed to membership of the European Community and to further integration. Opponents organised themselves, with an unofficial 'whip', in 1972 during the passage of the European Communities Bill (Norton, 1978) and organised themselves into the 'Fresh Start' Group during passage of the European Communities (Amendment) Bill – to ratify the Maastricht Treaty – in 1992 and 1993. The name was taken from an Early Day Motion signed by 69 Conservatives calling for a 'fresh start' on the issue of Europe. The group, claiming a membership of about 80 MPs, is now but one of several organised on the issue of Europe. In 1995 Prime Minister John Major was given such a bad reception at a meeting of the group that it was one of the key factors (if not *the* key factor) that convinced him to force a leadership election. A more reflective group of about 40 Euro-sceptics form the European Research Group. On the other side of the issue, about 40 Members belong to the pro-European Conservative Group for Europe. The Tory Reform Group is also prominent in supporting greater European integration.

What emerges from all this is a parliamentary party more crowded than ever before with groups pressing their views on leaders and on other Conservative MPs. At the beginning of the century the parliamentary party was organised in terms of leadership but not in terms of a back-bench infrastructure. Today Conservative MPs have a plethora of groups, both official and unofficial, that they can join (or, in some cases, be invited to join). The result is a more active body of MPs and one more organised to ensure that the views of MPs can be conveyed to party leaders. The organised nature of the groups also means that MPs are better placed than before to meet, prepare tactics and pursue their objections if they do not like the response of their leaders.

Party splits

The party in Parliament split badly on a number of issues in the early decades of the century, notably on free trade and, in the 1930s, on India and disarmament. Mostly, however, MPs were responsive to the pleas of the whips and voted loyally with their party. That loyalty became pronounced in the years after 1945. The party split on the issue of Suez in 1956, a number of back-benchers making clear their opposition to the occupation of the Suez canal zone by British and French forces, but that opposition did not involve voting against the government in the division lobbies. That did not stop opponents running into trouble with their local parties. Conservative MPs voted with their own side usually because they wanted to. In any event, there was little obvious cause for internal conflict. In the 1950s the party was in government and the country was enjoying relative economic prosperity. If there was any disagreement, it was expected to be expressed privately. Voting against the whips was discouraged by the fear of jeopardising the position of the government and by concern for the reaction of the local party (Norton, 1991: 221–2). Under the Maxwell-Fyfe reforms local parties achieved greater control of candidate selection. Candidates could no longer contribute significant amounts to local party funds and, in effect, purchase their candidatures. The candidate was now dependent on the local association, rather than the other way around. 'The trouble with the post 1950 situation', as Maxwell-Fyfe was himself to observe, 'was that many associations became more Royalist than the King, and assumed a control over their candidate which in some cases was tyrannical' (Maxwell-Fyfe, 1964). Some Conservative MPs ran into trouble with their local parties on issues such as capital punishment, one – Nigel Nicolson, in Bournemouth East – being de-selected by his local association.

During the 1950s voting cohesion in the House of Commons reached its peak. There were actually two sessions in which not one Conservative MP voted against the party. There was some cross-voting in the early 1960s, the occasional Conservative MP voting with the opposition, but this took place in a Parliament in which the government had a large overall majority and therefore had little effect. Cohesion remained the norm. A government with an overall majority knew it could get its way if it pressed ahead.

All this was to change during the years after 1970. In the Parliament of 1970–4 Conservative MPs voted against their own side more often than before, in greater numbers, and with greater effect (Norton, 1975, 1978). During the Parliament, there were more than 200 votes in which one or more Conservative MPs voted against their own side. Sixty-four of these votes involved ten or more Conservatives voting against the government. Given that the government had been returned with a modest overall majority (of 30), its majority was vulnerable on occasion to being wiped out. It was defeated six times, three of the defeats taking place on three-line whips. The issues creating divisions within the party's ranks were wide-ranging, including membership of the European Community, the economy, Northern Ireland and the siting of a third London airport. As we noted in Chapter 3, the leading dissenter on the Conservative benches was Enoch Powell (Conservative MP for Wolverhampton South-west) who voted against the government 113 times in the Parliament. The second most frequent dissenter was the MP for Oswestry, John Biffen, later to be a member of Margaret Thatcher's Cabinet.

There was little relationship between this behaviour and a 'new breed' of Conservative MP entering the House. (Enoch Powell, for instance, had been elected in 1950.) Rather, the trigger for MPs to take their disagreement to the voting lobbies has been identified as the Prime Ministerial style of Edward Heath (Norton, 1978). He forced through radical measures, insisting on their expeditious passage without amendment, and without being prepared to listen to objections voiced by back-benchers. Back-benchers felt excluded and

Table 8.1 Divisions witnessing dissenting votes in the House of Commons 1945–92

Parliament (number of sessions in parentheses)	Number of divisions witnessing dissenting votes			Number of divisions witnessing dissenting votes expressed as % of all divisions
	Total	Lab	Con	
1945–50 (4)	87	79	27	7
1950–1 (2)	6	5	2	2.5
1951–5 (4)	25	17	11	3
1955–9 (4)	19	10	12	2
1959–64 (5)	137	26	120	13.5
1964–6 (2)	2	1	1	0.5
1966–70 (4)	124	109	41	9.5
1970–4 (4)	221	34	204	20
1974 (1)	25	8	21	23
1974–9 (5)	423	309	240	28
1979–83 (4)	261	169	164	20
1983–7 (4)	280	88	209	22
1987–92 (5)	326	157	202	20

NB: The data for the period 1979–92 are provisional. They assume complete accuracy on the part of *Hansard* and a number of possible errors have yet to be checked.

Sources: Norton (1980) for 1945–79 and data from ESRC-funded research project being conducted by the author for the period 1979–92.

Heath made little attempt to generate goodwill: he made sparse use of his power of patronage and would often snub back-bench MPs, who felt that they had no way of expressing their opposition other than through the division lobbies. Once they had voted against their own side it became – in the words of one of them – so much easier to do it a second time. MPs soon discovered that government defeats did not jeopardise the continuance of the government in office and, as long as they maintained reputations as good constituency Members, they did not incur many (if any) problems with their local parties.

Once the genie of back-bench independence – albeit a rather modest genie – had been let out of the bottle, there was no way of putting it back. Cohesion remains a central feature of parliamentary life, but MPs are more prepared than before to vote against their own side. The change of the early 1970s has been maintained. This is apparent from Table 8.1. The data in the table are fairly crude, identifying simply the number of divisions in which one or more MP voted against the whips. Most occasions involved a small number of MPs. In the period between 1979 and 1992 the size of the government's overall majority meant that the Thatcher and then, from 1990 to 1992, the Major government, could absorb most occasions of cross-voting by dissident back-benchers. The effect, if not the incidence, of cross-voting was thus less than in the 1970s, when governments had more fragile or non-existent majorities.

Even so cross-voting by Conservative MPs, or the threat of it, was not al-together without effect. Various instances of back-bench dissent embarrassed the government, and concessions were variously made to assuage the doubts of back-bench critics (Norton, 1985: 33–5). On two occasions policies were dropped under the threat of defeat and on one celebrated occasion the Thatcher government went down to a humiliating defeat – on the Shops Bill, to deregulate Sunday trading – in April 1986 when 72 Conservative MPs voted with the opposition to defeat it on second reading (Regan, 1988; Bown, 1990). Such occasions were exceptional but sufficient to demonstrate that even an apparently powerful leader could not take her own back-benchers for granted. Letter writing by constituents to Conservative MPs also served to undermine back-bench support for the poll tax in 1990 (Cowley, 1995) and, as Margaret Thatcher remained committed to the tax, served to undermine her position as leader, a position that now depended on the annual support of Conservative MPs.

The government of John Major returned to office in 1992 was vulnerable in a way that Edward Heath's had been in 1970–4. It had a modest majority and there was a central issue – that of Europe – that split the party. The government suffered an embarrassing defeat on the issue in 1993 and then, in November 1994, when eight Conservatives failed to support the government in a declared vote of confidence, the whip was withdrawn from the offending eight – an action unprecedented in the history of the parliamentary party. In the period between 1900 and 1942, the whip was withdrawn from a Conservative MP on only five occasions, sometimes for a very short period. Between 1942 and 1992, no Conservative MP had the whip withdrawn, although some resigned it on occasion in protest. In the period 1992–4 ten Conservatives had the whip withdrawn: John Browne (1992) after deciding to contest the election as an independent Conservative (his local party had de-selected him), Rupert Allason (1993), after failing to vote for the government on two votes of confidence on the Maastricht Treaty in 1993 (it was restored a year later) and the eight in November 1994 who failed to support the government in a vote of confidence on the European Finance Bill (Norton, 1995: 10–11). The eight were joined by another Conservative MP, who resigned the whip in protest. The whip was restored to the eight the following April (the MP who resigned the whip, Sir Richard Body, chose not to ask for its return). In November 1994 the government suffered an embarrassing defeat on the imposition of VAT on domestic fuel and remained vulnerable to defeat as its overall majority dwindled as a consequence of seats lost in by-elections. The fraught situation within the parliamentary party, not least on the issue of Europe, resulted in the Prime Minister John Major resigning the party leadership in order to trigger a leadership contest.

The situation was exacerbated by a feature not present during the Heath era: the greater access to media coverage by back-bench rebels. Television cameras began covering proceedings in the House of Commons in November 1989. Clashes between ministers and dissenters, as well as between party leaders, were attractive to the cameras. Stinging attacks such as that by the former Chancellor of the Exchequer, Norman Lamont, in his resignation speech in 1993 – accusing the government of being in office, but not in power – were caught on screen, and the proximity of a new building housing broadcasting channels – at 4 Millbank, a couple of hundred yards from the Palace of Westminster – also made it easier for the media to interview rebels. Ministers and rebels now troop regularly into the building. With more news programmes being broadcast, the greater the media appetite for such coverage. The 'whipless nine' Conservative MPs in the period from November 1994 to April 1995 attracted considerable coverage on television and radio, achieving more attention than the average member of the Cabinet.

In sum, then, the Conservative Party in the House of Commons has often been internally divided on issues of public policy. However, doubts have traditionally been confined to party gatherings or expressed privately to the whips. Party committees have provided the means for dissent to be fanned but more often to be absorbed. Recent decades have seen a greater willingness on the part of backbenchers to 'go public' with their disagreement, a disagreement that now attracts more television coverage than before. Cohesion remains a feature of the parliamentary party – with each Conservative MP likely to support the party in at least nine out of every ten votes (and, more often than not, every ten out of ten votes) – but it is now frayed at the edges in a way that it was not before 1970.

Complicating the picture is the fact that Conservatives in the other chamber cannot be taken for granted, either. Despite a Conservative preponderance in the Upper House, Conservative peers cannot always be persuaded to be present in sufficient numbers to stave off defeats and on occasion have contributed to them. In the 12 parliamentary sessions following the return of a Conservative government in 1979, the government suffered 173 defeats (Drewry and Brock, 1993: 87). Although virtually all the defeats took place on amendments to bills, rather than core items of government policy, they were nonetheless irritants to government. In the early 1980s the Conservative chief whip took the remarkable step of removing the whip from one Conservative peer (former minister, Lord Alport), an action undertaken in order to send a signal to other Conservative peers. In 1995 another Conservative peer was seen as so unsupportive in his voting behaviour that similar consideration was given to withdrawing the whip. There are few sanctions that can be deployed against peers and independent voting behaviour on the part of Conservative peers is difficult to deflect, other than by concession. Dissent in the Lords attracts less attention than in the Commons – unless the chamber is being used as a platform by leading figures, such as former Prime Minister Lady Thatcher, for expressing disagreement – but it can add to the woes of the party leadership.

Career politicians

The party in Parliament is more organised but less cohesive than before. It has also seen a change in its social composition. Conservative MPs have become more middle class and more career orientated. These changes overlap with one another but are not necessarily related causally. Claims that an increase in independent voting by Conservative MPs is attributable to a new breed of MP entering the Commons have been found to have little empirical support (Franklin *et al.*, 1986). The biggest changes in social composition came *after* a notable change in the voting behaviour of Conservative MPs. Some of the most notable occasions when MPs voted against their own side were, as we have noted already, led by long-serving Members.

The shift in terms of the background of Conservative MPs has not been great (Rush, 1979) but it has been notable, especially in more recent years. The move has been away from a body of MPs drawn from fairly grand and privileged backgrounds (Eton, Oxbridge, company directors/barristers) to a more solidly middle class (grammar/minor public school, university, company executive) background: a shift, according to one analyst, 'from estate owners to estate agents' (Criddle, 1994: 161).

Up to and including the two 1974 general elections, half or almost half of all Conservative MPs had been to public school and then to Oxford or Cambridge universities. In 1979 the proportion dipped by a few percentage points to 43 per cent and by the time of the 1992 general election had fallen to 32 per cent. Until 1979 about three-quarters of Conservative MPs had been to public school. The proportion decreased notably after 1979. In 1945, one in four of Conservative MPs had been to Eton. By 1992, the number was one in ten (Criddle, 1994: 161).

In terms of occupation, Conservative MPs are also more likely now to have served as company executives rather than company directors. The number drawn from 'grand' backgrounds has decreased during the course of the century. By 1945, less than 3 per cent of Conservative MPs were deemed to survive on the basis of private means (Rush, 1979: 101), compared with 15 per cent at the turn of the century. The biggest change in recent decades has been the move from the upper middle class to more solidly middle class occupational backgrounds. More Conservatives are entering the House after a short spell as a company executive or after a period in a predominantly political post. The number in the latter category has grown over the decades. The number of MPs having pursued careers wholly independent of political activity – what Peter Riddell has termed 'proper jobs' – has decreased markedly. 'The total number of full-time politicians (for both the Tories and Labour) rose from 11 per cent of new MPs in 1951 to nearly 31 per cent in 1992. By contrast, the proportion of new MPs in "proper" jobs fell from 80 per cent to 41 per cent between 1951 and 1992' (Riddell, 1993: 22). There appears to be a clear underlying trend. The proportion of the new intake of MPs drawn from political posts increased in each of the four elections after October 1974.

The change in the social composition of the parliamentary party has been described graphically by one of their number. According to Julian Critchley:

Today, the Conservative Party in the House contains the party conference of ten years ago . . . small-town solicitors, garage owners and estate agents with flat, provincial accents, are now among its members. Essex Men selected by Suffolk women. . .

Thirty-five years ago you could tell a Tory just by looking at him . . . A Tory MP was well suited. The party still retained some of its pre-war sleekness; elderly gentlemen in Trumper's haircuts, wearing cream silk shirts and dark suits, Brigade or Old Etonian ties. They were called Charlie; today, they all seem to be called Norman. In those days, everyone appeared to be related to everyone else . . .
(Critchley, 1994: 64)

With this social change has marched a change in attitude towards the job. There has been the rise of the career politician (King, 1981), that is, someone who longs to be in Parliament and who enjoys the political game; in Weber's terms, someone who lives for politics, but not necessarily someone who lives off politics. Career politicians are not a phenomenon of recent decades or even of the twentieth century, but the argument advanced by both King (1981) and Riddell (1993) is that their number has grown in recent decades. Career politicians are crowding out those with other interests in life. This makes for a more active House of Commons, with career politicians keen to be involved in the intrigues of parliamentary life and usually eager for advancement.

The change in the nature of the 'typical' Conservative MP appears to have had a number of consequences. One, which may be considered positive, is greater constituency activity. For the career politician, election and continued re-election to the House of Commons is vital. Given greater electoral volatility since the 1960s such MPs are attentive to constituency needs in order to bolster their support (see Norton and Wood, 1993). Another development, attracting less positive publicity, has been a tendency to supplement parliamentary salaries by serving as consultants to organised interests or to lobbying firms. Given a lack of other professional skills to offer, career MPs can only supplement their income by such consultancy work. Such consultancies are marked on the Conservative side of the House. An analysis of the 1995 Register of Members' Interests found that 168 MPs – virtually all of them Conservatives – held between them 356 consultancies (Committee on Standards in Public Life, 1995: 22). The alleged willingness of some Conservative MPs to accept money from outside bodies to table parliamentary questions contributed to public perceptions of 'sleaze' within the Conservative Party and led in 1994 to the appointment of the Committee on Standards in Public Life. Some of the committee's recommendations to limit the acceptance of some consultancies faced opposition from a number of Conservative MPs.

The Conservative MP has thus changed over the years, and especially in the years since 1974, now being more middle class and more politically active than before. Where the greater activity has been in pursuit of constituency interests it has attracted positive comments. Where it has been in pursuit of apparent personal gain it has attracted publicity than has helped neither the Conservative Party nor the House of Commons.

CHAPTER 9

The party leader

Philip Norton

> The loyalties which centre on number one are enormous. If he trips he must be sustained. If he makes mistakes they must be covered. If he sleeps he must not be wantonly disturbed. If he is no good, he must be pole axed. (Winston Churchill)

The Conservative Party places great emphasis on the position of the leader. The leader is deemed to be the fount of all policy. Other bodies within the party may advise the leader, but party policy is ultimately the responsibility of the leader. The leader consults, reflects and decides. The leader also decides who will occupy important positions within the party organisation and who will form the Conservative front bench in the House of Commons. 'When appointed, the Leader leads and the party follows' (Lowell, 1908: 457). If the leader fails to lead the party to success – which, in essence, means electoral success – then the leader must, in Churchill's words, be pole-axed.

The relationship thus stated emphasises the power of the leader and some degree of detachment between leader and led. On this basis one could construct a *Hobbesian model* of power within the party. Under this model, there is a contractual relationship between leader and led in which all power is vested in the leader, but with the led having power to remove the leader in the event of failure to provide the protection required under the contract. In terms of the Conservative Party, the removal takes place when the leader appears unable to offer the prospect of electoral success. There was, at least until 1965, another parallel with Hobbes' *Leviathan*: no clear and stipulated means by which the leader could be removed.

This model, however, derives from the formal status of the leader within the party. In practice, power is not so concentrated as the model – and Churchill's description – implies. Indeed, the dispersal of power within the party has led Richard Rose to suggest that a more appropriate model is that of *baronial authority*, in which bargaining takes place between territorial barons, as in the case of American parties (Rose, 1976: 154–5, 161). One can see the plausibility of this model. Although the leader has great powers vested in him, there are many prominent figures within the party who have their own power base. That was certainly true in the nineteenth century and has remained true in this. Some leading figures enjoy territorial strength, having wealth and support in particular regions (such as, for much of the party's history, the Earl of Derby and, earlier this century, Sir Archibald Salvidge in Lancashire), while others have support within the House of Commons (in post-war years, for example, R. A. Butler and William Whitelaw). The leader has to mediate between competing barons and may be brought down by those barons if they combine against him.

The reality of the relationship between leader and led is such that neither model provides a good fit. They each operate at a particular extreme and, most important of all, assume a constant in the relationship between leader and led: the leader is all-powerful or the leader has to balance continuously the demands of competing figures within the party. The relationship between leader and party is more complex and shifting than either implies.

To capture this shifting and complex relationship, a *family model* has been utilised (Norton and Aughey, 1981: 242–3). This posits a relationship of mutual dependence, shared trust, but with leadership from the head of the 'household', other members of the family deferring but not necessarily automatically complying with that leadership. 'As in most families, there may be occasional discord, but the members of the family remain bonded to one another by ties of loyalty, respect and kinship. Over time, some members of the family may leave, there may be new arrivals, but the family entity remains' (Norton and Aughey, 1981: 242). The family analogy is also apt in that there is an emphasis on a natural hierarchy and on deferring to the wisdom of the head of the family, rather than reliance on mechanistic head counting by members of the family. There is also, as Arthur Aughey has already noted (Chapter 5), an emphasis on resolving problems within the family home rather than in public, although discord within a family does not preclude some members from making public their disquiet. In this model, the parliamentary party can be taken as partner to the head of the household. Since 1965 a formal mechanism has existed for achieving a break – in effect, a divorce – between the two.

The model, therefore, appears to have some utility. The fit is not precise, but it is useful in giving some shape to the relationship between leaders and led and especially for conveying the dynamics of the relationship. As in families, there are ups and downs in the relationship and at times the prospect of a family break-up. At other times, harmony prevails. The power – the capacity to achieve desired outcomes – of the head of the household is not a constant. As Richard Neustadt observed about presidential power in the United States, '"powers" are no guarantee of power' (Neustadt, 1990: 10). Formal powers may be vested in a leader but the capacity of the leader to achieve desired outcomes may not be commensurate with those formal powers. At times, the leader is in a strong position to achieve what he wants. At other times, he finds it difficult or near impossible. Power, in short, is variable not constant.

The variability in the relationship between leader and led is apparent when one considers the three basic features of the leader's powers: security of tenure, the power of appointment, and making of party policy (McKenzie, 1964). The formal position does not quite the match the reality; but, then again, the divorce between the two is sometimes not as great as critics claim.

Security of tenure

For most of its history, the party has been distinctive because of the means by which the leader has been selected and removed as well as subjected to uncertainty in the period between. Much has been written about selection and removal, but the uncertainty while in office has been less analysed, even though constituting the most significant feature of the leader's relationship to the party.

In terms of the leader's security of tenure there are two principal schools of thought. Both focus on the element of removal. The first, derived from the formal status of the leader, asserts the security of tenure. Until 1975, the leadership was held on a freehold, not leasehold, basis. There was no formal mechanism to remove a leader who did not wish to go. The second emphasises the opposite: the insecurity of tenure. Political pressures have been brought to bear to get rid of politically ailing leaders. According to McKenzie, there was 'ample precedent' for the withdrawal of support by the party. The pole-axe has not only been wielded but wielded with a regularity not matched by other political parties.

The reality, as we shall see, lies somewhere between: the leader is rarely forced out but is subject often to criticism or demands to go while in office. Far from being a *Leviathan*, the leader is – following the family model – more akin to the long-suffering head of a frequently disputatious household. Critics are prepared to talk more often than they are to strike.

Let us consider, first, the development of the leader's position in terms of selection and removal.

Selection
Until 1965, the party leader was not elected, but instead 'emerged'. There was normally a successor waiting in the wings and when the leader stepped down that successor was then formally endorsed by a party meeting, comprising (from 1937 onwards) MPs, peers, prospective candidates, and members of the National Union Executive Committee. If the party was in power the heir apparent was normally summoned to Buckingham Palace to 'kiss hands' as Prime Minister, and the endorsement by the party meeting then followed. Bonar Law in 1922 was an exception, insisting that he be endorsed as leader before going to the Palace.

So much for the formal position. The political reality has been different. As we have seen in Chapter 2, the succession has not always been smooth.

Table 9.1 Conservative leaders since 1902: their coming and going

Leader	Selection	Reason for departure
Arthur Balfour (1902–11)	Unchallenged	Exasperation/age
Andrew Bonar Law (1911–21)*	Compromise	Ill
Austen Chamberlain (1921–2)*	Unchallenged	Collapse of coalition
Andrew Bonar Law (1922–3)	Unchallenged	Fatally ill
Stanley Baldwin (1923–37)	Challenged	Retirement
Neville Chamberlain (1937–40)	Unchallenged	Ill**
Winston Churchill (1940–55)	Unchallenged**	Retirement
Sir Anthony Eden (1955–7)	Unchallenged	Ill/failure of Suez
Harold Macmillan (1957–63)	Challenged	Ill
Sir Alec Douglas-Home (1963–5)	Challenged	Exasperation/pressure
Introduction of election by the parliamentary party		
Edward Heath (1965–75)	Challenged	Beaten in ballot
Margaret Thatcher (1975–90)	Challenged	Failed to clear hurdle in first ballot
John Major (1990–)	Challenged	

* Balfour and Chamberlain were officially leaders of the party in the House of Commons, not of the whole party.

** Churchill's succession to the premiership in succession to Chamberlain was contentious, but Chamberlain retained the party leadership for a few months before resigning; by which stage, Churchill's succession to the leadership – although unpopular with many Conservatives – was not challenged.

Table 9.1 shows that, of the 10 leadership successions between 1902 and 1963 inclusively, four of them did not conform to the pattern prescribed. If we include the unusual circumstances of Churchill's accession to the leadership in 1940 (Chapter 2), then in only half the cases could the leader be said to have 'emerged' in the way the party expected.

There were problems in selecting a leader in 1911, a ballot – as we saw in Chapter 2 – only being avoided by the emergence of a compromise candidate. In 1923, 1957 and 1963 there was no obvious single successor. Given that the party was in power on each occasion, the monarch was left to make a choice. Involving the monarch in this way was an embarrassment to the party and, coupled with the public vying for support by leadership contenders in 1963, encouraged the new leader – Sir Alec Douglas-Home – to instigate a review of the method by which the leader was chosen. Credit for the introduction of new rules is often given to a Conservative back-bencher, Humphry Berkeley, who pressed Sir Alec to change the rules, but the review was already in train when Berkeley wrote to the leader requesting a change.

The new rules instigated by Sir Alec involved election of the leader by Conservative MPs. Although the views of the party outside the House were to be reported to the MPs, the votes of MPs alone were to determine the outcome. A Prime Minister rested on the confidence of the House of Commons, so it was deemed appropriate that the leader should be chosen by those on whose confidence he depended when in office. There was also a practical case for confining the electorate to MPs: they were the ones best able to judge competing candidates, since they were able to observe them at close quarters on a regular basis.

To be elected, a candidate had to receive an absolute majority of votes and a majority that constituted 15 per cent of those voting. If no candidate fulfilled those requirements, a second ballot was to take place. Nominations from the first ballot were to be declared void and new nominations invited (which could include candidates from the first round), thus allowing for compromise candidates to come forward. On the second ballot, an absolute majority alone was necessary for election. If no candidate achieved that the two leading candidates then proceeded to a third ballot.

The rules were employed for the first time in 1965 following the resignation of Sir Alec Douglas-Home. The results are shown in Chapter 3. Edward Heath was elected leader.

Since 1965 the rules have been variously amended. The most significant change took place in 1975. The 15 per cent requirement on the first ballot was changed to constitute 15 per cent of all those eligible to vote. Most significantly of all, they were changed to provide for the annual election of the leader. Since and including 1975, there have been four contested elections. Not one has been to choose a successor to a leader who has retired.

Removal

Until 1975 the leader enjoyed security of tenure. There was no formal method for removing the leader from office. He served until the hand of God, or a desire for a peaceful retirement, intervened. In practice, pressure sometimes built up within the party for the leader to go and the leader sometimes gave in to those pressures. However, a stubborn leader could not always be dislodged and in 1974 there was – as we saw in Chapter 3 – considerable pressure from Conservative MPs for Edward Heath to give up the leadership or at least offer himself for re-election. Heath agreed to a revision of the rules and the result was the introduction of the provision for annual election. Heath was challenged and was beaten by Margaret Thatcher in the first ballot.

The rules that allowed Margaret Thatcher to take the leadership were also to be used to bring her down. The unsuccessful challenge by Sir Anthony Meyer in 1989 was followed a year later by a challenge that did topple her (see Chapter 3). John Major became leader. In June 1995, frustrated by back-bench criticism and persistent talk of a challenge to his leadership in the autumn, he resigned the leadership in order to trigger a leadership contest. He was re-elected and the 1922 Committee agreed that there would be no contest allowed in the autumn. There was also pressure within the 1922 Committee for a radical overhaul of the election rules. The rules, it was felt, allowed too much leeway to the leader's critics and did the party's image no good.

This perception gives some credence to the school of thought that stresses the insecurity of the leader. Indeed, the argument is that the leader is becoming even more insecure. The provision for annual election has made the leader more vulnerable, both of John Major's predecessors being removed involuntarily from the leadership.

In practice, the leader is not quite so vulnerable to being removed from office as this approach argues. Proponents of this school of thought appear to believe that, before 1965, a failing leader was seen by a delegation of party grandees and told it was time to go. It was never thus. Occasionally there were mumblings in the 1922 Committee and – as we shall see – in 1931 and 1947 a number of leading figures did suggest, through intermediaries, that it was time for the leader to step down, but that was the extent of it. There was no leader who resigned following a delegation from 'the men in grey suits'. Usually there had to be some factor other than pressure from within the party for the leader to go. As Table 9.1 shows, that factor was often poor health. Bonar Law resigned after he was diagnosed as having cancer of the throat. Eden never fully recovered from botched surgery in 1953 and was already showing signs of mental strain during the Suez crisis. After a recurrence of abdominal pain at the beginning of January 1957, his doctors announced that his 'health gives cause for anxiety. . . . In our opinion, his health will no longer enable him to sustain the heavy burdens inseparable from the office of Prime Minister' (*News Chronicle* 10 January 1957). Within hours of getting the doctors' report, Eden saw the Queen and resigned. Macmillan was ill in hospital, resigning when he believed himself to be far more seriously ill than in fact he was. Once he realised that his condition was not as bad as he originally thought he regretted his decision (Sir Knox Cunningham, Macmillan's parliamentary private secretary, to author, 1972). Excluding the unique circumstances of the departure of the two Chamberlains, only Balfour and Douglas-Home appeared to go following criticism within the party. Balfour was subject to a 'BMG' (Balfour Must Go) campaign but carried on for some years after it got under way and indeed held the leadership for six years after resigning the premiership. When he resigned the leadership, he was able to cite age as a factor (he was 63), but in reality simply appeared 'sick of the struggle', not over his leadership but over the Parliament Bill (Thomson, 1980: 171). Sir Alec Douglas-Home appeared to decide that it was not worth carrying on.

However, the degree of insecurity appears to have increased as a consequence of the rule change providing for annual election. Since and including 1975 there have been four leadership contests, each one challenging the incumbent. (There was a technical vacancy in 1995, John Major having resigned to force an election, but he was fighting *de facto* to retain his leadership.) Of the four contests, two resulted in the incumbent failing to be re-elected.

Against this has to be set an analysis concerning length of tenure. One of the more remarkable facts to emerge from Table 9.1 is the length of tenure of leaders. Leaders have often enjoyed long stints in the office, with those being elected to the post (that is, leaders since 1965) serving longer stints than their immediate predecessors who 'emerged' and who served relatively short terms. Of individuals to have been party leader before the present holder of the office, six of them each held the leadership for nine years or more. Of the rest, two – both Chamberlains – went in circumstances that do not permit of generalisation. Of the remaining three, two resigned when they were clearly ill.

What emerges from this is that, before 1975, it was actually quite difficult to remove a leader who retained his health, nerve and determination to carry on as leader. After 1975 the same applies but with the added factor of having to avoid complacency. In the 1975 and 1990 leadership contests, the leader's campaign was characterised by complacency and mismanagement. In 1975 a more rigorous and efficient campaign by Heath's supporters may well have given Heath a lead in the first ballot – he trailed Margaret Thatcher by 11 votes. In 1990 a more determined campaign, not least by Margaret Thatcher herself – in Paris at the time of the contest – would almost certainly have been sufficient to clear the hurdles necessary to win on the first ballot. She was only four votes short. In 1995, John Major's campaign team made sure that the mistakes of his predecessors were not repeated.

Criticism in office

The real problem for the leader is not so much the likelihood of being removed from the leadership, but rather the likelihood of being criticised during one's tenure of it. The degree of detachment suggested in Churchill's opening observation is not borne out by experience – not least by his own experience. His succession to the leadership continued to rankle with many of Chamberlain's supporters (see Roberts, 1994) and he was subject to sniping by various back-benchers after the party went into opposition in 1945. One, Robert Boothby, told him to his face he should retire (Lord Boothby to author 1973). As we noted in Chapter 2, it was also claimed that some younger members wanted Churchill to step down in favour of Harold Macmillan or Quintin Hogg (Nicolson, 1971: 32; *Sunday Pictorial* 25 November 1945). According to the *Daily Herald* (on 21 November 1945), 'the identity of his successor is now a daily subject of speculation'. In 1947, the Chief Whip was deputed by some senior front benchers to tell him it was time to go (Stuart, 1967: 146–7; see also Moran, 1966: 308). The matter also came up at the 1922 Committee. 'Churchill listened to the dissidents, but was so moving in replying to them that we were almost all reduced to tears. His line was that he was the servant of of the party and that he would stand down any time the party wished him to do so, and against such a disarming reply the opposition melted away' (former Conservative MP to author, 1973).

The rumblings during Churchill's leadership, however, pale into insignificance against those during the leadership of Stanley Baldwin. He was subject to a bitter struggle with the press barons and with some of his own supporters (see Jenkins, 1995: 110–21). At one meeting of MPs and candidates in 1930, one MP moved a motion proposing a change of leadership. Although the motion was defeated by 462 votes to 116, the fact that it was moved at all – at a meeting summoned by Baldwin – demonstrated the conflict within the party. The following year several leading figures made clear their view that it was time for Baldwin to go (Lindsay and Harrington, 1979: 98). A Conservative stood in a by-election on a platform opposed to Baldwin's leadership: the fact that he was defeated by a pro-Baldwin candidate helped to save Baldwin's leadership.

Leaders in more recent decades have also encountered criticism from supporters, albeit rarely on the scale and persistence of that experienced by Baldwin. Eden was already encountering difficulties in 1956 before the Suez crisis, stung by complaints of poor leadership. Sir Alec Douglas-Home faced a whispering campaign from some back-benchers, especially those wanting Edward Heath to succeed to the leadership. Heath himself encountered some hostility, particularly after his U-turns on economic and industrial aid policy in 1972. Margaret Thatcher was criticised and in a vulnerable position in 1980 and 1981 – there was talk of a candidate being put up against her for the leadership in 1981 – and again during the Westland crisis in 1986, Michael Heseltine attacking her style of Prime Ministerial leadership. John Major faced constant sniping from some back-benchers from 1992 onwards, with public contemplation of a leadership contest in 1994 and 1995, the latter made real by his own action.

Such criticism is not necessarily a constant. For much of their periods of leadership incumbents enjoy the support of their back-benchers and the party in the country, but circumstances can and do combine to undermine that support. The leader is usually secure in the leadership. At other times, the leader occupies a throne that is subject to being rocked, but only rarely overturned.

Policy making

The leader of the Conservative Party enjoys extraordinary power in determining party policy. This power derives from the combination of two factors. One is the broad nature of the basic tenets of Conservative thought (Chapter 4). This offers great latitude to whoever is vested with the responsibility of translating principles into policy. The other is the fact that the responsibility for that translation rests solely with the leader. The leader is *the* policy-making body within the Conservative Party. No other element within the party is vested formally with the power to determine party policy. The leader can, and does, draw on others to assist but their role is advisory only.

In practice the leader draws heavily on other bodies within the party. From a purely party perspective, the principal activity is devoted to preparation of the party manifesto and occasional policy documents. The growth of organised interests and the ratchet effect of party competition have meant that party manifestos have become more detailed than before. At the turn of the century manifestos were essentially short statements by the party leaders. Today, they are extensive and detailed documents, stating the party's proposals in most sectors of public policy. The very nature of the document precludes the leader from preparing it personally. The result has been a reliance, especially in recent decades, on policy groups.

An Advisory Committee on Policy was set up in 1949. This brought together a small number of representatives of the different sections of the party (1922 Committee, peers, National Union and leading figures in Central Office) and was serviced by the Conservative Research Department. It met, usually monthly when Parliament was sitting, to consider reports from study groups and from CPC discussion groups, and also – in government – to discuss trends in departmental policies. The Committee continued in existence until the 1980s but basically fell into disuse during Margaret Thatcher's tenure of Downing Street. It met in 1983 to give, in the leader's words, 'the Party's final seal of approval' to the manifesto (Thatcher, 1993: 283), but appears to have been little used thereafter. By the end of Margaret Thatcher's tenure it was effectively in abeyance. The emphasis remained on policy groups, but reporting directly to the leader.

The policy groups set up to prepare material for the manifesto have varied over time in composition and remit. From 1964 to 1970, for example, there were about 30 groups, each comprising about 12 people, made up of the front bencher (who chaired the group), representatives of the different sections of the party and a few outside experts. Reports went to the Shadow Cabinet and a steering committee, usually after being channelled through the Advisory Committee and Research Department. Edward Heath is reported to have read every report. Margaret Thatcher – as we saw in Chapter 3 – retained a similar arrangement in opposition, but with more groups and a wider remit, looking more at the principles than at the detail. In government, she modified the practice. The Advisory Committee, which had played a useful, but limited, role as a co-ordinating body and sounding board, declined in importance and the use of groups varied from Parliament to Parliament. The Research Department, distrusted initially by Thatcher, also declined in significance, the leader being prepared to look outside the formal party structure for policy initiatives.

The emphasis since 1979 has remained on policy groups but practice has varied in terms of drafting the manifesto. For the 1983 manifesto, Sir Geoffrey Howe co-ordinated group responses but the final manifesto was drafted by the head of the No. 10 policy unit (Ferdinand Mount) and the final document agreed by some senior ministers and party advisers (Thatcher, 1993: 282–3). For the 1987 election Margaret Thatcher played a more direct role, but relied heavily on the chairman of the research department (Robin Harris) and head of the No. 10 policy unit (Brian Griffiths), who produced an initial paper based on group reports. After the main lines of the manifesto had been discussed with senior ministers, the leader then set up a small manifesto committee which reported directly to her. The group was chaired by John MacGregor (chief secretary to the treasury) and comprised Harris, Griffiths, the PM's political secretary (Stephen Sherbourne) and John O'Sullivan, a member of the policy unit, who drafted the manifesto (Thatcher, 1993: 571–2). Under John Major a key role has continued to be played by the head of the No. 10 policy unit. For the 1992 election, material from policy groups was worked on by the head of the policy unit, Sarah Hogg, and the Party Chairman, Chris Patten, in order to get it into a shape approved by the Prime Minister. Not all the material found favour (some was considered too insubstantial) and some individual ministers were utilised to provide fresh ideas. In 1995 the Prime Minister again established a range of policy groups. Although drawing on representatives of the voluntary wing of the party, an officer or officers of the relevant back-bench committee and one or two outside experts, the principal membership was ministerial; in practice, what this often meant in the case of ministers not chairing the groups was their special advisers. The ultimate responsibility for drafting the manifesto rested, as always, with the leader.

The determination of party policy remains the greatest strength of the leader in terms of policy making. Translating that policy, when in office, into government policy – and then ensuring its effective implementation – is more difficult. The size and complexity of government, and the demands made of it, mean that a great deal of policy making takes place at ministerial, and often subministerial, level. Prime Ministers do not have the time to delve into the detail of ministerial policy; or, if they seek to, to be effective they have to concentrate on particular policies. Interfering in several departments achieves little and engenders resentment; it was a notable feature of Sir Anthony Eden's tenure of the office. Indeed, given the demands on government, much of the role of the Prime Minister can be seen as a co-ordinating one (see Jones, 1985). However, a determined Prime Minister such as Edward Heath or Margaret Thatcher can be much more than that, being able to utilise the authority derived from the combination of party leader and Prime Minister to set the agenda of government.

Margaret Thatcher was an exemplar of the strong leader and she was able to draw on the resources of the No. 10 policy unit – a small body of policy advisors covering the different sectors of public policy – both for advice and to monitor departments. John Major has continued to use the policy unit, with the head (Sarah Hogg until the end of 1994, and Norman Blackwell since) playing an important advisory and co-ordinating role. Policy announcements from ministers have to be cleared with No. 10 and policy proposals going before Cabinet committees are checked by the policy unit. Ministers have variously found policy initiatives blocked by No. 10 or found themselves promoting policies that have their origins in No. 10, sometimes policies that they themselves have opposed. Two government policies announced in 1995, for example – on competitive sports in schools and the use of vouchers for nursery education – were the product of Prime Ministerial pressure; neither emanated from the Department for Education, where successive ministers had been cautious about or opposed to the proposals.

The Prime Minister is not all-powerful and depends on the support of Cabinet and, as we have seen, the parliamentary party. The Cabinet may not always endorse the Prime Minister's preferred stance. Margaret Thatcher did not get her way, for example, on trade union reform. Nonetheless, the Prime Minister is demonstrably the most powerful figure in the Cabinet. The Prime Minister may depend on the members of the Cabinet as a collective entity, but *each* member of the Cabinet is dependent usually on the confidence of the Prime Minister.

The party leader will thus, in office, normally – albeit not always – achieve desired policy outcomes, gaining the approval of Cabinet and Parliament. Achieving the successful implementation of that policy is another matter. Lack of support from the public or affected groups can undermine the successful implementation of policy and may undermine the political position of the leader. Edward Heath's U-turns on economic policy on 1972 failed to achieve the intended outcome and undermined his support among Conservative MPs (Norton, 1978). The poll tax in 1990 proved to be spectacularly unpopular and was a contributory factor in Margaret Thatcher's loss of the party leadership later that year (see Norton, 1993). From a Conservative perspective that is entirely as it should be. Powers have to be tempered with responsibility. The leader is the fount of all policy and must take responsibility for that policy. The sign on the desk of US President Harry S Truman could equally be placed on the desk of the leader of the Conservative Party: 'The buck stops here'.

Power of appointment

When in power, the leader enjoys the prerogative of the Prime Minister to recommend ministerial appointments to the Crown. In opposition, the leader also enjoys the power to appoint members of the front bench. These are themselves considerable powers. They are complemented by the power to appoint the leading figures in Central Office. The principal appointment in the leader's gift is that of Party Chairman.

The leader thus enjoys powers of patronage not matched by any other political leader. As Prime Minister the leader may also, and does, use the powers of the premier to recommend the award of a honour – a peerage, knighthood or lesser honour – to political supporters. Such patronage may be used to encourage and to reward loyalty. Although Labour leaders recommend peerages for supporters, the recommendation of knighthoods for Labour MPs is rare. Conservative leaders when in Downing Street make frequent use of the power and it is rare for a long-serving Conservative MP not to be rewarded with a knighthood.

The power to appoint to office and to reward with honours is thus a considerable one. Edward Heath appointed a Cabinet noted for its loyalty to him. Margaret Thatcher dropped some leading Heath supporters from front bench positions (and from Central Office) when she took over the leadership. In Downing Street, she made sure that like-minded neo-liberals occupied the key economic ministries.

The power, however, is not undiluted. It can rarely be wielded with a completely free hand. Although the model of baronial authority is not an appropriate one, there are nonetheless leading figures in the party whom a leader may find it difficult to exclude from office. Not to include them may generate resentment among MPs or the party in the country. Once in office the leader may prefer to keep them there rather than dismiss them and have them cause trouble on the back-benches. As Margaret Thatcher conceded, 'not only must the Cabinet to some extent reflect the varying views in the parliamentary party at a particular time: there are some people that it is better to bring in because they would cause more trouble outside. Peter Walker and, to a lesser extent, Kenneth Clarke are examples, precisely because they fought their corner hard' (Thatcher, 1993: 418).

Reshuffles can also prove something of a poisoned chalice. Moving ministers about can cause problems in terms of ensuring some continuity in programmes and getting on top of portfolios, but it serves to bring in some fresh blood to the front bench. The problem is that moving some ministers, especially with support on the back-benches, to posts they do not want or regard as demotion can generate bad feeling, as happened in 1985 when Mrs Thatcher moved Sir Geoffrey Howe from the Foreign Office to the post of leader of the House of Commons. For every new minister appointed, there are a number of other MPs who regard themselves as even better qualified to fill the post. After John Major's re-election as Conservative leader in July 1995 he carried out a reshuffle. His Cabinet dispositions, not well received by right-wing MPs, attracted headlines. Less commented on publicly, but causing just as much resentment on the back-benches, was the promotion of some back-benchers (first elected in 1992) to junior office ahead of longer-serving, and widely regarded as more able, MPs.

Nor can leaders always make the most advantageous use of the appointment power, simply because of the other demands made on their time. Margaret Thatcher was so preoccupied with policy and other matters when she was in Downing Street that she paid little attention to new ministerial appointments. A consequence was that many able MPs on the party's left achieved ministerial office, while some of her most ardent supporters never made it even to the first rung of the ministerial ladder (Norton, 1993: 47–8). After she lost the leadership she once asked one of her back-bench supporters 'Why was it that you were never given ministerial office?' to which she received the stunned reply 'I was rather hoping, Margaret, that you could tell me' (Norton, 1993: 48).

Even the appointment of the Party Chairman is not always problem free. The chairman has, in effect, two masters – the leader who appoints him and the voluntary wing of the party, on whose support he depends in order to be successful (Norton and Aughey, 1981: 254). As Philip Tether noted in Chapter 7, the party in the country likes the chairman to be a senior figure, someone with clout in the party in their relationship with the leader. Appointing someone who has senior or some independent status may prove difficult. Cabinet ministers are often reluctant to give up departmental posts or to combine those posts with the demanding position of Party Chairman. As Michael Pinto-Duschinsky recorded in 1972, 'recent party leaders have met several refusals before finding willing appointees' (Pinto-Duschinsky, 1972). Michael Heseltine, appointed deputy Prime Minister in John Major's 1995 reshuffle, was variously reported to have turned down the Party Chairmanship. And if a senior figure is appointed, this may mean that the leader may not always be able to rely on his (never yet her) loyalty. There were some tensions in the relationship between Baldwin and Neville Chamberlain when the latter – Baldwin's likely successor – was Party Chairman. Margaret Thatcher's first chairman, Lord Thorneycroft, a former Cabinet minister and party grandee, proved successful but, after several years in post, made some independent comments on the state of the economy that contributed to his departure. There were tensions between Margaret Thatcher and Party Chairman Norman Tebbit during the 1987 election campaign; at one point they had a 'ding-dong row' (Thatcher, 1993: 584). If a less senior figure is appointed, such as junior ministers John Selwyn Gummer in 1983 and Jeremy Hanley in 1994, this may ensure a chairman loyal to the leader but one who may lack clout with the party in the country or may not be taken seriously by leading party figures (or, in the case of gaffe-prone Hanley, the media). If the chairman performs badly this may reflect on the leader who made the appointment.

More often than not, the leader is able to rely on the chairman and to work well with him. There have been some chairmen who have clearly enjoyed the confidence of the leader *and* party activists. Cecil Parkinson, chairman from 1981 to 1983, was a good example. The leader relies on the chairman for advice on other Central Office appointments. The leader may make a personal choice in the appointment of Director of the Research Department, but will frequently look to the chairman to recruit him and to appoint other officers. In July 1995, for example, the incoming chairman, Brian Mawhinney, removed two existing deputy chairmen and brought in a politician who had close ties to him.

The leader can thus use the power of appointment to give some sense of direction to Central Office, but beyond that the power is limited (Pinto-Duschinsky, 1972). The leader has no direct control over the voluntary wing of the party and has to use persuasive rather than coercive powers to ensure the support of the National Union.

Leadership in context

The leader of the Conservative Party is clearly a powerful figure. That position of strength derives not from the formal powers vested in the office but from the party's view of leadership that produces those powers. The leader is placed at the apex of the party and bestowed with powers that allow the leader to lead. There is thus scope for the leader to dominate and, indeed, as is clear from our opening three chapters, the history of the party is in large part the history of the leader. There have certainly been some dominant leaders, from Peel and Disraeli in the nineteenth century through to Edward Heath and Margaret Thatcher in the latter half of the twentieth. Cobden said of Peel, 'I treat him as the government, as he is in the habit of treating himself' (Gilmour, 1971: 207). One can imagine politicians – and not just opposition politicians – making similar assertions about either Heath or Thatcher.

Yet the leader, as we have seen, is powerful without being all-powerful. The relationship between the leader and the party is far more subtle and inter-dependent than is implied by an analysis that focuses solely on the formal powers of the office. The relationship, as suggested by the family model, is one of mutual dependence and shifting attitudes. There is deference to the leader but it is not unconditional. The followers look to the leader – the head of the household – to fulfil particular tasks and the leader looks to the followers to assist in what, following our family analogy, can be characterised as household chores.

Above all, the leader, although vested with seemingly mighty powers, occupies a political environment in which the party – front bench, parliamentary party, Central Office and the voluntary wing – cannot always be taken for granted. The leader on occasion has to cajole and persuade in order to ensure a desired outcome. Even the most determined and powerful of recent leaders had to resort to nods and winks and occasional prodding. During the 1987 election campaign Margaret Thatcher made some public comments about education reform that put her at odds with her Education Secretary, Kenneth Baker:

> what was really behind the dispute was that, as I often did in government, I was using public statements to advance the argument and to push reluctant colleagues further than they would otherwise have gone. In an election campaign this was certainly a high-risk strategy. But without such tactics Thatcherism would be merely a theoretical viewpoint. (Thatcher, 1993: 579.)

Nor did Thatcher take party activists for granted. She laboured over her speeches to the party conference. As Philip Tether has noted (Chapter 6), the conference is not quite as supine as some commentators suggest. It serves a role of two-way communication and can reflect the mood of the party. Margaret Thatcher worked hard to keep party activists on her side. As her one-time Party Chairman, Kenneth Baker, recalled: 'Margaret looked upon her annual speech to the Tory Party Conference as one of the major events of the year. She spent days working on her speech . . .' (Baker, 1993: 270). The speeches were designed 'to commune with the Party faithful and to consolidate Margaret's grip over the Party' and to ensure that her agenda led the day's news (Baker, 1993: 270). Both she and her successor have had to use the conference to try to keep the party faithful on side when the political going got tough.

When in Downing Street, the Prime Minister also has to face a more crowded national and international environment. Power is more fragmented – more pressure groups, membership of the European Union – and there is the problem of a widening gap between resources and expectations. It is increasingly difficult for political leaders to deliver the goods expected of them (see Butler, 1995: 48–65; Waldegrave, 1995: 173–7). When Margaret Thatcher returned from the Rome Summit of European leaders in October 1990, where she had been outvoted by eleven-to-one on the timetable for implementing stage two of the Delors' Report, her declaration of 'no, no, no' at the dispatch box – in response to Jacques Delors' vision of European institutions – was a sign of frustration as well as the trigger for a process that removed her from the leadership of the Conservative Party (Norton, 1993: 52).

The Conservative leader is thus a powerful figure, but one occupying a more complex political environment than before. During the history of the party some leaders have faced difficult party conferences, some have faced a divided parliamentary party, some have had problems keeping their lieutenants on board, and some have had difficulty ensuring the implementation of policy once approved by party and Parliament. What renders the contemporary leadership of the party distinctive is the apparent confluence of these variables and the fact that they now appear to be constants. Add to this the annual election of the leader by Conservative MPs and one has a situation where the leader – the head of the household – has in effect to work harder to get his or her way. Get their way they normally will, but the outcome is not always assured.

In his seminal work on the US presidency, *Presidential Power*, Richard Neustadt argued that the power of the president was essentially the power to persuade: he got his way by persuading others that what was in his interests was in their interests as well (Neustadt, 1960, 1990). The leader of the Conservative Party has powers beyond those of persuasion but, with a disputatious household, the power to persuade is an important and arguably ever more central weapon in the leader's arsenal.

CHAPTER 10

Party finance

Justin Fisher

The financing of the Conservative Party is periodically one of the most con-troversial issues both within the party and in the wider context of British politics (Fisher, 1994a). The topic has been brought into sharp focus during the last decade for three principal reasons: first, the passing by the Conserva-tive government of the Trade Union Act 1984, which was widely interpreted as being an attack on Labour's main source of income; secondly, the 1993 Select Committee investigation into the funding of political parties; and thirdly, the large debt that the Conservative Party has accumulated. In this chapter, we examine developments in Conservative Party income and expen-diture which will help explain how the party is funded, how it spends its money and what financial problems it faces.

Income

The development of Conservative Party finance

In his study of British political finance from the early nineteenth century, Pinto-Duschinsky identifies three phases of development in party fund-raising; the aristocratic era, characterised by the bribing of voters (Pinto-Duschinsky, 1981: 15–24); the plutocratic era, characterised by the sale of honours to individuals in return for party funds (Pinto-Duschinsky, 1981: 30–56) and the modern era. As we shall see, there have been important developments in recent years which suggest that a new era of political finance may well be upon us: the post-modern era.

The beginnings of the modern era of Conservative Party finance lie with the formation of the Labour Party. The move towards corporate institutional funding by the Conservative Party, although by no means immediate, was largely a response to the growing labour movement. Donations were sought from the business community which was concerned about the rise of socialism and organised labour (Pinto-Duschinsky, 1981: 112). Developments were also

Table 10.1 Estimated sources of Conservative Central Office income (%)

	1950–64	1967/8–1973/4	1974/5–1977/8
Institutions	67.4	62.5	56.3
Individuals	16.9	15.6	14.1
Constituency quotas	11.9	19.2	21.5
Other	3.9	2.8	8.0
Total	100.0	100.0	100.0

Source: Pinto-Duschinsky, 1981: 139.

spurred on by a desire within the Conservative Party to distance itself, in image and probably practice, from the dealings in honours. (There is some debate as to when dealing in honours actually ceased, summarised in Pinto-Duschinsky, 1981:104–11.) This pattern continued and the three main pillars of Conservative central party income became constituency association quota payments, corporate donations and, to a lesser extent, individual donations.

While we have long been able to ascertain the proportion of income that comes from the constituency organisations, we can only speculate as to the proportion of donations that come from corporate sources and from individuals. The reason for this is that published Conservative Party accounts give little detail and do not distinguish between corporate and individual income. Pinto-Duschinsky, however, made some estimates for the post-war period until 1978 (see Table 10.1). It has been difficult, however, despite these estimates, to be clear about the extent of the sources of income since company donations have apparently declined in importance in recent years (Pinto-Duschinsky, 1989a; Fisher, 1994a). This trend was confirmed by the Conservative Party in the Select Committee on Home Affairs' investigations into the funding of political parties and it was here that the then Party Chairman, Sir Norman Fowler, revealed greater detail for the financial year 1992–3 (see Table 10.2).

Table 10.2 Proportion of Conservative Central Office income comprised by institutional and individual funding 1992–3

	£000s	% of total
Corporate donations	4,300	37.3
Individual donations	3,516	30.5
Total central income	11,520	100.0

NB: The figures here differ from previous published information in the light of new information.

Sources: Oral evidence to the Select Committee on Home Affairs, 16/6/93, Conservative Party Accounts 1993, private information

The proportion of companies making direct political donations is small. In surveys covering the late 1980s and early 1990s, only around 12 per cent of the top 1000 companies and 6 per cent of the top 4,000 companies made a political donation (Fisher, 1995: 182). Moreover, British companies do not make large political donations relative to what they could potentially make available. The mean donation during 1991–2 was £16,085 and donations as a proportion of profit have tended to be very small (a mean of 0.1 per cent) (Fisher, 1994b: 691).

State funding

In addition to these forms of income, the Conservatives also benefit from the limited state funding available in Britain. The earliest example of this was the introduction of the payment of MPs in 1911, which relieved the parties of their main source of expenditure (Pinto-Duschinsky, 1981: 66–7). Today parties also receive free mailing, free use of public halls and for the larger parties, free broadcasting. Opposition parties additionally receive 'Short' money for their work in Parliament. One might also add state security at party conferences which has increased significantly since the bomb at the 1984 Conservative Party Conference in Brighton. This might seem a contentious point, but it is worth pointing out that at football matches the costs of policing are borne by the football clubs. Although these subsidies are modest compared with those of many other Western countries (Nassmacher, 1993) the free broadcasting was worth an estimated £7 million to all three major parties in the 1987 general election and overall state subsidies provided an estimated £13.2 million to each major party (Pinto-Duschinsky, 1989b: 26–7).

Recent changes in Conservative Party funding

In recent years, however, there have been important developments in techniques of party fund-raising which indicate not only a shift away from institutional sources of finance, but also possibly a new era of Conservative Party finance (see Table 10.3). First, a trend that has been apparent in recent years has been the re-emergence of personal donations in the finances of the Conservative Party to the extent that some individual donations have exceeded any made by a corporation (Pinto-Duschinsky, 1989a: 210; Fisher, 1994a). Moreover, in 1994–5 the growth in donations was largely brought about by individual direct mail contributions as well as a 'substantial legacy'. This meant that contributions from individuals accounted for two-thirds of all donations (Conservative Party, 1995: 8). Additionally, there has been an apparent growth in donations emanating from individuals abroad (Fisher, 1994a).

Secondly, there has been a growth of other forms of income (classified in Table 10.3 as sundry income) which largely comprises commercial activities

Table 10.3 Conservative Party central income 1988/9–1994/5

| | 1988–9 | | 1989–90 | | 1990–1 | | 1991–2 | | 1992–3 | | 1993–4 | | 1994–5 | |
	£ 000s	% of total central income	£ 000s	% of total central income	£ 000s	% of total central income	£ 000s	% of total central income	£ 000s	% of total central income	£ 000s	% of total central income	£ 000s	% of total central income
Donations	6,718	77.7	7,090	77.5	10,556	80.9	20,044	85.5	7,816	67.8	9,372	66.5	12,729	83.2
Constituency quota income	1,191	13.8	1,211	13.2	1,281	9.8	1,288	5.5	1,051	9.1	745	5.3	865	5.7
Sundry income	736	8.5	851	9.3	1,205	9.2	2,117	9.0	2,653	23.0	3,977	28.2	1,713	11.2
Total central income	8,645	100.0	9,152	100.0	13,042	100.0	23,449	100.0	11,520	100.0	14,094	100.0	15,307	100.0
Net assets/ (liabilities)	NA		NA		NA		(17,347)		(19,200)		(17,402)		(15,018)	

NB: Donations: all corporate and individual; sundry income: primarily from conferences, sales, services and other. NA: not available.
Source: Conservative Party accounts.

manifesting themselves through financial services, conferences and sales. These forms of fund-raising provide a selective benefit for the institution or individual contributing money in these ways. This is opposed to direct donations which are seen as providing collective benefits (Fisher, 1995). This technique of fund-raising has grown quickly, providing 28.2 per cent of Conservative central income in 1993–4; a growth of more than 300 per cent in five years. However, in 1994–5 the amount raised was apparently much lower, although this can be partially explained by changes in accounting practices (Conservative Party, 1995: 8).

Thirdly, the proportion raised from constituency quota income has fallen considerably. This is compounded by the continuing and projected fall in Conservative Party membership which, as Whiteley *et al.* note in their study of Conservative Party members, is itself a vague concept (Whiteley *et al.*, 1994). This is illustrated well by the fact that membership of the Conservative Party carries no set fee. Whiteley *et al.* found that 2 per cent of party members paid nothing for their membership. Of the majority that did pay some fee, the median figure was £10. However, members' annual financial input is often greater since local parties indulge in many rounds of additional fund-raising. When that is included, the median member's contribution was £20 (Whiteley *et al.*, 1994: 75–6).

We have seen that income from constituency quota income has decreased as a proportion of central income. However, this decline has not necessarily been uniform across all constituency parties. Pattie and Johnston, for example, found that there were some distinct variations in the amount that constituency parties contributed and their success at meeting the quota targets set by Conservative Central Office. Moreover, not all local Associations make contributions every year. Pattie and Johnson show that between 1984 and 1994, an average of 15 per cent of local Associations did not contribute at all in any one year (Pattie and Johnson, 1995: 7). However, this itself was subject to some variation, mirroring the economic fortunes of the country. Thus in 1984–5 the figure was 19 per cent, in 1988–9 it was 9 per cent, but with the recession of the early 1990s the figure had moved back to 18 per cent by 1993–4.

Other factors, however, also appear to have influenced the amounts contributed by constituency parties. Notwithstanding the variable quota amounts which are fixed for constituencies by the central party, three factors appear to have accounted for differing levels of constituency contributions. First, the electoral strength of a constituency has affected the level of contributions. Constituencies where the Conservatives were electorally strongest raised the most money for central party finances. This was not a constant pattern. During the late 1980s not only did electorally strong constituencies return the most money, they also continually increased the amount sent to the centre. In the 1990s, however, while electorally stronger constituencies continue to pay more money, the gap between their contributions and those of electorally weaker constituencies is narrowing (Pattie and Johnston, 1995: 14–15).

The marginality of a constituency has also had an effect. Conservative Central Office quotas recognise this to an extent and require less money to be sent from marginal constituencies and vice versa. Again, in the late 1980s, the expected pattern occurred where, as constituencies were less marginal, so they contributed more money to central funds. However, in the 1990s this pattern has altered. While less marginal constituencies still contribute greater amounts than more marginal ones, the difference between the amounts has been declining (Pattie and Johnston, 1995: 15).

Finally, while any broad effect of region appeared to disappear after controlling for electoral strength and marginality, Pattie and Johnston did find that the local economy represented by house prices also had some effect on constituency party remits. In short, the higher the average house price in a constituency, the more money that constituency gave to the national party. Again, this relationship varied over time. As the recession of the early 1990s began to affect the more affluent South, the difference between average house prices and constituency remits declined. So, while the house price differential remained, this was decreasingly reflected in constituency remits (Pattie and Johnston, 1995: 21).

Regarding corporate donations it is apparent that these may also be under threat from a growing trend of corporate political independence. Although companies are not formally politically affiliated to the Conservatives as some trade unions are to the Labour Party, the bulk of corporate political donations do go to the Conservative Party (Fisher, 1994b: 691). However, there is evidence to suggest that companies may question the reasons for their political donations (Fisher, 1994b: 691). Secondly, there are indications that confidence in the Conservative Party may not be a constant view held by contributors. It is clear that some companies have ceased donations through disillusionment with the Conservative government's policies. Moreover, there is continuing criticism of government policies from the business community and recent reports indicate a continuing fall both in level and number of corporate donations (*Guardian* 5 November 1994, 2 December 1994). (See for example attacks from the Institute of Directors in 1993 which criticised the government's attempts to claim credit for economic recovery while failing to deliver economic stability (*Guardian* 28 April 1993.))

There are also other trends which threaten corporate donations. First, political considerations may be a factor. There are few public relations advantages in making donations, and with the periodic focus on Conservative Party finances the position becomes even more unfavourable (Fisher, 1994a: 69). In periods of financial pressure poor publicity arising from donations is more difficult to justify. Secondly, changing structures of corporate ownership indicate that there will be more multinational corporations which can pose a threat to donations through parent company disapproval (Ewing, 1992: 98).

Thirdly, there is the growth of professional lobbying organisations. These offer businesses political contact with all parties. Should a future Labour government be elected, lobbying organisations may prove to be a better way for companies to spend money in the political arena. Finally, previous research has illustrated the importance of key personnel in decisions concerning political donations (Fisher, 1994b: 695–6). Thus the point is worth making that when this personnel changes, so may the views on donations.

Expenditure

Forms of expenditure

There are two ways in which we can examine party expenditure: first by looking at the overall picture of how the party spends its money and secondly by looking at the ways in which the Conservative Party spends money at general elections. Tables 10.4 and 10.5 look at the overall picture of central party expenditure. There are two tables because in 1993, the Conservative Party radically changed its accounting procedures, making direct comparisons with previous years problematic. Nevertheless, a broad picture is painted in Table 10.4 and a more detailed one in Table 10.5.

Table 10.4 shows us that running a political party is an expensive business. In every year, including that of the 1992 general election, routine and research spending dwarfs that spent upon campaigning. Thus, while the proportion spent on routine expenditure has declined overall, it still generally constitutes around 80 per cent of Conservative central expenditure. This is an important point since, if greater measures of state funding were to be introduced, they would clearly not only be spent upon advertising (which might generate negative views about state assistance: certainly, previous opinion polls upon the concept of state funding for political parties have yielded generally negative responses) (Fisher, 1994a: 69; Linton, 1994: 99) but on the very maintenance of the parties themselves which is arguably necessary (Fisher, 1995: 194).

The second point to note is that while most campaigning is still undertaken in general elections, it is clear that a significant amount occurs between elections. Thus, £2.2 million was spent in the non-general election year 1993–4 (18.9 per cent of all central spending) and £4.4m (33.5 per cent of all central spending) in the European election year of 1994–5. This emphasises that party organisations do not only operate and campaign at general election time and it makes less sense to talk of an electoral cycle, and more of a constant. For the Conservative Party, however, there is the problem that donations have in the past tended to follow the cycle. This is undoubtedly one of the reasons why large deficits were commonplace during this period. Between 1989–90 and 1992–3 alone, the party accumulated a deficit of £17,387,000. Deficits might have been expected in a general election year, when victory may be seen as more important than balanced budgets (Pinto-Duschinsky, 1989b: 16). However, notwithstanding the refurbishment undertaken at Conservative

Table 10.4 Conservative Party central expenditure 1988/9–1994/5

	1988–9		1989–90		1990–1		1991–2		1992–3		1993–4		1994–5	
	£ 000s	% of total central exp	£ 000s	% of total central exp	£ 000s	% of total central exp	£ 000s	% of total central exp	£ 000s	% of total central exp	£ 000s	% of total central exp	£ 000s	% of total central exp
Routine and research	7,637	91.5	10,996	81.3	15,556	86.2	17,368	59.4	11,562	84.3	9,760	81.1	8,837	66.5
Campaigning	709	8.5	2,532	18.7	2,499	13.8	11,888	40.6	2,149	15.7	2,271	18.9	4,450	33.5
Total central expenditure	8,346	100.0	13,528	100.0	18,055	100.0	29,256	100.0	13,711	100.0	12,031	100.0	13,287	100.0
Surplus/(deficit) for the year	299		(4,376)		(5,013)		(5,807)		(2,191)		2,063		2,020	

NB: In 1993, the Conservative Party changed its classifications of expenditure activity detail. Thus years 1991–2, 1992–3 and 1993–4 are calculated on the basis of the new classifications. The new accounting procedures afford greater and more accurate detail. However, in order that comparisons can be made with years calculated upon the old accounting methods, some necessary adjustments have been made by the author. The classification used in this table are as follows:

Routine and research (1988/9–1990/1): Party Headquarters, expenditure on areas and constituencies, Conservative Political Centre, international, research and Parliamentary Services, National Union Headquarters, general administrative expenditure, interest payable, exceptional costs.
Routine and research (1991/2–1994/5): research and political support, National Union constituency services, offices in England, Scotland and Wales, conferences, fund-raising, publications and general services, exceptional costs, net interest payable, taxation.
Campaigning (1988/9–1990/1): publicity, press relations and broadcasting.
Campaigning (1991/2–1994/5): campaigning, direct political support costs, European elections.

Source: Conservative Party accounts.

Table 10.5 Conservative Party central expenditure 1991/2–1994/5 (with greater detail)

	1991–2		1992–3		1993–4		1994–5	
	£ 000s	% of total central exp	£ 000s	% of total central exp	£ 000s	% of total central exp	£ 000s	% of total central exp
Routine	13,622	46.7	9,025	65.8	7,425	61.7	6,232	46.9
Research	3,746	12.8	2,537	18.5	2,335	19.4	2,605	19.6
Campaigning	11,888	40.6	2,149	15.7	2,271	18.9	4,450	33.5
Total central expenditure	29,256	100.0	13,711	100.0	12,031	100.0	13,287	100.0

NB: *Routine*: National Union constituency services, offices in England, Scotland and Wales, conferences, fund-raising, publications and general services, exceptional costs, net interest payable, taxation.
Research: research and political support.
Campaigning: campaigning, direct political support costs, European elections.

Source: Conservative Party accounts.

Table 10.6 Conservative Party central election campaign spending activity 1983–92

	1983		1987		1992	
	£ 000s	% of total central campaign spending	£ 000s	% of total central campaign spending	£ 000s	% of total central campaign spending
Press advertising	1,725	49.3	4,523	50.9	4,000	35.9
Poster and leaflet advertising	843	24.1	1,834	20.6	1,800	20.2
PEB production costs	306	8.8	366	4.1	2,250	20.2
Opinion research	96	2.8	219	2.5	242	2.2
Tour and meetings	52	1.5	417	4.7	972	8.7
Publications	212	6.1	714	8.0	730	6.6
Administration	262	7.5	818	9.2	1,145	10.3
Total	3,496	100.0	8,891	100.0	11,139	100.0

NB: Each election may not necessarily be exactly comparable due to alterations in accounting methods and some estimated expenditures (see original texts for details).

Sources: Pinto-Duschinsky, 1985: 331; 1989b: 17; Pinto-Duschinsky, quoted in Linton, 1994: 23.

Central Office during 1990 and 1991, the fact that substantial deficits were experienced four years running indicates a longer term problem.

Table 10.5 allows us to break down routine and research spending as well as campaigning. It shows further that the routine costs of running a party are by far the most significant. Importantly, however, while the proportions spent upon research appear to be increasing, the actual amounts of money spent have generally declined, despite a slight increase in 1994–5. The proportion of central expenditure spent by the Conservative Party on research does, though, far outweigh that spent by other parties (Home Affairs Select Committee, 1994: xxiii). Clearly, if the Conservative Party is to maintain a function of political education which requires research, both the proportion and money spent upon it must be maintained. Again, it seems that without more reliable sources of income, this function may be threatened.

Table 10.6 illustrates the forms of central expenditure undertaken in the general elections of 1983, 1987 and 1992. A number of patterns are apparent. First, press advertising still forms the largest item of expenditure, though the proportion spent declined significantly in 1992. Indeed, it is worth noting that the public sector union NALGO (now part of UNISON) took out more press advertisements during the 1992 election campaign than the Conservative and Liberal Democrat Parties combined (Conservative Party, 1993b, Appendix B). Secondly, while the level of poster and leaflet advertising has remained relatively constant, the cost of producing party election broadcasts (PEBs) has increased considerably. It is interesting to note that the proportion spent declined in 1987 when Labour mounted a very successful campaign and then rose dramatically in 1992, presumably in part as a response to the more professional campaigning undertaken by the opposition parties. Finally, it is worth noting that the amounts spent upon tours and meetings appear to be on the increase, suggesting that the more apparently old-fashioned modes of election campaigning have not yet died out.

Local expenditure

We can also examine local expenditure patterns at general elections. The total amounts spent are easier to gauge since this is regulated by law, although it is commonly thought that returns can be subject to occasional elements of creative accounting. Notwithstanding that, it is apparent that the Conservatives have spent most on average per constituency, although the range of spending varies considerably (Johnston and Pattie, 1995: 262). It makes little sense to compare actual amounts spent, since the amount parties are able to utilise is dependent upon the numbers on the electoral roll in a constituency. Suffice to say that on average the Conservatives have spent 74.06 per cent, 78.26 per cent and 79.22 per cent of the maximum permitted in the 1983, 1987 and 1992 elections, respectively. By contrast, the figures for Labour were 66.53 per cent, 70.87 per cent and 70.63 per cent (Johnston and Pattie, 1995: 263).

This is all very well provided that, first, the money is spent where it is needed most, and secondly that it can be shown that the level of spending makes a difference to the electoral outcome. In fact the Conservatives, like other parties, are apparently rational in their constituency expenditure, spending most in marginal and defendable seats and least in unwinnable ones (Johnston and Pattie, 1995: 263–4). As far as making a difference is concerned, the fact that we can assess with reasonable accuracy the actual amounts spent within a certain period and with a defined electorate enables us to evaluate the likelihood of increased spending being reflected in improved electoral performance at constituency level. In fact there is a statistical relationship indicating (for all parties) that increased spending at constituency level always improves electoral performance within that constituency (Johnston and Pattie, 1995: 269). However, since the vast majority of this money is raised locally the decline in Conservative Party members is likely to raise problems for a party that likes to spend generously and successfully at local level.

Deficits

In recent years the Conservative Party has faced the problem, at a central level at least, of a considerable net deficit. By 1994–5 this stood at £15,018,000, having reached £19,200,000 in 1992–3. The party has only published details of net liabilities since 1993 (see Table 10.3), so we cannot be sure for how long they have experienced this problem. Nevertheless, it does appear that much (although not all) of the deficit has been brought about by the overspending discussed above (see Table 10.4). The considerable amounts involved have not only dwarfed those run by other parties, but have proved embarrassing for a party that has campaigned for, and implemented policies on, sound financial practices in the public sector.

However, the party has had some success in reducing its liabilities. This reduction owes something to the review of Conservative Central Office begun in 1992. A Director of Finance was appointed and a new Board of Management created to oversee expenditure budgets. The management of Conservative Central Office was also overhauled and the post of Director General created to assume managerial control. Additionally, there have been reductions in the numbers of staff employed by the party. At Central Office, for example, there were on average 224 employed at any one time during 1991–2. By 1994–5 that figure had fallen to 159. Similarly, the numbers of regional office staff fell. These measures have proved to be 'very cost effective' in the subsequent local and European election campaigns (Conservative Party, 1994: 6) although there were considerable electoral losses.

Despite the efforts to restructure the financial management of the party, a question that has been raised is how the party has been able to develop and maintain such a large deficit. To be sure, the party has made considerable interest payments to its bankers, the Royal Bank of Scotland. In 1993–4, for example, these amounted to more than £1 million. However, some have questioned whether this forms the full picture. For example, in the two years prior to the election year, the party had accumulated a deficit of more than £9 million. By conventional standards, the party was able to operate remarkably successfully, spending more than £11 million on the 1992 election, despite what might have been seen as crippling debts. Suggestions have been made, then, that some form of security may have been offered in order for the bank to permit such spending. In particular, there were suggestions that the party held overseas funds which were being used as security (Fisher, 1994a: 66). Notwithstanding these unproven claims, the question must surely arise as to whether the Conservative Party has received preferential treatment in its financial affairs.

Conclusions

In general the Conservatives, like the other main parties, are diversifying their sources of income. Notwithstanding the surprisingly large level of donations registered in 1994–5, they are generally becoming more commercial in their approach and relying less upon traditional sources of income which have generally been made available through ideological or sociotropic commitment. Indeed, the growth in direct mail donations, while not a new technique, also reflects this more businesslike approach. However, the party still faces financial problems and remains in debt to the tune of £15 million.

In terms of expenditure it is clear that the party faces some difficulty in simply maintaining its current level of organisation. Moreover, while it has successfully exploited constituency spending at general elections this may come under threat should the level of membership continue to decline. State funding would seem a possible solution to these problems. However, the recent report of the Select Committee on Home Affairs rejected increased state funding and a new enquiry is unlikely in the near future. That said, a commitment to the state funding of political parties is Labour Party policy. If the next general election yields a change of government, then we may yet see further developments in Conservative Party finance.

CHAPTER 11

Electoral support

David Denver

There is no doubt that the Conservative Party has been highly successful for more than a century: that is clear from the opening chapters of this volume. That success has been notable in post-war general elections. This is a period for which data exist that allow us not only to chart that success but to consider some of the explanations for it. As explained in the Introduction to this volume, some of the explanations for Conservative success are not amenable to empirical verification. Others, primarily the sociological and political explanations, are amenable to such testing through the use of survey material and voting data.

There have been 13 general elections since 1950 and, in what is conventionally described as a competitive two-party system, the Conservatives have won eight and lost a further three by very narrow margins – in 1950, when they won 16 seats fewer than Labour, in 1964, when they had 11 fewer, and in

Table 11.1 National distribution of votes, 1950–92 (%)

	1950	1951	1955	1959	1964	1966	1970
Conservative	43.5	48.0	49.7	49.4	43.4	41.9	46.4
Labour	46.1	48.8	46.4	43.8	44.1	47.9	43.0
Liberal	9.1	2.5	2.7	5.9	11.2	8.5	7.5
Others	1.3	0.7	1.1	1.0	1.3	1.6	3.1

	Feb. 1974	Oct. 1974	1979	1983	1987	1992
Conservative	37.8	35.8	43.9	42.4	42.3	41.9
Labour	37.1	39.2	37.0	27.6	30.8	34.4
Liberal, etc.	19.3	18.3	13.8	25.4	22.6	17.8
Others	5.8	6.7	5.3	4.6	4.3	5.8

NB: In 1951 the Conservatives won a smaller share of the vote than Labour but more seats. In February 1974 they had a larger share of the vote than Labour but won fewer seats.

Source: Butler and Kavanagh, 1992: 284–5.

February 1974, when they were only four seats behind. Their feat of achieving four consecutive (and very convincing) victories from 1979 to 1992 is unparalleled in the twentieth century. The Labour Party, in contrast, has only twice recorded clear wins since 1950 (in 1966 and October 1974). Table 11.1 shows the shares of the votes won by the major parties at each general election since 1950. Only the Conservatives have come very close to winning 50 per cent of the vote (in 1955 and 1959). Moreover, in the four elections from 1979 their lead over Labour ranged from 6.9 to a massive 14.8 percentage points.

Electoral success of this kind clearly demands explanation and, in order to explore the sources of Conservative support, it is useful to distinguish two periods. The first, which may be called the era of alignment, stretches from 1950 to 1970 while the second – the era of dealignment – covers the period from the elections of 1974 to the 1990s.

The era of alignment 1950–70

Our knowledge of voting behaviour in the 1950s and 1960s is based on analyses of election results themselves and on public opinion polls, local survey studies of voting behaviour and the first studies of the electorate based on nationwide surveys (see Butler and Stokes, 1969, 1974). The picture of British voters that emerged from these various sources was very consistent. Broadly speaking, the electorate was divided into two large blocs, which provided reliable and stable support for the Conservative and Labour Parties, respectively. In two connected ways there could be said to be an alignment between voters and parties. First, voters in different social groups aligned themselves with different parties and secondly, voters aligned themselves psychologically with parties by thinking of themselves as party supporters. Someone born into a middle class family, for example, would usually be brought up to believe that the Conservatives were the party for the middle class and would also come to have a Conservative Party identification, to think of himself or herself as 'a Conservative', rather than simply someone who voted Conservative from time to time. Voters generally paid little attention to the policies, performance or leaders of the parties. Indeed, to think of a voter 'deciding' to vote for one party rather than another in an election during this period would be somewhat misleading. Rather, a voter's family background and social characteristics would lead him or her to have an ongoing identification with a party, and when an election came along this would produce an almost automatic vote for the party concerned. An analysis of the sources of Conservative support in this period, therefore, involves looking at the main social influences on party choice – class, age, sex, religious denomination and geographical location.

Table 11.2 Conservative support in different occupational classes, 1964–70 (%)

	Professional/ managerial			Intermediate non-manual			Manual working class		
	1964	1966	1970	1964	1966	1970	1964	1966	1970
% Conservative	68	67	65	57	54	56	26	25	34
Con. lead over Lab.	+52	+49	+41	+30	+21	+23	–39	–45	–23

NB: The figure for Conservative lead is % Conservative minus % Labour, among the class concerned.

Source: Table 1.12 in Crewe *et al.*, 1991.

Class and party support

Of all the possible social characteristics that might influence party choice, social class was consistently found to be the most important between 1950 and 1970. As Butler and Stokes noted, 'Its pre-eminent role can hardly be questioned' (1974: 77). Table 11.2, which is based on the relevant BES (British Election Study) surveys, shows levels of Conservative support in three occupational classes at the elections of 1964, 1966 and 1970 and the relationship between class and party is clear. In these elections, around two-thirds of professional and managerial workers voted Conservative as did more than half of those with other non-manual occupations. In both groups the Conservatives had large leads over Labour. In the manual working class, on the other hand, Conservative support varied between a quarter and a third and Labour was clearly in the lead. Occupation is a relatively crude indicator of what we mean by social class – and there is some debate about how occupations should be assigned to class categories – but figures of this order were regularly found in polls and surveys during this period. Not surprisingly, similar differences were found when researchers investigated the effects of other class-related characteristics such as level of education, income, housing tenure and trade union membership.

The pre-eminence of class as a determinant of party choice was such that, when investigators wished to claim that some other social characteristic apparently unrelated to class affected party choice, they had to demonstrate that it had an effect within social classes. There would be little point in becoming excited about the fact that Scottish voters were more likely to vote Labour than English voters if this simply reflected the fact that Scottish voters were (and are) more likely to be working class. A number of variables passed this test and the four most important are considered here.

Age and party support

During the 1950s and 1960s, academic surveys and polls regularly found that younger people – especially the youngest eligible age group – were more

Table 11.3 Conservative lead over Labour by age and class, 1964–70 (%)

	1964		1966		1970	
	Under 35	54+	Under 35	54+	Under 35	54+
Professional/ managerial	32	84	36	68	6	60
Intermediate non-manual	25	45	5	37	2	42
Manual working class	–43	–31	–49	–36	–22	–9

NB: The figure in each cell is % Conservative minus % Labour, among the class/age group concerned.

Source: Calculated from Table 1.15 in Crewe *et al.*, 1991.

inclined to vote Labour while older voters consistently favoured the Conservatives. Table 11.3 presents some summary figures for a younger and an older age group and it can be seen that in every class, at each of the three elections concerned, the Conservative lead is much greater, or the Labour lead smaller, among older voters. When age groups are analysed in more detail the steady increase in Conservative support from the youngest to the oldest group is very clear (see, for example, Rose, 1974: 521).

Two main explanations have been offered for this phenomenon. The first suggests a 'life cycle' effect. Young people tend to be idealistic and want to change the world. As they grow older, however, people acquire more responsibilities, more of a stake in society and become more cautious and conservative in their attitudes. The second explanation concentrates on political generations, or 'cohorts'. In this view, it is not a person's chronological age that is important, but when he or she was young and beginning to experience politics. As each generation enters the electorate it is influenced by currently important political events – the election of the first majority Labour government in 1945, for example. This helps to explain the strength of Conservative support among older people in the 1950s and 1960s since someone aged over 60, in, for instance, 1959 would have become politically aware in the early 1920s, when Labour was a relatively new party, so that their earliest influences were unlikely to have been in a pro-Labour direction.

Sex and party support

Writing in the 1960s Peter Pulzer claimed that 'sex is the one factor which indubitably counter-balances class trends' (1967: 107). In all classes, women were more likely to vote Conservative than men. This is illustrated in Table 11.4. Although the differences are neither as large nor as consistent as those found for age, the general pattern is clear. What is not clear is why women

Table 11.4 Conservative lead over Labour by sex and class, 1964–70 (%)

	1964		1966		1970	
	Male	Female	Male	Female	Male	Female
Professional/managerial	48	56	47	46	36	45
Intermediate non-manual	30	33	19	34	23	23
Manual working class	−39	−34	−48	−41	−29	−16

NB: The figure in each cell is % Conservative minus % Labour, among the class/sex group concerned.
Source: Calculated from Table 1.14 in Crewe *et al.*, 1991.

provided a stronger source of support for the Conservatives than men. It may have been due to the fact that in this period women were very much more home-centred than men, and were thus insulated from industrial con- flicts and community pressures. Alternatively, women may be more hesitant about radical politics because they prefer a stable environment in which to bring up their families. It may even be that women are simply more socially aspiring then men and prefer to associate themselves with the more middle class and respectable party.

Religion and party support

In the late nineteenth and early twentieth centuries religious denomination strongly influenced political loyalties. The Church of England was described as 'the Tory party at prayer', while the Liberal party was strongly supported by non-conformists. Although the influence of religion had declined in general and in relation to politics by the 1950s and 1960s, its effect on party choice was still evident. Relevant BES data of the form used in previous tables are not easily available, but Table 11.5 presents figures showing the relationship between denomination and vote in the 1970 election. In the middle class groups the Conservative lead over Labour was clearly greater among adherents of the Church of England than it was among non-conformists and people with no religious attachment. Roman Catholics in the lower middle and working classes were much less inclined to vote Conservative than other groups.

Explanations for the varying strength of the Conservatives among different denominations have tended to focus on the fact that the Church of England, as the established church, is identified with the social and political establish- ment while religious dissent goes hand in hand with political dissent. Catholics in Britain are, to a considerable extent, descendants of Irish immigrants and their antipathy to the Conservatives reflects the historical opposition of the Conservatives to Irish Home Rule, as well as the close links between the Conservatives and the Ulster Unionist party in this period.

Table 11.5 Conservative lead over Labour by religious denomination and class, 1970 (%)

	Church of England	Non-conformist	Roman Catholic	Other/none
Upper middle class	+57	+26	+43	+21
Lower middle class	+26	+10	−4	−3
Working class	−9	−9	−32	−19

Source: Calculated from Rose, 1974: 518.

Geographical location and party support

It is very easy to demonstrate geographical differences in party support simply by looking at election results. In election after election in this period there were clear regional divisions – the Conservatives were stronger in the South of England (excluding London) and weaker in the North, Scotland and Wales. Indeed, Richard Rose (1974: 490) has shown that these regional patterns stretch back to 1918 with little alteration. In addition, the Conservatives were stronger in rural areas than in urban areas, especially the large cities. In part this simply reflects the fact that there are large concentrations of working class voters in cities and in Scotland, Wales and the North, but the differences remain even when class is controlled. Thus, Heath *et al.* (1991: 108) report that among working class voters in 1964, 15 per cent voted Conservative in Wales, 17 per cent in Scotland, 24 per cent in the North, 27 per cent in the Midlands and 29 per cent in the South of England. Similarly, a calculation based on Rose's data for the 1970 election (1974: 512) shows that middle class groups in rural areas gave more support to the Conservatives (68 per cent) than those in more urban areas (58 per cent).

Explaining working-class support for the Conservatives

Support for the Conservative Party in the era of alignment was, then, located in a series of social groups – the middle class, older voters, women, Anglicans, people living in rural areas and in the South of England. The class divide in party support was by far the most important and it was thought by students of electoral behaviour to be almost natural. There was nothing to explain about why middle class people voted Conservative and working class people voted Labour, since the parties clearly represented and advanced different class interests; but this raised a problem, since there were many people who 'crossed over' and voted for the party of the opposite class. Most attention centred on working class Conservatives, rather than middle class Labour supporters, however, since numerically and historically these were a more important group. As Philip Norton has mentioned in the Introduction, the working class in this period was much larger than the middle class and the

Conservatives could not possibly have won elections without working class support. Labour, on the other hand, would never have been out of office if all working class voters had supported them. Five main theories were put forward to account for working class Conservatism.

The first concentrated on the 'cross pressures' that working class people may experience. As well as belonging to the predominantly Labour working class, they may also have been part of other social groups which were predominantly Conservative – Anglicans and rural dwellers, for example. This weakened their basic class identity and, as a result, they were more likely to vote in a class-deviant way. One problem with this approach is that it offers little guidance as to why some people should defect from their class party while others in the same position do not.

The second explanation suggested that working class Tories simply misperceived their class position (see Runciman, 1966: ch. IX). Manual workers who described themselves as 'middle class' were more likely to vote Conservative than those who said that they were 'working class', but this still leaves unexplained why some members of the 'objective' working class failed to identify themselves as such, and why there was still considerable support for the Conservatives among those who thought of themselves as working class.

A third explanation concentrated on attitudes of deference among working class Tories (McKenzie and Silver, 1968; Nordlinger, 1967). The idea is that those who were deferential towards authority and socially superior leaders were strongly predisposed to favour the Conservatives. The problem here, as explained in the Introduction, is that many working class Conservatives were not particularly deferential and many working class Labour supporters were just as deferential as their Conservative counterparts.

A fourth explanation for working class support for the Conservatives, which was very popular during the 1950s, is the so-called *embourgeoisement* thesis. After Labour lost its third election in a row in 1959, many commentators argued that Labour was losing out because the working class was becoming more affluent. As they acquired the trappings of middle class life – becoming more *bourgeois* – workers were increasingly adopting middle class life styles and attitudes and, in consequence, supporting the Conservatives. This approach tells us nothing, of course, about the reasons for Conservative support among the working class before relative affluence became widespread but, in any case, when the thesis was tested in the 1960s it was found that, contrary to expectations, more affluent workers were more likely to be Labour supporters than were working class people in general (see Goldthorpe *et al.*, 1968).

Perhaps the most convincing explanation for working class Conservative support in this period was that put forward by Butler and Stokes (1974). They use the idea of political generations or cohorts to argue that, since party loyalty is largely passed on from generation to generation within families, Labour's problem was that it was a relatively late arrival on the political scene. By the 1920s, when Labour first became a serious contender in elections, many families had already established patterns of support for other parties. Consequently, many people alive in the 1950s – especially older people – could not have been socialised into supporting Labour because their parents and grandparents had developed a party loyalty before Labour was on the scene. Although there was, of course, some 'leakage' to Labour as time passed, the importance of family socialisation is such that Conservative loyalties continued to be transmitted and to have a tenacious hold in a large segment of the working class. Nonetheless, Butler and Stokes suggested that as the lines of transmission lengthened in the 1970s and 1980s working class support for the Conservatives would steadily decline. As we shall see, they could hardly have been more mistaken.

The electoral successes of the Conservatives in the 1950s rested, then, upon their appeal to most middle class voters and to a significant segment of the 'objective' working class. Among the latter, older voters, women, Anglicans and those living in the South of England or in rural areas were more likely to have been socialised into holding pro-Conservative attitudes and values, and there were enough of such people to make the Conservatives the 'natural' majority party. What is striking about this summary is that it says nothing directly about Conservative policies or performance in government, about political issues or perceptions of the party leaders. This is because such matters did not figure very strongly in voters' calculations about which party to support. Social location and family socialisation were the main determinants of party support.

The era of dealignment: 1970s–90s

In the period after 1970 the model of aligned voting, involving two solid blocs of support for the major parties, came to be increasingly at odds with reality. The figures in Table 11.1 show that their support varied much more from election to election, and that there were also marked increases in support for the Liberals and their successors and for 'others'. In England the two-party duopoly was eroded by the 'centre' parties, while in Scotland and Wales the nationalist parties became important and permanent features of the political landscape. Voting studies revealed that what seemed to be going on among voters was a two-pronged 'dealignment'. In the first place, there was a marked decline in the strength with which voters identified with the major parties. This 'partisan dealignment' affected both parties and Table 11.6 shows the relevant figures for the Conservatives. The first row of the table shows that there was very little change in absolute levels of Conservative identification. Indeed, in 1992 – possibly because the order of the relevant questions in the BES survey was changed – there appeared to be a sharp increase in identification with the Conservatives. In contrast, the proportion of the electorate

Table 11.6 Trends in Conservative Party identification (%)

	Average 1964–70	Feb. 1974	Oct. 1974	1979	1983	1987	1992
With Conservative identification	38	35	34	38	36	37	45
'Very strong' Conservative identifiers	19	11	9	9	9	9	9
% of Conservative identifiers 'very strong'	49	32	27	24	25	23	21

Source: Figures to 1979 are from Sarlvik and Crewe 1983: 334–6; those for 1983 to 1992 have been calculated directly from the relevant BES survey data.

which had a 'very strong' identification with, or commitment to, the Conservatives was much smaller after 1970 and did not recover in 1992. The third row shows that, whereas just under half of all Conservative identifiers classed themselves as 'very strong' in the 1960s, the proportion declined steadily to just over a fifth by 1992.

The second prong of dealignment is 'class dealignment'. The interpretation of the evidence is more controversial in this case and the topic has generated a considerable literature (see Denver, 1994 for a summary). Nonetheless, most electoral analysts agree that the level of class voting – the extent to which working class voters supported Labour and middle class voters supported the Conservatives – declined markedly after 1970. Some summary figures showing support for the Conservatives in different occupational classes are given in Table 11.7, and it can be seen that the proportion of middle class (non-manual) voters supporting the Conservatives declined, while working class support for them increased. It is important to understand that it is not claimed that class no longer affects party support, simply that the effect of class is significantly smaller than it used to be.

Together, the processes of class and partisan dealignment are the most striking developments in British electoral behaviour during the last 30 years. They explain a move from a situation in which party choice was generally stable and predictable to one in which voters are volatile and unpredictable in

Table 11.7 Occupational class and Conservative support, 1964–92

	Mean % Conservative		
	1964–70	1974–9	1983–92
Non-manual workers	62	55	55
Manual workers	29	28	35

Source: Calculated from data in Denver, 1994: 61.

their behaviour. Nonetheless, the Conservatives have continued to be very successful in elections and so new explanations for Conservative support must be sought. These have generally focused on voters' opinions, but before considering this approach it is worth looking at the effects of voters' social characteristics in this period.

Social characteristics and Conservative support

Throughout the dealignment period the overall influence of social characteristics on party choice declined (see Rose and McAllister, 1990). By the 1980s the 'gender gap' had all but disappeared for example and, although the Conservatives were still stronger among older age groups, the clear relationship between age and party choice had diminished. There were still traces of a religious effect, especially among more middle class groups (see Heath *et al.*, 1991: 85–8) but in an increasingly secular age it is difficult to gauge the importance of this. On the other hand, party choice was increasingly associated with geographical location. From the 1959 general election, the Conservatives steadily strengthened their position relative to Labour in the South of England and more rural areas and became relatively weaker in big cities outside London, and in Scotland, Wales and the North of England. These divergences accelerated sharply during the 1980s and, despite a slight reversal of the regional trends in 1992, Conservative support is now highly concentrated. The regional concentration of support in the 1992 election is apparent in Table 11.8. The Conservatives won more than half of all votes and 80 per cent of the seats in the South. In Scotland, Wales and the North, in contrast, they won only 70 seats (26 per cent of the total). The division between urban and rural parts of the country is illustrated by the fact that, in the six former metropolitan counties in England, the Conservatives won only 34.9 per cent of the votes and 34 of the 129 seats, whereas in non-metropolitan

Table 11.8 Regional variations in party support, 1992

	% Share of votes			Seats won		
	Con.	Lab.	Lib. Dem.	Con.	Lab.	Lib. Dem.
Scotland	25.7	39.0	13.1	11	49	9
Wales	28.6	49.5	12.4	6	27	1
North	36.9	46.0	16.1	53	107	3
Midlands	46.6	36.3	15.9	74	46	0
South	50.4	24.9	22.9	192	42	7

NB: Percentages do not total 100 because votes (and seats) for other parties and candidates are not shown.

Source: Butler and Kavanagh, 1992: 286–7.

counties they took 49.1 per cent of the vote and 237 (out of 311) seats (*The Times* 1992). In a string of Northern and Scottish cities – Glasgow, Newcastle upon Tyne, Sunderland, Liverpool, Manchester – they won no seats at all.

In so far as social characteristics still influence party choice, the social changes of the past 30 years have favoured the Conservative Party. Groups favourably disposed to the Conservatives have increased in size and this has given them a long-term advantage. The most notable change in this respect is the growth of the middle class – a majority of voters are now middle class – but other changes, such as the growth in the proportions of home owners and share owners, the movement of the population from the North to the South and from the cities to suburbs and the countryside, have also tended to in-crease the size of the pool of 'naturally' Conservative supporters. There are trends working in the opposite direction – the growth in the number of ethnic minority voters, for example – but it has been calculated that simply because of changes in the social structure since 1964 the Conservative share of the vote was four percentage points higher (and Labour's five points lower) in 1992 than it would have been had the sizes of the most important social groups been unchanged (see Heath *et al.*, 1994: 281–4). Social changes alone cannot account for the string of Conservative victories from 1979, however. To do so we need to take more account of voters' opinions.

'Judgemental' voting

As the social underpinnings of party choice have crumbled and partisan attach-ment weakened, more attention has been paid to the opinions of voters. Research has focused both on opinions about relatively short-term matters, such as party policies, party performance in government and the party leaders, and on longer-term attitudes relating to the parties' ideologies and images. What all of these approaches have in common is that they view the voters as making some kind of judgement about the parties. We might, therefore, use the term 'judgemental' voting to describe the various approaches and it is clear that, in the dealignment period, such judgemental voting has increased in import-ance, as long-term influences such as class or family socialisation have declined.

The picture that is drawn of the modern 'dealigned' voter – unpredictable, unstable, hesitant and moved by short-term influences – appears to be contra-dicted by the Conservative performance in the four elections from 1979. As Table 11.1 shows, their share of the vote hardly changed. It would be a mistake, however, to regard the 40-odd per cent of the vote that they gained in these elections as constituting a solid bloc of core supporters. The party identification data suggest that the real core vote – very strong Conservative identifiers – amounts to only about 9 per cent of the electorate. Rather, the interpretation consistent with dealignment is that the Conservatives have been successful in putting together a sort of temporary coalition at each

Table 11.9 Issues in elections 1979–92

	1979		1983	
	Salience	Preferred party lead	Salience	Preferred party lead
Prices	42	Lab +13	20	Con +40
Unemployment	27	Lab +15	72	Lab +16
Taxes	21	Con +61	–	
Trade unions/strikes	20	Con +15	–	
Law and order	11	Con +27	–	
Defence	–		38	Con +54
NHS	–		38	Lab +46
	1987		1992	
	Salience	Preferred party lead	Salience	Preferred party lead
Unemployment	49	Lab +34	36	Lab +26
Defence	35	Con +63	35	Con +63
NHS	33	Lab +49	41	Lab +34
Education	19	Lab +15	23	Lab +23
Prices	–		11	Con +59
Taxes	–		10	Con +72
Defence	–		3	Con +86

NB: The table reports issues mentioned by more than 10% of voters at any of the elections. The preferred party lead is % saying the party most preferred on the issue had the best policy minus % saying the same of the next most preferred party.

Sources: Gallup data reported in Crewe, 1981, 1985, 1992a, 1992b.

election. To understand their success, therefore, we need to examine the short-term factors that enabled them to do this.

One such factor is the popularity of party leaders. The evidence concerning the relative popularity of the Conservative and Labour leaders in the 1979 election is somewhat ambiguous, but James Callaghan led Margaret Thatcher as the most popular choice for Prime Minister. In the next two elections, however, Mrs Thatcher far outscored her Labour counterparts (Michael Foot in 1983 and Neil Kinnock in 1987), while in 1992 John Major was strongly preferred over Neil Kinnock. It used to be that party leaders did not count for much electorally, but Mughan (1993) has shown that their impact began to increase in the mid-1970s and became much more significant in 1987 and 1992. The greater electoral appeal of Conservative leaders seems to be part of the explanation for the party's success.

A second line of explanation is to look at elector's opinions about the best party to handle issues that are prominent at the time of an election. Table 11.9 shows the figures that Crewe has reported on issue salience – the frequency with which voters said that the issue was an important one – and the party preferred on salient issues. Taken overall, the data suggest that the Conservatives have consistently benefited from favourable ratings from the voters on matters connected with defence, taxation and prices. Looking at individual elections, however, it appears that, although the combination of issue salience and party preferred on the issue might satisfactorily account for the Conservative victories in 1979 and 1983, it does not work for 1987 and 1992. If voting had been entirely on the basis of the figures given here, then Labour should have won both elections. This has led commentators to include another dimension in the analysis of issues – the credibility or competence of the party on the issue – and here the Conservatives have had a decisive advantage.

Most commentators agree that the state of the economy is the central issue as far as voting is concerned. This is not a 'position' issue like privatisation, for example, on which people take views for and against. Everyone wants prosperity, and the issue is how well the parties have performed, or might perform in future, in delivering it. In general the electorate has had more faith in the economic competence of the Conservatives. In the 12 months before the 1992 election, for example, when asked by Gallup which party was best able to handle the problem of Britain's economic difficulties, on average 45 per cent of respondents opted for the Conservatives and 30 per cent for Labour, despite the fact that the Conservatives had been in office for 13 years and were presiding over another economic recession. Similarly, during the election campaign 42 per cent believed that Britain as a whole would be worse off under Labour and 44 per cent believed that their families would be worse off, compared with 38 per cent and 30 per cent, respectively, who thought things would be better. In all four elections from 1979, the Conservatives were the preferred party on economic issues, with the exception of unemployment. Labour had large leads on this issue but the electorate had doubts about Labour's ability to do anything about it. It would appear, as Newton (1993) and others have argued, that the electoral impact of unemployment declined very substantially during the 1980s as people came to believe that it resulted from market forces which governments could do little to control.

The most detailed work on the impact of the state of the economy on support for the parties in recent years has been carried out by David Sanders (see, for example, Sanders *et al.*, 1987; Sanders, 1992). He finds that the level of personal economic optimism – itself conditioned by changes in the level of inflation and changes in interest rates – is a good predictor of support for the Conservatives from 1983 to 1992. In this analysis, explaining the Conservative victories is not difficult: once in government they were able to manage the economy to ensure that, when an election came round, personal economic optimism outweighed pessimism among the voters, even if only temporarily, and thus reaped an electoral reward.

The fact that electors' judgements have become more important since 1970 suggests two other factors which might help to explain Conservative success. Electors must have information on which to base their judgements and are also more open to persuasion than they were when party choice was almost automatic. It might be, then, that the Conservatives have been more adept at marketing themselves in campaigns and that the predominantly (and, in some cases, violently) pro-Conservative position of the national press has been a substantial advantage. The evidence as far as campaigning is concerned is variable, however. There is no doubt that in 1983 Labour had a truly awful campaign, but things were tightened up and most observers agree that in 1987 and 1992 Labour had very professional national campaigns, probably better than those mounted by the Conservatives. Recent evidence also suggests that in 1992 Labour ran more effective local campaigns than the Conservatives (see Denver and Hands, 1993).

On the other hand, the Conservatives have enjoyed a massive advantage over the other parties in terms of support from the national press in recent elections. In the 1950s and 1960s the advantage was smaller and, in any case, the strength of party identification ensured that readers were not greatly influenced by their newspaper. More recent research has found readers to be more open to influence. Sanders *et al.* (1993) show that the perceptions that voters have of the state of the economy is influenced by press reporting. Miller (1991) reports that, in the run-up to the 1987 election, Conservative support increased dramatically among readers of pro-Conservative tabloids, especially among those who were not strongly committed to a party. Curtice and Semetko (1994) are more cautious in their conclusion with reference to the 1992 election, but say that there is evidence of a press effect over the longer term. Overall, evidence that voters are influenced by the papers they read remains somewhat patchy and open to doubt – partly because researching the topic is extremely difficult – but the weight of opinion, in these and other recent studies, is that the Conservatives have derived some advantage from the backing they have received from most of the national press.

The perils of government 1979–92

Between elections there is a regular cycle of support for the governing party. Immediately following an election there is usually a brief 'honeymoon' and the popularity of the party increases. There then follows a long decline in popularity and during this period the party is likely to do badly in parliamentary by-elections and local elections, as well as in the opinion polls. As another election approaches, however, popularity increases and by the date of the election the party is back in serious contention. Sometimes the pattern is affected by a 'random shock', such as the Falklands War or the resignation of

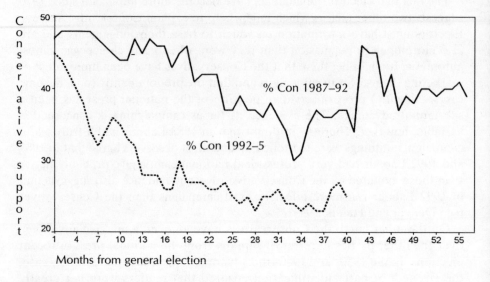

Figure 11.1 The cycle of Conservative support

Mrs Thatcher as Prime Minister, but generally the effect of these does not last long and the basic pattern is soon re-established. The Conservatives have experienced a cycle of popularity broadly following this pattern between each pair of elections since 1979 (see Norpoth, 1992). Data charting the cycles for 1987 to 1992, and for 1992 to late 1995, are shown in Figure 11.1.

The cycle for 1987–92 illustrates the familiar pattern (and also demonstrates very effectively the argument that the Conservatives' election winning coalitions of voters are very temporary). After a brief 'honeymoon', the Conservative share of voting intentions declined steadily until about three years after the election and thereafter there was a recovery. The very sharp rise between months 41 and 42 reflects public reaction to Major's replacing Thatcher as Prime Minister, but the effects of this soon faded and the basic upward trend continued. All of the parliamentary seats lost in by-elections during the trough of unpopularity were regained at the 1992 general election.

In the current cycle, the Conservatives have fallen faster and further in popularity than ever before. Formerly safe seats have been lost in spectacular fashion in by-elections, and local elections have been disastrous. The cumulative effect of four terms in government and four cycles of unpopularity has been that the Conservatives are now extremely weak in local government. In 1980 they had over 10,000 local councillors and controlled almost 200 authorities; after the 1995 local elections they had just under 5,000 councillors and controlled 13 councils – fewer, in both cases, than the

Liberal Democrats. Across large areas of urban Britain they have hardly any councillors, while in the whole of Scotland they hold only 82 council seats out of 1,161.

All this may not matter very much. It may be that when voting in local elections and in parliamentary by-elections, and when stating their voting intentions to opinion pollsters, electors are merely indulging in 'protest' politics to a greater extent than normal, and that when they are faced with actually voting for a government they will return to the Conservative fold. In other words, the normal cyclical pattern – even if more accentuated than usual – will be repeated. It is possible to argue, on the other hand, that things are different this time around because there have been changes in the factors which have helped the Conservatives to maintain their electoral dominance since 1979. Philip Norton addresses these, including some pervasive and potentially long-term changes, in the Conclusion. Here we simply identify three decisive changes that have taken place in recent years and which bear upon our preceding analysis.

The first concerns the party leaders. Just five months after the 1992 general election, there was an economic crisis as the government was forced to suspend sterling from the European exchange rate mechanism (ERM), and John Major's popularity plummeted. Despite a slight recovery in the summer of 1995, he remained very unpopular with the electorate. In contrast, Tony Blair became leader of the Labour Party in 1994 and proved to be extremely popular, easily outscoring Major in the polls when voters were asked to nominate the best person to be Prime Minister. It seems likely, therefore, that the considerable electoral advantage accruing to the Conservatives from the relative popularity of their leaders will not occur at the next election.

Secondly, since 1992 national newspapers have not been as supportive of the Conservatives, nor as hostile to Labour, as they were before. It is likely that they will return to their traditional allegiances in the heat of the next election, but the evidence suggests that such influence as they have among voters is long term, so that it will be difficult for them to erase the effects of a lengthy period during which they have virulently attacked John Major and his government.

Thirdly, and most importantly, the Conservatives appear to have lost their reputation for economic competence. The key event here was, once again, the fiasco over the ERM. Since then, according to Gallup, the 'normal' ratings of the parties on their ability to handle the economy have been reversed. During 1993, the average proportion choosing Labour as the best party to deal with Britain's economic problems was 40 per cent, compared with 27 per cent choosing the Conservatives. In 1994 the figures were 46 per cent and 22 per cent, respectively, and in the first half of 1995 they were 49 per cent and 21 per cent. These figures reveal considerable Conservative weakness in what has usually been one of their strong suits.

Writing about trends in party support in the middle of an interelection cycle is always problematical. With a dealigned and volatile electorate anything can happen. It does seem, however, that the developments discussed in the previous paragraph make the current cycle different from those that have gone before, and that the long period of electoral hegemony enjoyed by the Conservatives is about to come to an end.

PART 3

Party and policy

CHAPTER 12

The party and economic policy

Andrew Gamble

Managing the economy has become a key attribute of political leadership in the era of mass democracy, and trust in the Conservatives' ability to manage it successfully has been a key factor in ensuring their political dominance of British politics. The reputation which governments and parties have for 'economic competence' with the electorate is an important determinant of their popularity, or lack of it. Voters may disagree with a party's policies on many other issues but will still vote for it if they trust it to deliver prosperity.

The situation of the party after 1992 was therefore both unusual and uncomfortable for the Conservatives. They seemed to have lost their magic touch. Not only did the party trail the Labour Party by more than 20 percentage points, but the party also lost its superior rating for economic competence. In previous times of unpopularity, and at the General Election of 1992, the party had generally retained its advantage. However, the events of Black Wednesday in September 1992 when Britain was forced to suspend sterling's membership of the European Exchange Rate Mechanism (ERM) destroyed Conservative credibility in a way which had still not been remedied three years later in 1995, despite a considerable improvement in the performance of the economy.

Why should a sterling devaluation have such an impact on voters' perceptions of the government? One reason has to do with the national prestige which still tends to be associated, however illogically, with the level of the exchange rate. A forced devaluation is seen to entail national humiliation. It is an important political fact that previous major crises in the financial markets which precipitated devaluations of sterling in this century have taken place under Labour governments (1949, 1967, 1976) or could be blamed on the immediately preceding Labour government (1931).

A second reason why Black Wednesday has had such an adverse effect upon the Major government is that the government was forced to reverse a central plank of its economic policy which up to that moment it had been asserting was essential for economic recovery. The report that the Chancellor was 'singing in his bath' after the exit from the ERM because the straitjacket on the conduct of economic policy had been removed did little for the government's reputation. The long economic recession which had hurt large numbers of Conservative voters, particularly because of the collapse of the housing market, was now seen to have been prolonged by the government's insistence on maintaining very high interest rates to keep sterling within the ERM at the agreed parity. This was then followed by the raising of taxation to reduce the growing public sector deficit. The imposition of VAT on fuel was particularly resented (see Chapter 3) but what really damaged the Conservatives was that for so long they had presented themselves as the party of low taxation. It was the Conservatives' ability to play on voters' fears of how Labour might raise taxes if it was returned to office that proved one of its strongest arguments in the 1992 election.

These events also raised questions about Conservative success in the 1980s. The economic record which had been so confidently advertised by Nigel Lawson and other ministers in the 1987 general election as proving that the British economy had decisively turned the corner and was now the strongest economy in Europe no longer looked so convincing by 1992. The overheating of the economy and the credit boom which reignited inflation and brought the economic expansion to an end was seen by many Conservatives – including Margaret Thatcher – as economic mismanagement, for which Nigel Lawson was specifically blamed. It dented the claim of the Thatcher government to have made a decisive difference, liberating Britain from economic decline, inflation, and recession. The electoral backlash against the Major government was in part a result of the disillusion many voters felt following the high expectations of economic success which the Thatcher years had created.

Nevertheless, despite its tribulations the Major government continued the policies which it had inherited from the Thatcher government. In 1995 the Conservative Party was still the party of the free market, committed to free movement of goods and capital, low taxation, deregulation and privatisation. There were elements in the government, most notably concentrated in the Department of Trade and Industry and the new Department for Education and Employment, which attempted to pursue a more interventionist strategy aimed at boosting the competitiveness of particular firms and sectors, through initiatives on training and technology transfer. However, the general pattern of the government's economic policy was not very different from what it had been under the Thatcher government in the 1980s.

Wets and dries

The economic policy which the Conservatives adopted under Margaret Thatcher was, however, highly controversial within the party. There was a long and bitter argument between two groups in the leadership who became known in the media as 'wets' and 'dries'. The wets were Keynesians who favoured giving a high priority to measures to reduce unemployment and maintain growth, and therefore also favoured maintaining a large public sector and good relations with the trade unions. Leading wets in Thatcher's early cabinets were James Prior, Ian Gilmour, Christopher Soames and Peter Walker. Several of them almost resigned from the Government when they heard the contents of the 1981 budget, which applied further deflationary measures to an economy already deep in recession.

The dries, by contrast, were monetarists who saw the first duty of government to be the maintenance of sound money, and who therefore made the prevention of inflation the top priority for government economic policy. The level of unemployment and the rate of economic growth were not regarded as proper targets for government policy. If the government concentrated on keeping inflation under control and removed obstacles to the working of free markets it would create conditions which would be conducive to high employment and economic growth.

The argument between wets and dries was always more than a disagreement over the best technical means of managing the economy. There was a technical argument between Keynesian and monetarist economists about macroeconomic policy and the best way of controlling inflation and reducing unemployment, but in the Conservative Party the argument was always much more political than that. The debate expressed two different ways of conceiving the role of the state in the economy and two different attitudes to government.

The Tory tradition

These divisions cut across more conventional left/right divisions. The dominant tradition in the Conservative Party in relation to the economy and economic policy has been Tory and collectivist, concerned with the welfare and security of the national economy. Economic policy was traditionally subordinated to the requirements of the party's statecraft. The party has often portrayed itself as steering a middle course between the excesses of liberalism and socialism, *laissez-faire* and central planning. Both derive from rigid ideological doctrines which are adhered to regardless of the consequences. The Tory virtue by contrast is flexibility and pragmatism, taking the best from both liberalism and socialism, but having primary regard to the policies which best promote the general welfare of the community.

This idea became known as the Middle Way, expounded among others by Harold Macmillan (Macmillan, 1938). The role of the Conservative Party was always to hold the balance. It had to curb the excesses of *laissez-faire* liberalism in the nineteenth century and the excesses of state socialism in the twentieth, but in doing so it was prepared to work within the framework of policy which each of these doctrines established. The Conservatives accepted free trade in the nineteenth century and they accepted the welfare state and the managed economy in the twentieth century.

This famous adaptability of the Conservatives was often criticised by its opponents, who saw it as a lack of firm principle and opportunistic. The Conservatives would do anything to stay in office, and were prepared to compromise their principles if that was necessary. In his essay 'Why I am not a Conservative' F. A. Hayek, who was later to become an important influence on Margaret Thatcher and Keith Joseph, argued that the main problem with Conservatism was that it offered no set of principles against which to evaluate the current drift of policy and events (Hayek, 1960). The Conservatives' attachment to office and to the nation-state meant for Hayek that they were not reliable defenders of the principles of a market order. In certain circumstances they would be quite happy to drift towards collectivism. This is what had happened in the 1930s. The liberal principles which had governed British economic policy for so long were abandoned by the National government which was dominated by the Conservatives. With the abandonment of the gold standard national protectionism, industrial subsidies and restrictions on free markets multiplied. Hayek saw modern societies in danger of slipping down a road to serfdom, steadily losing economic liberty and creating the conditions for totalitarianism (Hayek, 1944). In Britain this process began in the 1930s under the Conservatives.

When Hayek wrote his postscript in 1960 Harold Macmillan was Prime Minister and the philosophy of the Middle Way was in the ascendancy. However, Hayek's views were to become increasingly influential as a growing number of Conservatives began to question many of the underlying principles of post-war economic policy. A different approach to government was advanced, based on the doctrines of economic liberalism, and not on accepting what was politically possible. The Conservatives, it was argued, needed to wrest the ideological initiative and the moral high ground from Labour. They should not be content simply to be good managers of the economy. They should seek to change the relationship between the state and the economy.

This attitude was often presented by its opponents in the party, such as Ian Gilmour, as a turn to dogma and a shift away from the Conservative concern with governing a community (Gilmour, 1992). The growing appeal of economic liberalism within the party was seen as the intrusion of an alien dogma, and not only by Tory wets like Gilmour. Roger Scruton, from his High Tory stance, has also emphasised that the fundamental purpose of the Conservative Party was to maintain the conditions for authority and order. Economic policy should be subordinate to that end, and he praised Keynesianism as an economic policy which was primarily driven by political considerations. The relief of unemployment, the level of welfare provision, the question of incomes policy, relationships with the trade unions and the size of the public sector were all questions which need to be decided politically in the light of circumstances, and the overriding duty of Conservatives is to ensure the protection of the state. He criticised Conservative enthusiasm for economic liberalism because it threatened to subordinate government policy to a set of principles which promoted one-sided individualism, and eroded civic obligations and national identity (Scruton, 1980).

From their side, economic liberals have countered that they are the true Tory tradition, and that the philosophy of the Middle Way is an alien import-ation into the party, belonging more to a Whig conception of government of balancing interests and holding power. They argue that for too much of the twentieth century and particularly since 1945 the party has been on the defen-sive and failed to articulate a clear alternative to socialism. Keith Joseph diagnosed a ratchet of socialism (Joseph, 1976). Each period of Labour gov-ernment would increase government control over the economy; each period of Conservative government would accept the new level and not significantly reduce it. As the public sector expanded so the interests supporting its further enlargement also grew, and a politics emerged in which the Conservatives were in danger of being marginalised. This trend towards corporatism in which the economy would be managed through agreements between the government, employers and trade unions was regarded by economic liberal Conservatives such as Joseph as leading not just to the extinction of economic liberty but also to the extinction of the Conservative Party. For the economic liberals in the party the prime need was for a Tory statecraft which could reverse the ratchet of socialism, seize back the initiative from Labour and recreate the institutions for an individualist society and a market order which would support Conservative values and generate political support for the Conservative Party.

The post-war settlement

The origins of this dispute over the most appropriate role of the state in the economy can be traced back to the accommodation that the leadership made to the post-war settlement, set out in plans of the Coalition gov-ernment and implemented by the Labour government between 1945 and 1951. These changed the parameters of economic policy because of the substantial enlargement both of the public sector and of public spending and therefore of taxation. As a percentage of Gross Domestic Product (GDP) public spending increased from around 25 per cent before 1939 to more than 40 per cent. The programmes which showed the largest increases were social security, health, education, housing and defence. The implementation of the Beveridge Plan, the establishment of the National Health Service, the new school structure and new defence commitments, particularly through NATO, entailed very large percentage increases in expenditure. This in turn made a Keynesian approach to managing the economy both more feasible and also more necessary.

Post-war Keynesianism set out to achieve four targets – full employment, stable prices, a balance of payments surplus and economic growth. After the experience of the inter-war years when unemployment had been persistently high it is not surprising that especial importance was attached to the goal of full employment. Some inflation was thought acceptable if it allowed the goal of full employment to be reached. The aim of post-war governments was to use fiscal and monetary measures to alter the level of demand in the economy in a bid to ensure that recessions whenever they occurred were mild and that the economy kept expanding and that employment was as high as possible. In that way welfare would be maximised and the growing wealth of the society would allow public services to expand as the tax yield increased proportionately to the increase in national income, without any need to raise taxes.

Two other key features of the post-war settlement were Britain's place in the new world order and the relationship with the trade unions. The international financial system was reconstructed around the dollar and sterling became its junior partner, in a regime of fixed exchange rates, with the aim of moving all the economies within the US orbit towards convertibility of their currencies and multilateral free trade as quickly as circumstances allowed. These moves helped create the conditions for the remarkable period of economic prosperity in the world economy throughout the 1950s and 1960s.

The relationship with the trade unions was also placed on a new footing after 1945. The close involvement of the unions in the war effort, as well as the moves during the 1930s to involve them more closely in national economic policy, were developed in the post-war period. The unions and the employers became important partners with government in helping to implement national policy. The commitment to full employment considerably strengthened the influence and bargaining strength of organised labour, alongside the influence of the employers and the financial markets, and it meant that the unions were increasingly consulted on many aspects of policy.

The post-war world was considerably different from the inter-war years, and there was some scepticism as to whether the Conservatives would be able to adapt to it; but a vigorous set of new leaders rapidly repositioned the party. The 1947 Industrial Charter was an important symbolic gesture in seeking to bury past conflicts with the trade unions, and the party made clear its broad acceptance of many of the changes Labour was introducing (see Chapter 2). It also accepted most of the measures of nationalisation where these affected the public utilities, but it opposed vigorously any further extension of the principle into the profitable manufacturing sector.

Butskellism

When the party returned to office in 1951 it made few changes to the style of managing the economy established by Labour. Nationalisation was halted and limited denationalisation of steel and road haulage was undertaken, but the public sector was not otherwise reduced and the government accepted all the commitments on health, social security and education inherited from its predecessor. In some instances, such as housing, it increased them. The government showed itself totally committed to the goal of full employment. Replying to those economists who believed that the economy would perform better if there was a greater margin of unemployment, the Conservative Chancellor, R. A. Butler, retorted at the 1953 Conservative Party Conference that those who advocated creating pools of unemployment should be thrown into them and made to swim.

So little difference was there in the style of economic management between Labour and Conservative that the *Economist* coined the phrase Butskellism in 1955 to point up the similarity in philosophy and approach between the last Labour Chancellor Hugh Gaitskell and the then Conservative Chancellor, R. A. Butler. Relations with the trade unions were also very good. Churchill installed Walter Monckton as Minister of Labour with a brief to reassure the unions about government intentions. The new status of the unions as partners with government was fully accepted.

One reason for the success of Conservative economic management in the 1950s was that conditions in the world economy were highly favourable. The expansion was so rapid and so long-lasting that all the goals of economic policy were being fulfilled in the 1950s. Unemployment was minuscule – in many years less than 250,000. If it reached half a million alarm bells started ringing. Inflation, too, was never more than 2 or 3 per cent once the Korean war was over and economic growth, although poor compared to what was happening in the rest of Europe, was still much faster than it had been at any time in the twentieth century.

Keynesianism and the Middle Way appeared to deliver results and the Conservatives reaped the electoral benefit in 1955 and 1959. There were critics of the extent to which the government had accepted the reforms initiated by Labour but they were muted not least by the success which the Conservatives achieved, in the same way that in the 1980s critics of Thatcher's economic policy were disarmed when it seemed to be delivering economic success.

Modernisation

The success of Conservative economic policy in the 1950s was qualified by the increasing evidence towards the end of the decade that the British economy was not performing as well as some of its main competitors. The response of the Macmillan government was to launch an ambitious modernisation programme designed to increase the competitiveness of the British economy and raise its rate of growth. The programme involved significant extensions of public powers and public responsibilities. The use of the state in this way to improve economic performance was regarded by Conservatives as legitimate and right. Many of the initiatives the government took on regional aid, education, prices and incomes policy, investment incentives and indicative planning were continued and amplified by Labour after 1964.

The 1960s was another decade of exceptional economic performance in absolute terms; but the expectations which modernisation had unleashed and the comparisons with performance abroad made British achievements appear extremely inadequate. A cycle of disillusion set in with governments and politicians who promised great improvements and then failed to deliver. After the Conservatives' 13 continuous years in office government changed hands four times between 1964 and 1979. Inability to manage the economy successfully was not the only factor in this regular rejection of the incumbent government but it was an important one.

The inability of governments of either party to deliver economic success and reverse economic decline became still more marked in the 1970s. The failure of the Heath government left deep scars in the Conservative Party and provided the opportunity for Thatcher to seize the leadership and for a sea change to take place in the party's thinking about economic policy and the role of the state in the economy.

The experience of the Heath government was pivotal to this reassessment because it was seen as having set out with a set of economic policies which in important respects were a departure from the collectivist and corporatist policies of the 1960s. The Heath government proposed a new industrial relations law to curb the growth of strikes, it planned to scrap many of the interventionist boards and agencies which had been established under previous governments and it sought to rely on competition and market disciplines rather than state direction and support to improve economic performance. Heath in particular believed that a substantial increase in economic efficiency was necessary if the British economy was to be able to compete successfully in the European Economic Community (EEC).

These new Conservative policies, however, did not reflect a fundamental change in the thinking of the leadership about economic policy or the principles on which it should be based. When the policies ran into trouble, particularly labour unrest, and did not seem to be bearing fruit the government changed tack and proposed instead a major extension of the powers of government over the economy in order to achieve the objectives it sought. A new Industry Act, conferring sweeping powers on the Secretary of State, a compulsory prices and incomes policy and major new spending programmes were introduced as part of an expansionary package to propel the economy into faster growth.

The economy did grow exceptionally fast in 1973, the year in which membership of the EEC was finally achieved, but the policy suffered spectacular shipwreck because of events in the world economy – the oil price hike by

OPEC (Organisation of Petroleum Exporting Countries) – and the resistance by the miners to stage three of the pay policy. The sense of crisis created by the imposition of a three-day week and the spectre of a world recession was the backdrop against which Heath called an early election in 1974 and lost.

This defeat proved a fateful one for the Conservatives. The reaction in the party to their failure in government created a climate in which it was not only possible for Margaret Thatcher to challenge for the leadership but allowed a debate to develop which questioned the adherence of the Conservatives to the policies of the post-war years and advocated that the party should adopt a very different attitude in future to the role of the state in the economy.

Thatcherism

The debate was aided by the worldwide recession and by the increasing signs that a watershed had been reached in post-war economic policy. The post-war international financial system established at Bretton Woods had collapsed, and the sources of the post-war expansion were exhausted. Inflation had accelerated to dangerous levels as governments sought to maintain prosperity and expansion, employment and growth had declined and the dangers of protectionism and trade wars had increased. All economies needed radical restructuring to make them more competitive, but for the weaker economies like Britain's this was a daunting political prospect.

The division in the Conservative Party over how to handle this crisis was complicated by the dominance within the Shadow Cabinet of ministers who still adhered to the One Nation, Middle Way outlook of Macmillan and Heath. Those around Thatcher and active in the 'think tanks' pressed for a much more radical policy to deal with fundamentals – the size and scope of the state, the power of the trade unions and a return to sound money.

The result while the party was in opposition was a compromise. The main policy documents *The Right Approach* and *The Right Approach to the Economy* were bland and vague and contained statements which were satisfactory to both sides of the argument. They ruled little out and little in. There were no specific pledges for example on Conservative tax policy, on privatisation or on trade union reform. Behind the scenes more work was being done preparing for a radical change of policy, but there were few public signs of it. Political caution and the need to maintain unity within the Shadow Cabinet meant that the main effort was devoted to attacking the record of the Labour government.

The Thatcher government

Once the Thatcher government was elected, however, it quickly became clear that this would not be like previous Conservative governments. It is easy to exaggerate the extent of the radicalism of the Thatcher government and the coherence of its policies, but what emerged from its 11 years of office was a determination to make radical changes when circumstances permitted. The result was not the triumphant roll-back of the state which many of the supporters of Thatcherism were hoping for, but there was a significant change in the agenda of government and in the relationship between the state and the economy.

The Thatcher government generally sought to reduce the role of the state and to promote individual self-reliance. The state should no longer be responsible for such things as the level of unemployment or the rate of growth, or the provision of many public services. The Thatcherites wanted to reduce what was expected of government. They wanted the state to become enabling rather than directive. The state could help to create the conditions for prosperity but it could not create the prosperity itself.

The dilemma the Thatcherites encountered in government was that there was no simple way to roll back the state. The accumulation of institutions, agencies and special interests in the course of the twentieth century meant that government action was highly constrained. In many areas free markets did not exist and any attempt to create them would encounter fierce opposition. In pursuing its objective of reducing the size and the scope of government the Thatcher government was obliged to strengthen the powers of the state in order to defeat the interests which impeded the creation of a market order.

In order to restore a free economy the state had to be made strong. The state of post-war social democracy had been a weak state because the autonomy of the executive had been eroded by the power of special interests. One of the main political tasks of the Thatcher government was therefore to assert its autonomy of all special interests. Monetarism was useful here, because it was a technique of economic management which by concentrating on the control of inflation through the setting of monetary targets allowed the government to disengage from entanglement with trade unions and employers in the determination of prices and incomes. The government simply declared that unemployment was not its responsibility. It had a duty to maintain sound money; it was then up to trade unions and employers to adjust their costs accordingly and price their members into jobs.

This approach was justified as a return to the sound liberal principles which had governed Britain in the past. Its opponents saw it as a return to the policy regime of the 1920s and 1930s under which the power of organised labour was held in check by the market disciplines of bankruptcy and unemployment. The Thatcher government did not set out deliberately to create higher unemployment, but its monetarist policies intensified the impact of the world slump on the British economy in 1980 and 1981, which saw a dramatic reduction in British industrial capacity and the rise of unemployment to over three million. The government made full use of this opportunity to preach the need for a radical change of attitudes and for a reorganisation of industry. It pushed through in stages a comprehensive reform of trade union law which removed many of the privileges and immunities which had been granted to the trade unions since the 1906 Trade Disputes Act.

One of the government's most successful economic policies turned out to be privatisation, but it was a policy which happened by accident rather than design. The first major privatisation was British Telecom, which was undertaken primarily because its investment programme could not be funded through the Treasury. The success and ease of this privatisation encouraged the government to plan many more. By the end of the decade much of the old nationalised public sector had been dismantled.

The Thatcher government undoubtedly had big successes in relation to privatisation and the trade unions, but its wider strategic objectives proved harder to achieve. Although direct taxation, particularly the higher rates, were cut sharply the overall burden of taxation was not reduced because indirect taxes like VAT were increased. The government restructured public spending and cut many programmes severely, but it was unable to achieve an overall reduction in public spending. The public sector remained large and a constraint on government action.

From one angle a case can be made for regarding the Thatcher government as continuing the broad lines of post-war Conservative economic policy – widening property ownership through sales of council houses and nationalised industries, reducing the burden of direct taxation, encouraging enterprise, competition and consumer choice. It was also seeking to do more than this. Thatcher wanted to create a situation in which a return to collectivist policies and government interference in the economy would be impossible. Here she achieved some of her objectives but a great deal remained to be done. The Major government has continued with the broad thrust of Thatcher's policies, but the crusading tone of the radical free market enthusiasts has disappeared. Thatcherites feared the return of collectivist intervention, particularly through the intervention from the European Commission. The dispute over domestic economic policy and the role of the state in the economy has become tied into the debate over Britain's future in the European Union. After his re-election as leader in 1995 John Major assembled around him a Cabinet which was more in tune with One Nation Toryism than radical Thatcherism. However, the Thatcherites remain a potent force in the party and believe that the agenda of the Thatcherite revolution is far from finished. The struggle between these two wings of the party over economic policy is set to continue.

CHAPTER 13

The party and foreign policy

Arthur Aughey

The Conservative Party has presented itself traditionally as the party with a unique grasp of, and a unique competence in, matters of foreign policy. This is a logical extension of its claim to be the natural party of government. In so far as one can argue that foreign policy is based on reasons of state and not on party ideology, then to think of oneself as the natural party of government is to think of oneself as uniquely qualified in foreign policy. The party, as we have seen, has been in office alone or as the most powerful element in coalition for 70 of the 100 years since 1895. It might be assumed that Conservatives would have a clear idea of foreign policy objectives. This is a debatable point.

It has been argued, for instance, that Churchill's notion of Britain's post-war foreign policy being defined by its location at the intersection of 'Three Circles' of world influence was only 'a masterly ideological mystification' (Gamble, 1974: 186). This has become an accepted wisdom. Its criticism of British foreign policy suggests that such 'ideological mystification' prevented the country in general and the Conservative Party in particular from recognising that the days of world power status had gone. The Three Circles notion, however, was a more accurate depiction of reality than retrospective judgement would allow, even if the hubris which assumed that Britain remained the hyphen which joined and the buckle which fastened these three circles together was quite a masterly overstatement. Britain was indeed a power intimately involved in each circle of influence – America, the Commonwealth and Europe – while at the same time overstretched by that involvement, economically, politically and militarily. Those who argue that Britain 'missed the bus' of leadership in Europe also fail to recognise that 'Europe' was not an exclusive option in the early post-war years (see, e.g., Charlton, 1983). The orientation of Conservative policy towards Europe which began hesitantly in the late 1950s and early 1960s was not and is not a straightforward process, nor was it historically inevitable. Then again, nor was the Commonwealth an exclusive option. American power was a deciding factor and it was quite rational for Conservative leaders to acknowledge its pervasive importance. The Suez crisis of 1956 clarified this if it had not been obvious previously.

The notion that the Conservative Party has been united and single-minded about the objectives of foreign policy is certainly an ideological mystification. On nearly every aspect of policy there have been dissenting voices, some significant and others insignificant. The present divisions on Europe are not without a history. They are a contemporary example of argument within Conservative politics about Britain's modern role in the world. Indeed, it could be argued that Europe is only central to Conservative politics today because many of its other post-war concerns, such as decolonisation, overseas military commitments or the Commonwealth, are no longer live issues. An understanding of contemporary policy demands an examination of how attitudes towards American, Commonwealth and European relationships have developed. Continuities are as important as discontinuities.

The American sphere

Official Conservative policy has consistently supported the value of the 'special relationship'. Indeed, Conservatives have claimed that it was their own creation, the result of a meeting of minds between Churchill and Roosevelt. This has been a recurring theme. Macmillan tried to play the Greek to Kennedy's Roman. Thatcher played the woman behind the great men of Reagan and Bush. Heath's attitude to the United States may have been distinctly cooler and Major may have experienced an often uneasy and uncertain relationship with an American administration. All Conservative leaders, however, have paid formal obeisance to the unique quality of the connection and its importance for Britain's role in the world. Below the surface formalities of Conservative fidelity towards the special relationship it is possible to detect three historic attitudes. The first reveals a distaste for America's post-war dominance and a suspicion that the broad lines of British foreign policy, even membership of the European Community, have been a consequence of this dominance. The second reveals a similar suspicion of such dominance but has translated this suspicion into firm advocacy of British membership of the Community as a means to counteract overweening American power. Both these attitudes have been expressed openly by few leading Conservatives, although they are held quite widely within the Party. The third attitude, which remains the authoritative voice of the Party, has been concerned to maintain the Atlantic Alliance under the leadership of the United States. It has no overtone of that anti-Americanism which has characterised the other two attitudes. The aim of policy has been to ensure that America stays coupled to Europe. This was one policy certainty of the Cold War, defined by the need to maintain a common front against Soviet influence. It is policy still, albeit a less certain one, in the very different circumstances following the collapse of the Soviet Union.

The first of these attitudes was characteristic of those who were pro-Commonwealth, an attitude influential until the early 1970s. Their grievance was that the Americans had used the principles of free trade and the post-war institution of the General Agreement on Tariffs and Trade (GATT) to deprive Britain of the opportunity to strengthen the political and economic unity of the Commonwealth. The feeling was that GATT had made the world safe for American exports at the expense of British political interests. As Ronald Russell argued, the success of the Commonwealth as an organisation for international stability 'did not deter the American Government from taking full adantage of our need for their help during the war and continually pressing for [Commonwealth] preferences to be abolished' (Russell, 1962: 48). Following Macmillan's application to join the Common Market in 1961 it was proposed that the Conservative leadership was following the dictates of Washington's grand design. This involved, among other things, detaching Canada from the Commonwealth once Britain was inside the Common Market and pushing the Caribbean Commonwealth members further into the American sphere of influence. It ought to be no part of the Conservative Party's policy to aid the Americans in depriving Britain of her global, seafaring role. As Lord Hinchingbroke put it dramatically at the Party Conference in 1961: 'The question is: do we ally ourselves with our history and all that we have done to maintain this enormous Commonwealth . . . or do we put obstacles in its progress, at the behest of the United States of America?' (NUCUA Conference Report, 1961: 56).

Such feelings did not so much die away as become resigned to defeat (see Chapter 5 for a discussion of pessimistic Toryism). By the 1970s the Conservative Party had joined the European Community, thus acting 'in line with all the promptings to sacrifice ourselves which America has given to us since 1945' (Montagu, 1970: 4). These feelings had by that time found a new voice in a distinctive British nationalism (sometimes misleadingly called 'Powellism') which may have had illusions about the character of the British people but which had no illusions about America or the Commonwealth and certainly no affection for Europe. Echoes of that voice are to be found today in the tones of Euro-scepticism. American motives are also suspected of having damaged British policy and Conservative Unionism in Northern Ireland (see Clark, 1994: 117).

The second attitude expressed the same antagonism towards American power and the same suspicion of its motives. It drew the opposite conclusion, however, about Conservative policy towards Europe. It was only as part of a strong European arrangement that Britain could exert its influence and develop a countervailing power to potentially damaging strategies proposed by American governments. Julian Amery argued this case forcefully throughout the 1960s and presented it in a way which suggested parallels with the cause of Tariff Reform which had so exercised his father. With more justice in his terminology than those who later applied it to Margaret Thatcher (who is an 'Atlanticist'), Julian Critchley called this tendency in the Party 'Gaullist'. There was indeed more than a sneaking regard for the determination of

General de Gaulle to advance French interests against the tide of American opinion. The purpose of Conservative policy, so ran this argument, should be to set itself against the 'continued subjection of our continent to outside influences, Soviet and American' (Cambridge Monday Club, 1965: 6). This attitude ranged wider than one would have expected. Jock Bruce-Gardyne was of the opinion that Conservatives needed to consider a new alignment to balance what he believed to be, in the fashionable contemporary terminology of convergence, 'the inevitable and growing collaboration of the two super powers' (*Spectator* 12 July 1968). Only thus could the Conservatives deliver some self respect to the British people. Edward Heath shared some, if not all, of these views and they informed his commitment to Europe (see Campbell, 1994). Europhiles within the party tend to hold these views today.

The dominant and still authoritative view in the party has been to build neither a cohesive Commonwealth nor a Third Force Europe but to maintain the closest possible relations between Britain and America within the framework of the Atlantic Alliance. 'Atlanticism' has been as much a consistent and solid element of Conservative policy this century as either imperialism or Europeanism, even though there have been rather different emphases. Macmillan's concept of the special relationship meant Britain playing the role of intermediary between America, Europe and the Soviet Union. By virtue of history, military interest – especially nuclear weaponry – and the habit of working together, the ties that bound London and Washington set in turn the bounds of foreign policy. Heath, on the other hand, was less committed to the Atlanticist tradition and was willing to prepare for the day when America could no longer fulfill the role of guaranteeing British and European security. The special relationship was to take on a renewed ideological significance under Mrs Thatcher's leadership. Her Bruges speech of 1988 was, among other things, a contemporary manifesto of Atlanticism. It was not personality which encouraged this renewal. It was concern about defence and the threat of war. The Cruise missile affair of the 1980s symbolised this. The very uniqueness of the special relationship which Thatcher had built up with Reagan and Bush and the closeness of British–American policy in the 1980s was always going to be difficult to sustain. So it has proved under John Major.

The Commonwealth sphere

The idea of the Empire as an extension of British greatness in the world had come, by the end of the nineteenth century, to play an important part in the imagination of Conservative politics (see, e.g., McKenzie and Silver, 1968). It continued to play that role in the first half of the twentieth century. With the transformation of Empire into Commonwealth its imaginative power began to diminish, slowly at first and then rapidly. A trend developed, and became more pronounced within the Party from the late 1960s onwards, to see the Commonwealth as being as much of a hindrance as a help to British foreign policy. Nevertheless, there did exist a vital Commonwealth lobby throughout the 1960s and into the 1970s which included figures such Sir Derek Walker-Smith, Robin Turton and Peter Walker.

In 1962 Walker-Smith and Walker had produced a pamphlet, *A Call to the Commonwealth*, which argued that the Commonwealth could provide a proper bulwark against international communism and that it should be the first objective of Conservative foreign policy to strengthen it. Communism, it noted, fed on the discontents of the less developed countries in the Third World. The Commonwealth, by developing institutions with 'teeth' could formulate constructive policies for political and economic co-operation to prevent these countries from succumbing. Imaginative exercises in statecraft through the medium of the Commonwealth would allow British governments to act as a bridge between the developed and the underdeveloped worlds. By doing so, Britain would bring advantage to both and would sacrifice neither the Commonwealth nor national sovereignty (*The Times* 15 June 1962). Such fond hopes never got beyond the 'imaginative' stage. The Commonwealth never seemed able, in the eyes of most pragmatic Conservatives, to provide Britain with the real basis for, as Peter Walker put it, 'responsible leadership in the world' (Walker, 1962: 51).

Indeed, the last thing the Commonwealth seemed to represent was unity and the ability to act with 'one voice'. While the party tended to pay formal obeisance to the value of the Commonwealth, the divisive experience of South Africa and then of Rhodesia created widespread disenchantment. There was a deep reluctance to deny the Commonwealth any place in Britain's foreign policy considerations. This had as much to do with Britain's role in the United Nations as it had to do with the relationship itself. By the 1960s, if not before, it was no longer possible to view the Commonwealth as central to Britain's world role. The Conservative leadership began to re-assert British freedom of manoeuvre in foreign policy unconstrained by deeper obligations to the Commonwealth idea. The Macmillan application to the Common Market in 1961 was something of a watershed. Thus Lord Home, sensitive though he was to Commonwealth feeling, set the tone which was to become more insistent in later years. In 1962, Home argued that 'the Commonwealth is no longer held together by authority and therefore it has developed in a way in which each Commonwealth country now has legitimate interests beyond its borders and beyond the Commonwealth circle' (cited in Conservative Central Office, 1962a: 4).

This implied a right to discount Commonwealth objections to a change in Britain's trading and political relationships. Home returned to the theme in delphic terms in 1966 when he noted in a speech to Conference that 'the modern Commonwealth and the multiracial Commonwealth is something we must cultivate with infinite patience so long as in doing so we do not ever compromise the principles in which we ourselves believe' (Conservative Central Office, 1966).

Those 'principles' appeared to be British 'interests' which might no longer find so congenial the obligations of the 'modern Commonwealth'. His leader, Edward Heath, was even more explicit. Speaking at Harvard in 1967, Heath expressed some exasperation with the restrictive atmosphere of the Commonwealth. It is now the British government, he told his American audience:

> which must approach Commonwealth Conferences with the fear that its freedom of action will be impaired. Many people in Britain might have been prepared in the past to accept a Commonwealth in which there was genuine pooling of sovereignty by all, though that vision never became a reality. But I doubt whether the present one-sided state of affairs can continue . . . (Heath, 1970: 65–6)

By the time of Heath's negotiations for entry to the European Community in 1970–1, the Commonwealth had been relegated to the lower divisions of Conservative foreign policy concerns. Speaking to the Party Conference following his election victory in 1970 Heath declared his own manifesto of independence by arguing that the Commonwealth could only thrive if Britain enjoyed full independence of action. 'As our freedom of manoeuvre increases', he told the party, 'we shall be more and more able to play a major part in seizing the opportunities which events open up for us' (NUCUA, 1970: 129).

Margaret Thatcher's leadership showed that she was of like mind on that point. The general trend within the party has been clear. By the 1970s the Commonwealth no longer had the old emotional power with Conservatives which had made Macmillan so cautious about his European policy a decade earlier. In the 1980s and 1990s its existence has become a shadowy, if lingering, presence in modern Conservatism.

The European sphere

In the 1960s the issue of membership of the European Community became a centrepiece of Conservative foreign policy concern and has remained so ever since. Those who advocated membership had a number of priorities which they believed overrode other factors, especially loyalty to or affection for the Commonwealth. The first priority was that Britain's political commitments should reflect the country's dominant economic interests. The second was that Britain *had* to make a decision about its international relationships and needed to find a role within a wider community which would enable it to remain a power of world stature. The justification for membership of the European Community was that this would not be an abdication of a world role as critics suggested but its re-assertion in a more realistic and constructive fashion. In 'choosing' Europe the party would not be abandoning its historic principles of patriotism and national interest but advancing them in a more relevant and modern form.

The first priority was, in short, the flag–trade argument. Wherever Britain's economic interests lay there too should Britain play an active political role. Conceiving of Europe in this way translated the imperial heritage which the party felt it held in trust into a new style of discourse. Lord Home provides an illustration of this direction of policy. 'Where', he asked, ' in the next twenty or thirty years are going to be the centre of markets and the centre of power?' (Conservative Central Office, 1962b). He was sure that they would be in Europe and America. 'If, as is certain, power is to lie in Europe, then I think it is there that Britain ought to be.' Macmillan had made a similar case in 1961–3 and Heath was to be even more emphatic on this point in 1970–3. (That economic argument, at least, was never disputed by Thatcher.) Sentimentalism, especially about Britain's imperial past, ought not to distort the party's grasp of the nation's real interests. Patriotism was really to be measured in statistics of growth and economic efficiency. Feelings of moral superiority about the multiracial Commonwealth could not provide the answer to Britain's decline in effective international influence; nor was it a substitute for being competitive in world markets and for sustaining technologically advanced industry.

On the second priority of 'choosing' Europe, Community advocates had to tread a careful line. On one hand, the argument that Britain would be weak and isolated outside the Community was a powerful one and fed on deep Conservative anxieties about Britain's world status. On the other hand, they had to be careful about appearing to denigrate Britain and undermining an article of Conservative faith which holds that Britain is indeed 'great'. The image of Britain as a prospective wretched 'offshore island' was always mitigated by an obligatory phrase of qualification. As Macmillan deftly put it: 'Supposing we stand outside. Of course we shall go on but we shall be relatively weak, and we shan't find the true strength that we have, and ought to have. We shan't be able to exercise it in a world of giants' (Conservative Central Office, 1962c).

The security of being part of a collective giant remained a persuasive theme of Community advocacy and was the basis of Heath's committed Europeanism. As he summed up in the debate on the principle of membership on 28 October 1971, Heath found it difficult to understand those who argued that joining the European Community represented a retreat from a world role:

> when the members of the Community itself are the great trading countries of the world; when the Community itself is the greatest trading bloc in the world; when, as the leader of the Liberal Party pointed out this evening, when the enlarged Community is created, it will have arrangements with 80 countries. Twenty nine of the Commonwealth countries and 19 dependencies will be associated with the Community. (*HC Deb.* Vol. 123, c. 2205)

Community membership would be an advance, not a retreat. There would be no betrayal of the party's historic principles. In the words of an early Bow Group pamphlet: 'The policy of joining Europe implies no change in British aims. These are what they have always been – the survival of the nation and the preservation and promotion of the freedom, peace and prosperity of the British people' (Bow Group, 1962: 5). Above all, it was argued, there would be no significant loss of sovereignty. Sovereignty, argued the pro-Marketeers, was about the capacity of governments to do things on the world and on the domestic stage. It was not to be defined exclusively in terms of legal or institutional integrity. Membership of the Community, it was proposed, would enhance the capacity of British governments to achieve their objectives. It was another aspect of Conservative *realpolitik*.

All of these arguments were consistently contested by opponents of British membership. On the economic case for Europe there were three phases of Conservative opposition to the (then) Common Market. The first of these phases, from the time of Macmillan's application to about the mid-1960s, emphasised the Commonwealth and the European Free Trade Association (EFTA) as the natural focus for Britain's trading relationships. The second phase saw the development of a new critique of the Common Market in a period in which most Conservatives recognised the Commonwealth's declining importance as a politico-economic association. This phase, from the mid-1960s to the early 1970s, stressed the importance of seeking alternative arrangements which would enable Britain to avoid the constitutional implications of the Treaty of Rome but which would also ensure Britain's participation in a larger trading bloc. The North Atlantic Free Trade Area (NAFTA) was one such alternative. The third phase witnessed a casting off of ideas about blocs, groupings and associations. Critics sought not to advocate 'alternatives' to Europe but to concentrate upon the value of Britain's political independence within the world trading system. This was an 'openseas liberalism' which was heavily influenced by the thinking of Enoch Powell even if its advocates would have rejected the common label of 'Powellite'. What was common to each phase of opposition to the leadership's European policy was the claim that the supposed benefits of Europe were illusory and not real, that they were based on faith and not on science. What the anti-Marketeers felt they needed to contradict (as Euro-sceptics do today) was the argument of inevitability. As Powell put it succinctly, Conservative support for Europe could be reduced to the belief that:

> since our commerce with the Commonwealth is becoming less important, our only compensation is to be found in Western Europe and the Common Market and that therefore, in short, we have no choice in the matter. There is no truth in this belief. (Croydon Chamber of Commerce, 27 September 1971)

It was on the issue of sovereignty, however, that the anti-Market case was most coherently and consistently focused. Three propositions were advanced.

First, since the idea that Europe would increase the capacity of British governments to achieve its economic objectives was fallacious, membership would ultimately undermine the traditions and practices of British democracy. Secondly, since British institutional sovereignty is intimately linked to British nationhood, membership posed a serious threat to the country's identity. Thirdly, the Conservative Party would lose its own identity and role as the defender of the British way of life and would betray both itself and the British people. These were powerful Conservative arguments and they were well argued (and are still argued today). Underlying them has been the belief that, despite the statements of Conservative leaders about the limits of concessions on sovereignty, there was actually no theoretical boundary to integration. Edward Heath, they thought, did not even believe there should be one. As Neil Marten argued: 'Once in the Common Market the pressure for Britain to become a state in the United States of Europe will be on. The Common Market of the Six only really makes sense if it be federal with a directly elected Parliament. It is time this nonsense stopped' (*The Times* 24 July 1969).

The Conservative Party did take Britain into the European Community under Heath's premiership. It did so against the stubborn resistance of a minority of anti-Market Conservative MPs. Equally, only a minority of Conservatives were truly enthusiastic Europeans. The majority were pragmatists and willing to follow the median position taken by their leadership. On Europe, the party followed its head and not its heart. Perhaps as a result the questions it raised would not go away. While the result of the referendum on membership in 1975 seemed to end the question as to whether Britain should be in or out, it could not resolve the question: of what sort of Europe is Britain a member? This is the question which has come to dominate foreign policy debate within the party in recent years and it has revealed some remarkable continuities of argument.

The Thatcher and Major years

Despite the obvious and central importance of Europe in Conservative debate, Britain's shadowy and lingering imperial legacy posed problems for Conservative foreign policy throughout the 1980s. For instance, the settlement of the Rhodesian question was, in the words of one of her fiercest critics, an indication that Mrs Thatcher (ultimately) did not allow her instinctive sympathies to overrule her calculation of British interests. Despite Gilmour's comment that Mrs Thatcher 'never seemed to realize that British interests were heavily involved and should not be ignored by any British government, let alone a Conservative one' he did acknowledge that she deserved credit for delivering a successful outcome to the 1980 negotiations (Gilmour, 1992: 283–5). As Mrs Thatcher herself put it, Britain had been able to demonstrate her ability 'to settle one of the most intractable disputes arising from her colonial past' (Thatcher, 1993: 78). Agreement on another issue from Britain's colonial past, Hong Kong, was reached with China in 1984. In the case of South Africa, the Conservative Government remained isolated within the Commonwealth because of its opposition to economic sanctions. Political change in South Africa itself removed the problem. John Major, as an informed commentator noted, has 'few emotional attachments or inhibitions over Britain's Commonwealth connections' (Wallace, 1994: 291). He is now representative of the party in this.

Furthermore, the remarkable events of the Falklands War of 1982 and, as it now seems in retrospect, the even more remarkable victory in that war, brought the circumstances of an obscure outpost of the British way of life to the forefront of government policy. The Falklands War was the result of a series of Argentinian miscalculations. The Argentinians miscalculated British military capacity. They miscalculated those foreign policy resources which Britain could use to influence America, Europe and the UN. They miscalculated the mood of the House of Commons. Above all, they miscalculated the will of the Conservative Prime Minister. The Falklands victory was the event which Mrs Thatcher believed symbolised the new vigour which Conservatives had brought to foreign affairs. After decades of self-doubt, Britain now had the confidence to re-assert itself in the world. At Cheltenham, 3 July 1982, she said:

> We have ceased to be a nation in retreat. We have instead a newfound confidence
> . . . we rejoice that Britain has rekindled that spirit which has fired her for
> generations past and which today has begun to burn as brightly as before. Britain
> found herself again in the South Atlantic and will not look back from the victory
> she has won. (Thatcher, 1993: 235)

That confidence and spirit was partly responsible for Mrs Thatcher's influence in Washington and partly instrumental in deciding the response taken by President Bush following Saddam Hussein's invasion of Kuwait in August 1990. The Gulf War, and the vital role played by British forces there, revealed both the potential scope of British commitments and the potential strength of the American relationship. By contrast, John Major has had a fraught relationship with an erratic President. President Clinton's judgement has been poor and his motivations have been suspect. The high moral criticism by Washington of the Major government's role in the Yugoslav crisis has been ill-conceived, given the reluctance of America to commit troops on the ground. The Clinton administration's interventions in the Northern Ireland 'peace process' have had the effect of taking pressure off the IRA and putting it on to the British government. Beyond the failings of individual leaders, however, the real change in Anglo-American relations is coming about as a result of the collapse of the Soviet Union and the new international environment.

Despite the political turbulence of Conservative divisions over European integration which has dominated public attention recently, the arguments are essentially a replay of those of the 1960s and 1970s (Barnes, 1994: 91). These continuities are sometimes masked by the dramas which have attended events such as the fall of Mrs Thatcher in 1990, Major's struggle with the Maastricht Bill in 1992 and 1993 and his persistent troubles with a small dissenting minority on the back-benches (Baker *et al.*, 1993a). Those within the Party who favour closer integration tend to restate propositions which became familiar two decades earlier. They propose that Britain's economic prosperity depends upon being at 'the very heart of Europe'; that Britain will be isolated from the main currents of political and economic power if it stands apart from movement towards European Union; that Britain's security in a competitive and dangerous world depends on full participation in the European bloc; that in the modern world parliamentary sovereignty is an outdated formal concept and that it is the capacity to achieve policy objectives which counts as real sovereignty; that traditional ideas of the nation state are outmoded because we live in an age of interdependence; and that the European Union represents the future and is inevitable.

Conservative opponents of a European 'vocation' do not, in the main, talk openly of withdrawal. Instead they continue to support the advantages of free trade and note the costs of such policies as the Common Agricultural Policy (CAP). They point to the calamity of Britain's experience in the Exchange Rate Mechanism (ERM) 1991–2 as evidence of the folly of moving towards a single European currency. They argue that a federal structure in Europe should be resisted because it would be centralising and inefficient, the principle of subsidiarity notwithstanding. They argue that a Europe of the nation states co-operating for mutual advantage is the appropriate political relationship. They defend parliamentary sovereignty as the symbol of nationhood and the guarantor of representative and responsible government. For them, the case for European Union, particularly on the model of a federation which they believe is implied by the Maastricht Treaty, is certainly not inevitable. Indeed it is a model, like the very different Soviet model, whose time has *not* come. It has gone (see Spicer, 1992). Once more the majority of the party remains in the pragmatic centre. While 'less than enthusiastic about membership of the EU, they can see no alternative to it, and would be ready to see Britain make the most of her membership given the right lead' (Barnes, 1994: 91).

It is not the arguments about Britain in Europe which are new. It is the circumstances. What Neil Marten claimed to be the federalist *potential* of the Common Market in the 1970s now appears to some to be the federalist *agenda* of the European Union in the 1990s. Euro-sceptics have been trying to define in policy terms the precise limits of the European enterprise. The historic importance of Mrs Thatcher's Bruges speech of 1988, the general content of which was not out of line with traditional Conservative views on Europe, was its attempt to establish such limits to European integration – 'We have not successfully rolled back the frontiers of the state in Britain only to see them reimposed at a European level, with a European super-state exercising a new dominance from Brussels' (Thatcher, 1988: 4). Having signed the

Single European Act, Mrs Thatcher had second thoughts about its implications. However, it was possibly too late:

> The first fruits of what would be called the Single European Act were good for Britain. At last, I felt, we were going to get the Community back on course, concentrating on its role as a huge market, with all the opportunities that would bring to our industries . . . The trouble was – and I must give full credit to those Tories who warned of this at the time – that the new powers the [European] Commission received only seemed to whet its appetite. (Thatcher, 1993: 556)

The Single European Act, which ended the national veto in the European Council on single market measures and gave the go-ahead to further consideration of economic and monetary union, had been sold to the Conservative Party as a measure of economic common sense. This is the basis upon which the party leadership has always promoted or resisted measures of European integration. It was the gathering pace of European political union – that is its transition from a foreign policy issue to an acute constitutional challenge – which alarmed Mrs Thatcher, fostered policy quarrels and encouraged back-bench dissent. Divisions within the Cabinet on the ERM were public knowledge and the Prime Minister herself had become alienated from her closest colleagues. Shirley Letwin has made the interesting observation that 'Europe is the mirror in which Thatcherism came most clearly to see itself as a Conservative doctrine – and, by a curious irony, it was that picture in that mirror which did not suit the Conservative party' (Letwin, 1992: 306).

Nigel Lawson has made a similar point:

> It was always clear to me that the Conservative Party could be successfully led only by someone who took their stand in the centre of the spectrum on this issue [Europe], where the silent majority dwelt. Margaret's evident determination to lead the Party from one of the two extremes of that spectrum spelled nothing but trouble. (Lawson, 1992: 923)

When Conservative MPs replaced Margaret Thatcher with John Major in November 1990 they appeared to be voting for someone from that centre of the spectrum. His election, however, has not made the party any easier to manage. It has been argued that Major's preoccupation since taking office has been with short-term considerations of party management rather than with the long-term objectives of Britain's foreign policy (Wallace, 1994: 291). That is a rather harsh judgement, for party management has been more of a pressing reality for John Major than ever it was for Margaret Thatcher.

Conclusion

The claim of the Conservative Party is that it has a unique understanding of the requirements of British foreign policy. The present crisis of Conservative politics concerns the extent to which the party may be seen to have lost the feel for 'what is best for Britain'. Kenneth Minogue has argued that the European process has distanced the government from the people in a way which no other foreign policy issue could possibly do. It has 'induced a rhetoric of deception which goes far beyond the ordinary equivocations of politics'. His conclusion is that it 'is not merely that this new situation runs contrary to the principles by which conservatives have hitherto navigated; it is also that this gap cannot widen much further before generating a quite explosive national resentment' (Minogue, 1992: 74).

Jim Bulpitt, on the other hand, has argued that the 'turn' towards European Union has a great deal to do with the political elite's deeply ingrained lack of self-confidence in the British state. Despite the impact of the Thatcher years of reassertion in foreign policy, Bulpitt has proposed that the speed of this 'turn' has been remarkable. 'It suggests, once again', he continues, 'that future resistance to Euro-Union amongst both Conservative MPs and leaders will be minimal' (Bulpitt, 1992: 267).

Such a view is debatable, however. Recent research has shown widespread resistance to the idea of ever further European integration at the expense of British parliamentary traditions. As this research suggests, the Conservative leadership could only take the party to a point, 'a Rubicon that Conservative MPs would refuse to cross' (Baker *et al.*, 1993b: 434). It is possible that John Major's leadership has reached that point. There are indeed those who are prophesying splits as serious as those over the repeal of the Corn Laws or Tariff Reform. Yet this is exactly what Macmillan had feared in 1961. We must wait to see if *plus ça change* is indeed a case of *plus c'est la même chose*.

CHAPTER 14

The party and social policy

David Willetts

Conservatives value the institutions which stand between the individual and the state. They shape and they nurture us. They enable us to co-operate with others, and they give practical expression to our moral obligations to others. The most important of these institutions is, of course, the family, but there are many others – schools, hospitals, clubs, churches – in which our country has been so rich. The aim of Conservative social policy is to sustain and strengthen those institutions so that they are able to address what Disraeli called the condition of the people.

Disraeli was but the first of a stream of leading Conservative politicians preoccupied with the condition of the people – Joseph Chamberlain (although strictly a Unionist), Neville Chamberlain, Rab Butler, Enoch Powell, Iain Macleod, Keith Joseph. However, despite the great Conservative contribution to social policy this century, the two most ambitious periods of expansion of the welfare state – the Asquith/Lloyd George programme after 1906 and the Attlee programme after 1945 – belong to others. This is no accident. Conservatives are too conscious of the damage which state action can do, too wary of the unintended consequences of intentional actions and too concerned about protecting the general taxpayer to embark on massive programmes of state action. As a result there is no crucial defining moment, no single programme, no canonical text to which Conservatives can point as defining a Conservative social policy. As always with British Conservatism, as both Philip Norton and Arthur Aughey have stressed already in this volume, the best way to discern the principles is to study the practice; hence the bulk of this chapter will focus on significant Conservative measures since the Second World War. In this period social policy has meant, above all, addressing the complex issues surrounding the 'welfare state'. But why should Conservatives have any sort of engagement with the welfare state at all? If it is, above all, the creation of the Lloyd George and Attlee governments, why should Conservatives have any truck with it? There are three answers to this challenge although each, in turn, reveals dilemmas with which Conservatives have to wrestle.

The first answer is that a modern welfare state can itself contribute to economic efficiency. Modern capitalism and some sort of welfare system go together. That is partly because only modern market economies can afford it; although the direction of causation goes the other way too – modern capitalist economies need geographical and labour mobility to operate efficiently and this in turn requires some sort of social safety net. The concepts 'unemployment' and 'retirement' are both inventions of modern industrial society. Firms need to be able to lay people off if demand for their goods or services is falling, or if the productivity of their employees is declining. That would be so brutal as to be impossible unless there were alternative provision for people to receive some income while out of work. Also, a well-educated and healthy workforce is an asset. This is not to say that any welfare system, however extensive and expensive, must inevitably contribute to economic efficiency. It may become an obstacle to economic change and drive up social costs so high that it exacerbates those very problems, such as unemployment, which it is supposed to ease.

Nobody would seriously argue that the *sole* purpose of the welfare state is to contribute to economic efficiency. A second role for the welfare state is to provide a nationwide mutual insurance scheme against some of the risks and vagaries of life. Everybody pays into the pot during their working lives and is entitled to draw on cash and services when the need arises. At any one moment there is a redistribution from contributors paying their National Insurance contributions and taxes to beneficiaries receiving their pensions or health care. Hence we think of the welfare state as redistributing resources to others; but if, instead, we think of our own relationship to the welfare state during the whole of our lives, it is clear that what it really does is to reallocate resources across different stages of the life cycle. Money is taken from us when we are earning and we are given command over resources when we are being educated, or unemployed, or sick, or retired. On this view, the welfare state is like fire insurance or car insurance. Indeed, Beveridge insisted on equal national insurance payments by everyone (calling them a sort of 'poll tax') because this was exactly his view of the welfare state.

This second role of the welfare state also raises some tricky problems, however. It depends on our believing that we are all in it together; that it is genuine mutual insurance. The mistake is that it easily becomes skewed – raising money from one section of the population to direct resources to another group to which the rest never expect to belong. The welfare state then begins to look very different. It becomes a device whereby 'we' pay taxes to 'them'. Moreover, there is always the problem of 'moral hazard' which occurs when the very fact that an adversity is insured may make us more likely to get into difficulties. Old age and ill health are not like this and hence they are particularly well-suited to a mutual insurance model; but this may be more of a risk in other cases.

This leads to the third function for a welfare state – a nationalised system of charity without any economic efficiency or mutuality to it. Such a system requires strict definitions of need, often with a means-test. But means-tests bring their own problems, notably the poverty trap (one's net income barely increasing as one's earnings rise) and the unemployment trap (being no better off in work than out of work). A Conservative worries that a thoroughly means-tested system could be a serious disincentive to personal improvement and advancement.

We have seen, therefore, that there are three specific roles which a Conservative may attribute to the welfare state: to improve economic efficiency, to provide mutual insurance for all members of the community and to be a form of charity to those in greatest need. Each of those arguments in turn prompts a question. Is the welfare state so expensive that it is an economic burden rather than a benefit? Is it indeed a genuinely mutual insurance arrangement? Is it trapping people in dependency? It is upon these questions that Conservative debate upon social policy has focused during the post-war period.

Housing

Housing was crucial to the Conservative election victory in 1951 and to defeat in 1964. It was probably the most politically important area of social policy in the 20 years after the Second World War when there was felt to be a straightforward physical shortage of housing. It also first reveals themes which have since become commonplace in other areas of social policy.

The 1950 Conservative Conference was the scene of one of the most famous grass roots rebellions in the history of the Party. Delegates demanded that a reluctant leadership commit the Party to a clear target for building more houses. It was only deft handling by the Chairman, Lord Woolton, which stopped the bidding at 300,000 houses a year – an apparently impossible figure, given that the Labour government was straining to produce 170,000 that year. However, the pledge to build 300,000 houses was one of the most vivid and eyecatching items in the election manifesto. In 1951 Macmillan was plucked out of obscurity to become Minister for Housing.

Macmillan brought in a dynamic industrialist, Sir Percy Mills, whose job was to 'cut out red tape and simplify procedures; to break bottlenecks; to overcome shortages' (Macmillan, 1969). Macmillan called this technique 'modified Beaverbrookism' and in his memoirs describes fraught arguments with the civil servants about the role of businessmen in government which have reverberated around Whitehall ever since. Business acumen and the latest management techniques were to be applied in the public sector to deliver social objectives. In 1954 Macmillan returned to the party conference in triumph with the target achieved. It was a powerful demonstration that Conservatives could get things done. This episode thus set one of the themes which can be traced through post-war Conservative policy: others may employ the rhetoric of compassion, but only the Conservative Party can deliver efficiently.

There was also an ideological edge to Macmillan's delivery of his programme. Under Labour, three-quarters of all new building had been council housing using direct labour; private houses required licences. By contrast, Macmillan worked by 'setting the builders free' and private sector building revived in 1951. Of the 300,100 houses built in 1954, 220,000 were still council houses – the highest post-war figure – but more of them were being built by private builders under contract. It was a prelude to the Conservative approach in other areas – private provision for public use. Ernest Marples, Macmillan's deputy, remarked: 'Technically private enterprise is a much superior instrument for actually building houses. Whether it is better for disposing of them is a matter of argument.' Capitalist enterprise was to be harnessed to public objectives. Macmillan was liberalising the supply of housing while keeping the demand side under strict control – a policy which surfaced later in, for example, the private finance initiative, the NHS reforms and private provision of nursing home care financed by the social security system.

This approach was not enough, however, for the Conservative free-marketeers of the One Nation Group (Macleod, Powell, Maude) who were behind a notable rightwards shift of Conservative social policy in the mid-1950s. Housing was still being supplied in a market which had been heavily rigged against private landlords. They could not put up rents and, as a result, were not able to afford to maintain their properties. Very few new private tenancies were being created. Macmillan himself had observed: 'It is all right to put up the houses. But the next job is to put up the rents.'

Duncan Sandys, the then Minister for Housing, and his deputy Enoch Powell therefore pushed through the 1957 Rent Act which deregulated rents at the top end of the market; allowed lower rents to be raised while remaining controlled; and deregulated rents on new tenancies. It was a stark ideological contrast with the views of the Labour Opposition which was committed to bringing private rented property under local authority control. In his final speech in the debate on the Bill, James Callaghan, Labour's opposition spokesman, argued: 'We dismiss the concept that housing and homes are a commodity that can be bought and sold in the marketplace' – another line of argument that has reverberated down the decades. It was setting the scene for the perennial post-war debate with Labour arguing that market prices were incompatible with any social function, while Conservatives stressed the central role of prices in allocating resources efficiently.

However, a London landlord, Peter Rachman, used the most appalling methods to drive out tenants and create new tenancies which would therefore be deregulated. Rachmanism entered the political vocabulary. Landlordism and housing became a major issue in the 1964 general election, Harold Wilson declaring: 'The plain fact is that rented housing is not a proper field for profit.' Labour promptly brought in the 1965 Rent Act which reimposed extensive rent controls and the private rented sector continued its steady decline.

The crucial issue, which had been evaded, was how poor people were to afford market rents in the private sector. This problem went back to 1915 when rent strikes broke out in Glasgow, spreading alarm in Asquith's government about domestic disturbances undermining the war effort. Worried officials and ministers quickly invented rent controls. By, in effect, expropriating landlords, this started the decline of the private rented sector. Conservatives argued that a vigorous private rented sector was desirable and only possible with deregulated rents. The obvious solution, eventually introduced in the 1972 Housing Finance Act, was to provide income-related housing benefits.

It was difficult to grasp this nettle since 'means-testing' was such an emotive concept for those steeped in popular hostility towards the old Poor Law. Also, Labour was more interested in ensuring direct public provision of housing than in enabling poor people to rent privately. Its 1965 Rent Act was seen as ending Rachmanite abuse; it was not a welfare measure to improve poor people's access to housing.

Conservatives were wary because inventing a new benefit meant there was a public expendure cost to free market reform. Taking the money from the landlords by rent control did not constitute public expenditure and was therefore a 'cheap' option even if, in the long run, a nonsense. However, had the panic-stricken ministers in 1915 allowed rents to remain free and invented housing benefit instead, the whole pattern of housing in the twentieth century might have been different – and much better.

The middle class and the welfare state: the case of pensions

Beveridge contributed to the design of two welfare states in his long and fruitful career. First was the Lloyd George welfare state, which emerged between 1906 and 1911. This provided insurance for specific risks (unemployment in certain industries, health care and pensions for the over-70s) and was restricted to specific sections of the population (people in employment with incomes below the upper earnings limit). The second model was designed for Churchill's Coalition government and implemented by Attlee. It very much captured the mood of the Second World War with an inclusive, universalist spirit; everyone, however affluent, was to participate in the National Insurance scheme, paying the same fixed contribution to obtain prescribed weekly benefits covering a variety of contingencies and also to help to finance the NHS. Some doubted the wisdom of this approach from the beginning: the then Chancellor, Kingsley Wood, minuted Churchill when the Beveridge report was published that: 'The weekly progress of the millionaire to the Post Office for his old age pension would have an element of farce but for the fact that it is to be provided in large measure by the general taxpayer' (Timmins, 1995).

That final remark about the cost to the general tax payer was the crucial problem with Beveridge: the figures never added up. The maximum standard contribution which could be afforded by everyone was not going to pay for a National Insurance benefit large enough to float people off means-tested National Assistance. The National Insurance fund was never going to balance without subsidies from the general taxpayer. This problem was exacerbated by the Attlee government's decision to pay pensions in full from the beginning rather than after the 20-year build-up which Beveridge had envisaged. But the underlying problem was fundamental and it destroyed all subsequent ambitious schemes for a universal benefit – the minimum amount necessary to get people off means-tested benefits cost more than could be raised not just in fixed contributions but acceptable levels of income tax as well.

Beveridge's original model of financing could not survive. It fell to the Macmillan government in 1958 to make the first significant break with Beveridge's doctrine by introducing earnings-related contributions in order to raise more revenue for the National Insurance fund; but it was thought earnings-related contributions had to be matched with some earnings-related benefit. Pensions minister John Boyd-Carpenter therefore introduced in 1961 his graduated pension scheme providing some top-up to the basic state pension for those who were paying larger National Insurance contributions. Boyd-Carpenter was worried that a full-blooded and ambitious earnings-related scheme, much closer to the Continental model of social insurance, would have been a significant threat to private occupational pensions (which are indeed much less common on the Continent). In a far-sighted move, Boyd-Carpenter therefore introduced a new concept to the language of the welfare state, a term which has reverberated down the decades since 'opting-out'. If an employee was a member of a suitable occupational pension scheme he need not participate in the state graduated scheme.

Boyd-Carpenter's 1961 scheme was too modest to generate a useful second pension for those without an occupational pension and was thus always vulnerable to a more ambitious scheme. Labour's Social Services minister, Richard Crossman, came up with such a scheme which he tried to implement during the 1964–70 Labour government. Sir Keith Joseph responded by developing an alternative set of proposals during the Heath government, which were also lost in election defeat. As Nicholas Timmins (1995) observes in *The Five Giants*, his classic study of the welfare state since the war:

> There had been some nice paradoxes in the Crossman and Joseph plans which illustrate that in social security Left/Right distinctions can fall in odd ways. Crossman's scheme had been fully earnings-related, with no flat rate basic pension, in an attempt to provide pensions that in all normal cases would end up above means-tested National Assistance. Up to a ceiling, therefore, it had proposed more for the better-off in return for a higher contribution. Joseph's, by contrast, was a flat rate basic pension plus a 'reserve' earnings-related scheme to be run by the State for those who employers did not provide even an occupational scheme on top. The aim behind that was to encourage private provision for the second pension. Under Joseph's scheme, however, the basic pension was to be

paid for by graduated contributions – in other words, higher earners would pay more for the same basic pension (p. 348).

As Timmins points out, Joseph's scheme was more redistributive than Crossman's while Crossman's scheme did much more for the middle classes in a desperate attempt to keep them within the state-financed system.

The furious argument on pensions which had lasted for nearly 20 years was muted after Barbara Castle's state earnings-related scheme (SERPS), introduced in 1978, which provided a top-up earnings-related pension in the state scheme for everyone who did not enjoy a contracted-out occupational scheme. It was an over-ambitious scheme which was radically changed in Norman Fowler's wide-ranging social security review of the mid-1980s. The value of future SERPS entitlements was cut back and, for the first time, it was possible for employees to opt out of SERPS into a personal pension scheme. The easy way of explaining the need for these reductions was to point to the enormous long-term cost of full SERPS pensions. Cost has always been a Conservative anxiety about the welfare state and nowhere do future public expenditure liabilities roll up so precipitously as with pensions. However, two further arguments were rather lost from view. First, Barbara Castle's SERPS, just like Crossman's before it, had the state mimicking what a commercial pension scheme would do. It was the state running a reverse means test in which those with higher earnings received a higher state pension. SERPS was so complex and ambitious because Labour wanted to include the middle classes in the welfare state even at the cost of running a reverse redistribution scheme. The Conservative response was to cut back on such negative redistribution and make it easier for people to save for themselves.

The second point was even more fundamental. Pension provision is about acquiring claims on future resources. The resources which will pay our pensions in 2020 do not physically exist now. By acquiring pension rights, we are registering a claim to some of the Gross National Product (GNP) that will be generated then. In a state-run system, that claim ultimately rests on the state's power to tax. National Insurance contributions or taxes will be levied then to pay out on the liabilities which the state is currently accumulating in respect of future pensions. But Conservatives feel uncomfortable with giving the state such a role in claiming future resources. Not only may it notch up excessive liabilities now which will push up future taxes (the cost problem), it is also more inflexible and, above all, means that decisions about pensioner incomes become totally politicised. Far better for those claims to be registered through private contracts so that, for example, people own shares giving them a right to a stream of dividends which will be generated by economic activity in the future. Such private contracts are one of the great strengths of the British pension system. As we enter the next century, Britain finds that more of those claims on future resources are genuinely privately funded claims and fewer rest on the state's power to tax than in Continental systems.

Education and health

The wartime Coalition government worked hard on plans both for education and health. Rab Butler's 1944 Education Act has rightly gone down in the history books alongside two other Conservative measures – Balfour's Act of 1902 and Baker's Act of 1988 – which between them have shaped education this century. The wartime Coalition also published, in 1944, a major White Paper, 'A National Health Service', proposing a nationwide tax-financed health service. It stated that everybody 'irrespective of means, age, sex, or education shall have equal opportunity to benefit from the best and most up-to-date medical and allied services available'; the service should be 'comprehensive' and should be 'free of charge'. It proposed grouping local authorities to run their own hospitals and also to contract with the voluntary hospitals 'for the performance of agreed services'. However, while Butler's proposals went straight into legislation and would thus be indelibly associated with Churchill's Coalition government, Henry Willink's proposals were over-taken by the arrival of the Attlee government. Bevan decided to nationalise both local authority and voluntary hospitals and bring them all under direct Whitehall control. This, together with his bitter arguments with general prac-titioners, meant that the creation of the NHS is attributed to him – while the Coalition government's sensible proposals, which show some striking similari-ties with the Major government's reforms, have been forgotten.

Bevan's take-over of local authority hospitals (against the opposition of the Labour deputy leader, Herbert Morrison), together with the nationalisation of many other previously municipal services, left education as one of local government's main responsibilities. The health service, by contrast, was run by a structure of committees and boards ending with the department in Whitehall. As Bevan observed, not a bedpan could fall in a hospital corridor without the sound being heard in Whitehall.

In education, the story was rather more complicated. The churches had been worried about what local education authorities might do to their church schools and pressed, successfully, for a residual role for the Department of Education in agreeing any changes in a school's 'character'. The commitment to equalising resources across local authorities meant that they were heavily dependent on central government for funds – which resulted in the De-partment obtaining extraordinarily detailed power over capital spending, individual applications by schools for capital spending going all the way up to the Department. This power was then used, especially by Labour govern-ments, to enforce comprehensive education without any Act of Parliament; it was simply made clear to schools that no applications for capital expenditure would be granted unless they were part of a plan for the local education authority to go comprehensive.

In practice, the Department for Health delegated decisions down its struc-ture of boards and authorities and thus tended to find itself rather less involved in, for example, the detailed planning of an individual hospital. Crossman compared the relation of the regional health boards to the DHSS as resembling the relations of 'semi-autonomous' satraps towards ancient Persian emperors (see Timmins, 1995: 294). Local government, therefore, could find itself closely supervised by central government, whereas central government might delegate its own responsibilities quite substantially; such are the paradoxes of 'centralisation' in this country.

Beveridge expected health spending to fall as the NHS became successful at dealing with health problems before they became acute. In fact, spending rose quickly and the Attlee government had to bring back prescription charges and spectacle charges to meet some of the costs. There was no new capital expenditure; hostpials were taken over, but not built. The incoming Conservative government of 1951 set up the Guillebaud Committee to identify savings in current spending but it concluded that actually the NHS was, if anything, under-resourced. Thereafter the themes were expansion and better management, as shown in Enoch Powell's *Hospital Plan for England and Wales* (1962) and then in Keith Joseph's management reforms implemented in 1974. In education this was evidenced in the Robbins Report, leading to the expansion of universities after 1963 and Margaret Thatcher's policy statement as Secretary of State for Education *Education: A Framework for Expansion* (1972). Expansion and better management were after all the common assumptions of the policy debates of the day and Conservatives were not immune to them. They were indeed given a Conservative slant, because of the argument that Conservatives were best able to manage the economy and therefore generate the resources necessary to pay for the expansion of the welfare state. It was also argued that Conservatives were not tied to the trade unions and understood how to run things, and so were best able to operate the services of the welfare state with maximum efficiency.

As the 1970s passed, this approach on its own no longer seemed satisfactory for education and health any more than for the rest of the welfare state. Sir Keith Joseph led the questioning during his intellectually fruitful time in opposition from 1974 to 1979. Many of the great services from the welfare state combined two crucial features. First, they were nationwide tax-based financing systems to ensure that schools, hospitals and so on were free at the point of use. This raised issues about how the welfare state was financed – the demand side of the equation. Secondly, they were nationalised organisations in the public sector delivering education and healthcare. This raised questions about how services were delivered – the supply side of the equation.

Free-thinking Conservatives, some of the think-tanks and even the government looked at various options for opening up the financing of health and education during the late 1970s and early 1980s. The most conspicuous example was an internal Whitehall working group on alternative methods of financing the NHS, which sat in 1980–1, and the prolonged debate on education vouchers which Keith Joseph sponsored and encouraged when he was

Secretary of State for Education. The challenge was to make it easier for people to top-up with their own money while remaining within the framework of a tax-financed service. This is what Margaret Thatcher regarded as the authentic Conservative middle way. It could be applied very effectively with pensions because public money can be topped up easily with private money, but when dealing with services such as education and health it was much more problematical. Politicians found it difficult to define a 'minimum' service above which people should pay for themselves. Indeed, the most rigorous attempt to do this with legislation – the 1988 Education Act – actually ended up restricting the services for which parents could pay, compared with previous custom and practice.

The voucher began life as an attempt to solve the under-financing problem by bringing new flexibility – everybody would be given a certain amount of spending power from the state and then be free to add more of their own money to top up the provision if they wished. But on close study some difficult issues had to be resolved. If people who were already paying privately were to be eligible for vouchers, there would be a significant 'dead-weight cost'. The question of the basic guaranteed level of service financed from taxation remained; and would organisations providing services be able to require that people paid extra on top of the voucher, or would they be obliged to accept the basic voucher on its own? The cautious response to these issues was not to allow the voucher to be used externally by people who had already opted out and to require that the voucher on its own should obtain a full range of services. This, however, hardly constitutes a radical new approach to financing. The government has recently announced a new initiative – nursery education vouchers. They will be available to all parents, including those who prefer to use the private and voluntary sectors. Those providers will be able to charge fees which exceed the voucher value, but in the *state* sector schools are prevented by law from charging for education.

Successive Conservative governments have ruled out radical options on welfare state financing. Instead, attention has shifted from financing to provision. A distinctive Conservative approach to social policy has emerged, aimed at bringing the best features of choice and competition into the provision of health services and education while keeping a tax-based finance system. The 'paperless' voucher described earlier may not open up the financing of the welfare state, but can be a very powerful instrument for bringing the good features of markets, competition and choice to the supply of public services. There is a striking parallel between the reforms of education and health here. Both were aimed at ensuring that the financing of schools and colleges, hospitals and GP practices depended rather more on the number of pupils or patients that they managed to attract. Instead of a new patient or student being seen as an extra cost, they would become an extra source of revenue and thus, instead of trying to keep them out, the incentive would be to try to attract them in.

By the early 1990s there was a much clearer distinction between a nation-wide, tax-based system of financing the great services of the welfare state – the purchasing function – and a much more diverse and competitive network of providers of services, competing to win public funds. The rather technical expression which emerged for this is 'the internal market' and it does at least describe accurately the point that the market is an internal one, within a publicly financed service. This had been established not only in education and health but in other branches of social services and was increasingly the philosophy which guided the government's approach to local government. This was a distinctive approach to social policy which both addressed the electorate's key anxiety that the financing base should not be destabilised and at the same time genuinely introduced greater competition and choice. The Conservatives were at last generating their own vision of the welfare state to rival and, indeed, to overtake those of Lloyd George and Attlee. It was not a moment too soon.

CHAPTER 15

The party and the Union

Arthur Aughey

Support for the Union has been a consistent policy of the Conservative Party and a central aspect of its identity for more than a century. However natural it may appear to those both inside and outside the party, Conservative unionism is quite a complex confluence of ideas, interests and historical circumstance. The Conservative nation, to use a phrase of Andrew Gamble's, is a distinctive union of Englishness, Britishness and constitutional patriotism (Gamble, 1974).

Conservatism and English political culture

Conservatives have traditionally understood the genius of the *English* people to lie in the capacity to fashion institutions which reconcile order with personal liberty. The English national genius has been bound up, therefore, with the political institutions of the United Kingdom. Constitutional celebration became a substitute for an ideology of English nationalism. Conservative thought made the 'constitution' and not the 'people' sovereign (see, e.g., Mansfield Jr, 1987: 55). A 'constitutional patriotism' was celebrated as the reflection of those leading traits of the English political character, a vigorous commitment to personal liberty on one hand and the practical wisdom of slow, piecemeal, gradual constitutional change on the other hand (Stapleton, 1993: 5).

It was Michael Oakeshott who continued that tradition of thought into the contemporary era. Reputable political behaviour, he wrote shortly after the end of the Second World War, is not the product of nor is it dependent upon sound philosophy, never mind ideology. 'In general, constitutional tradition is a good substitute for philosophy' (Oakeshott, 1948: 476). This English 'ideology' has become a recognisably Conservative ideology, not because it is the property of that party – it was not and is not – but because it was the Conservative Party which, at the end of the nineteenth century, seized the opportunity to present itself as the constitutional (and patriotic) party. That meant becoming the Unionist (British) party, a label which it still carries.

The Conservative nation

There is something of an irony here. The respected historian of the party, Robert Blake, has argued that from one aspect 'the Conservative Party could be regarded as the party of English nationalism' (Blake, 1985: 361). If one accepts Blake's description of these matters, how does one explain the Conservative Party's politically successful reconciliation of its English 'nationalism' and its British Unionism? Part of the answer would seem to lie in that complex construction, the 'Conservative nation'.

The Conservative nation has been a compound of two traditions within the party. The first of these traditions is rooted in the pre-modern notion of the authority of the Crown. It holds that the nation is founded on the allegiance of the people to the person of the monarch, an allegiance which obliges all subjects irrespective of their regional, cultural or national differences. 'One Nation', therefore, is this political community united in acceptance of the legitimacy of that obligation (see, e.g., Rose, 1982: 62). The second tradition of Conservative thought derives from the nineteenth-century concern to integrate the working class into the 'constitutional people'. It proposes a sense of belonging with those of one's own kind and assumes a popular unity (see, e.g., McKenzie and Silver, 1968). These two traditions might be termed the patriotic and the populist styles. Their practical significance for the success of Conservative politics was to come through their fusion, originally intimated by Disraeli, from the 1870s onwards (Vincent, 1990). What reconciled and regulated both of these traditions, especially when Whigs and Liberal Unionists were absorbed in the late nineteenth century, was the venerable, although refurbished, idea of the balanced constitution. The diverse elements of the Conservative nation were presented together in a seamless union (Norton and Aughey, 1981: ch. 1).

It is a political disposition which has associated the proper governance of the territory of Britain with the institution of the Conservative Party and with the particular competence of its parliamentary leadership. Conservatives, it is argued, are sensitive to the various traditions within the United Kingdom. The Union, they claim to recognise, involves unity in diversity. In the twentieth century Conservatives have argued that it is socialism which misunderstands that relationship and has centralising pretentions (just as the Liberals had misunderstood it in a different way during the Home Rule crisis at the beginning of the century). In Conservative thinking for most of this century, however, there has existed and continues to exist two Unions, linked of course, but rather distinctive. There is first the Union of England, Scotland and Wales. Secondly, there is the Union of Great Britain and Northern Ireland. It is necessary to consider both.

The Union: Great Britain and Northern Ireland

The original Irish (rather, Union) question in British politics meant, as Boyce summarised it: 'was the United Kingdom inhabited by a single nation, however much regional or even patriotic differences might distinguish its component parts' as the Conservatives and Unionists would have it; 'or, as the Liberals would have it, was it one whose national distinctions made it essential that they should be given some constitutional recognition?' (Boyce, 1988: 8–9). The Union of Great Britain and Ireland which Conservatives had defended was broken by the encounter of Irish nationalist separatism and Ulster Unionist loyalism. What remained of the Union in Ireland – the six counties of Ulster – became accepted as a place apart from the usual considerations of political life at Westminster. Northern Ireland was compelled to accept the sort of Home Rule which Conservatives up to 1914 had opposed for the whole of Ireland.

Ulster Unionist MPs at Westminster continued to take the Conservative whip (it was withdrawn from them after the February 1974 general election) and Ulster remained part of the constitutional people. Yet a crucial change had occurred. Before the First World War the cause of Ireland had pre-occupied the Conservative leadership and had absorbed the energies of its brightest and best (and worst). As we saw in Chapter 2, the party's opposition to Home Rule had actually threatened to destroy the settled civilities of British parliamentary life even to the extent of provoking civil conflict. After the war the issue had lost its passionate intensity. It lingered, of course, but mainly on the wings of Conservative politics. The devolution of legislative authority over most domestic matters to a parliament in Belfast seemed to have achieved the best possible of all possible worlds – it removed the Irish question from British politics while satisfying the demand of the majority in Northern Ireland to remain within the Union. Thereafter, as Boyce puts it, the Irish question 'was not what it had been between 1886 and 1922, an essential part of the education of a whole generation of British politicians' (Boyce, 1988: 11–12).

Therefore, when the Ulster crisis forced its way back into British political life in the late 1960s most Conservatives had little or no feel for the problem. For some it was a fearful anachronism and a tiresome distraction from the business of government (in the 'real' Union of Great Britain). However, there remained those within the party who were Unionist in the traditional sense. They constituted a relatively small number of MPs – about 30 or so – although not without influence in the party at all levels. Whereas the first group has tended to give almost uncritical support to the policy of the leadership on Northern Ireland (whatever its details) the latter group have shown a willingness to dissent on principle, not only voting against the government but resigning from it – as did, for instance, Nicholas Budgen, Lord Cranborne and Peter Lloyd in 1981 and Ian Gow in 1985. Nevertheless, there is common ground in the party. While Conservative and Labour have striven to maintain bipartisanship on Northern Ireland, the Conservative leadership has always had to pay due regard on the issue to the distinctive character of its party. Thus Conservatives have always been sensitive to traditional sentiment (for the Union, the British 'way of life'); to traditional purposes (law and order, opposition to terrorism); to traditional interests (the military, national security); and to traditional duties (protecting the lives and property of British citizens). It is too simple to dismiss these considerations as mere rhetoric for rhetoric is part of the reality of politics (Aughey, 1994a: 121–9).

Since 1972, when the government of Edward Heath prorogued the devolved parliament in Belfast, the consistent element of Conservative Northern Ireland policy has been a concern to 'balance' the right of unionists to remain part of the United Kingdom and the aspiration of nationalists to have a unified Irish state. The character of that 'balance', however, has changed over this period. The first Conservative Secretary of State for Northern Ireland, William Whitelaw, established two principles of 'power-sharing' devolution and the 'Irish dimension'. In other words, there should be balance between unionist and nationalist interests within Northern Ireland as part of the United Kingdom; and there should be a new institutional arrangement, a Council of Ireland, linking Northern Ireland and the Republic of Ireland. This comprehensive strategy, which was finalised in December 1973, collapsed just as comprehensively six months later when it was rejected by a large majority of unionists.

When in opposition in the late 1970s, the Conservative Northern Ireland spokesman, Airey Neave, shifted policy away from the comprehensive approach of Whitelaw towards an acceptance of reformed direct rule. He proposed changes in local government to democratise administration and eschewed any formal institutional arrangements between the two parts of Ireland. This formed part of the Conservative manifesto in the general election of May 1979 and drew the party closer to its old ally, the Ulster Unionist Party. Indeed, Margaret Thatcher proclaimed herself to be 'rock firm for the Union' of Great Britain and Northern Ireland (Biggs-Davison, 1979: 6). This trend away from support for devolution in Northern Ireland corresponded with changing Conservative attitudes to devolution for Scotland and Wales. Neave's murder by Republican terrorists in March 1979, and the Conservative election victory later that year, saw a move back to a half-hearted policy of devolution for Northern Ireland. There was no change of policy for Scotland and Wales.

In the early years of the Thatcher premiership the Conservative government pursued a course which stressed the priority of accommodation between the parties within Northern Ireland as a precondition of any 'Irish dimension'. At about the same time, however, another 'track' had been opened up between the British and Irish governments. Both governments were keen to maintain their own 'balanced' view of possibilities for progress in Northern Ireland. Indeed, the Anglo-Irish Agreement of November 1985 shifted the priority of Conservative policy to an intergovernmental balance as the basis

for an internal compromise. Power-sharing devolution was now to be a function of an Irish dimension – the Intergovernmental Conference and the
Anglo-Irish Secretariat – which gave Dublin both a direct and an indirect
influence on British policy in Northern Ireland. In March 1986, as a result of
the Agreement, Ulster Unionists severed their last remaining organisational
links with the Conservative party (Aughey, 1989: ch. 3).

Under John Major the Downing Street Declaration of December 1993 went
one stage further in attenuating the traditional unionism of the party. The
political balance now sought is still that between the democratic right of
unionists to remain part of the United Kingdom and the aspiration of nationalists to Irish unity, but the manner in which it is expressed has changed. The
language is much 'greener'. In paragraph 2 of the Declaration, 'Northern
Ireland's statutory constitutional guarantee' is reaffirmed; but it is paragraph
4 which sets out the government's position most clearly. Only in one line of
that labyrinthine formulation does the 'democratic wish of the greater number of the people of Northern Ireland' get a direct mention and even then in
the context of possible support for a 'sovereign united Ireland'. The statement
by Secretaries of State Peter Brooke and Sir Patrick Mayhew that the British
government has no 'selfish strategic or economic interest in Northern Ireland'
is repeated. It commits the British government to 'encourage, facilitate and
enable' agreement in Ireland. Further, it acknowledges that such agreement
'as of right' may be a united Ireland.

The next sentence is both the most striking and the most heavily qualified. It
states: 'The British Government agree that it is for the people of the island of
Ireland alone, by agreement between the two parts respectively, to exercise
their right of self-determination on the basis of consent, freely and concurrently
given, North and South, to bring about a united Ireland, if that is their wish.' As
if to confirm that Irish self-determination is to be exercised by a single people,
the paragraph concludes by referring to the 'people of Britain' and 'the people
of Ireland' as if they were entirely distinct and already constituting separate
entities. That is the sort of definitional politics Conservative unionism has traditionally denied, for it used to assume that the people of Northern Ireland are
definitively part of the British constitutional people (Aughey, 1994b: 276–9).
The joint Framework Documents, published in February 1995, propose institutions to give expression to the principles of the Declaration. The general
Conservative Party support for the Documents tends to confirm the extent to
which the Union of Great Britain and Northern Ireland has become peripheral
to the constitutional thinking of modern Conservatism.

The Union of England, Scotland and Wales

In his foreword to the White Paper, *Scotland in the Union: A Partnership for
Good*, John Major stated that: 'The Union is almost 300 years old. As I have

said before, no nation could be held irrevocably in a Union against its will and the way it works should be assessed from time to time, so that it continues to work for the good of all of us' (cited in Conservative Research Department, 1994: 4).

In its own pragmatic fashion, the Conservative Party has on occasion re-assessed the workings of the Union in Great Britain. It has done so with a sceptical view of the value of significant constitutional change and, as John Major suggests, with a principled assumption of the intrinsic good of the existing relationship between the nations.

It was a Conservative government which created the Scottish Office in 1885. A Conservative government upgraded the status of the Secretary for Scotland to that of a Principal Secretary of State in 1926. A Conservative-dominated government transferred the functions of the Scottish Office from London to Edinburgh in 1939. Conservative governments have indeed modified the procedures for the conduct of Scottish business on a regular basis and have done so more recently under John Major's 'taking stock' exercise. Conservatives were reluctant, however, to extend a similar sort of structure to Wales. It was a Labour government which did so in 1964 and the Conservative Party has adapted that system when in office. Reform of administration has not been a major problem in Conservative politics. What has been and remains contentious is the appropriateness of establishing devolved elected assemblies to manage the affairs of Scotland and Wales (Burch and Holliday, 1992: 386–98).

In May 1968 Edward Heath announced an initiative to the Scottish Conservative Conference which became known as the Perth Declaration. It was a pledge to 'give the people of Scotland genuine participation in the making of decisions that affect them – all within the historic unity of the United Kingdom' (Conservative Party, 1977: 518). A Scottish Constitutional Committee was established under the chairmanship of Sir Alec Douglas-Home to make proposals to that effect. Its report, 'Scotland's Government', was published in March 1970 and suggested the creation of a directly elected Assembly which would form, in effect, a third chamber of the United Kingdom Parliament. The Heath Government of 1970–4, however, was both committed to a general reform of local government throughout the United Kingdom and was also pledged to await the recommendations of the Royal Commission on the Constitution set up by Harold Wilson in April 1969. Overwhelmed by other pressing matters, devolution was not a Conservative priority although it continued to have strong Scottish advocates such as Alick Buchanan-Smith, who became shadow Scottish Secretary following the Conservative defeat of February 1974, and Malcolm Rifkind.

Margaret Thatcher, the new leader after February 1975, had little sympathy for devolution. In this she was in tune with the general sentiments of her party. However, while opposing the arrangements for Scotland and Wales proposed by the Labour Government in 1976 (which provoked the resignation of

Buchanan-Smith), the Conservatives were still officially committed to devolution for Scotland on the lines tentatively established in 1970. Most English Conservative MPs were opposed to the idea, as were their Welsh colleagues. Scottish Conservative MPs were deeply divided. In the referendum campaign on Labour's Scotland and Wales Acts, the Conservative Party argued for a 'No' vote. This, it was made clear in Scotland, did not mean that the party would not consider an appropriate form of devolution in the future. There was some relief when the Acts failed to generate sufficient public support in the referendum vote of 1 March 1979. Bogdanor sums up well the party's position at this time: the party, he argued, supported 'devolution in theory while opposing it in practice' (Bogdanor, 1980: 93). In Conservative terms that meant not supporting it at all, a position confirmed when the party won office in May 1979.

There has been something of a consensus among critics of Conservative government since 1979 that the traditional order of the United Kingdom has been damaged because of the course of recent policy. In particular, there has developed the notion that (Conservative) England no longer feels obliged to consider seriously the interests of (non-Conservative) Britain. Conservative criticism of socialists and liberals (their lack of practical knowledge) has now been turned against them. For instance, Bernard Crick, with a certain ironic nostalgia for the *ancien régime*, has argued that:

> The old English governing class were historically-minded and had considerable knowledge, strengthened indeed by landowning interest, of Ireland and Scotland. Our present masters are largely ignorant and dismissive of the territorial politics of the United Kingdom, are Anglocentric in mentality and Home-Counties suburban or mid-Atlantic in culture. (Crick, 1990: 111)

The reasons for this could not be ascribed to the electoral geography of Britain. As Robert Blake pointed out, the distribution of Conservative strength in the last quarter of the twentieth century would come as little surprise to a Tory Rip Van Winkle who went to sleep in 1840 (Blake, 1985: 361). Of course, by the 1980s things had become much worse in Wales and quite disastrous in Scotland (Miller *et al.*, 1981: 203–13). This was bound to cause difficulties for the Thatcher administration whatever its policies. Perhaps, as she herself believed, there was not much she could have done anyway about the recrudescence of nationalist sentiment, particularly in Scotland. Did her attitude, however, encourage it?

An indication of her attitude is to be found in Mrs Thatcher's appeal to the Conservative Philosophy Group: 'We must have an ideology. The other side has got an ideology they can test their policies against. We must have one as well' (cited in Gilmour, 1992: 8). This was a rather different emphasis to the traditional Conservative belief that the constitution was an adequate substitute for a philosophy; for the trouble with an ideology is its incentive to make things clear cut when the secret of the Conservative nation has been to rely on convention. There would appear to have been two things which Mrs Thatcher wanted to clarify and which were to cause problems for Conservative unionism. They were first, the superiority of individualism and secondly, the doctrine of parliamentary sovereignty.

Mrs Thatcher has been rather candid about one failure during her term of office. 'There was no Tartan Thatcherite revolution.' This was always a surprise to her for 'Scotland in the eighteenth century was the home of the very same Scottish Enlightenment which produced Adam Smith, the greatest exponent of free enterprise economics till Hayek and Friedman' (Thatcher, 1993: 618). Scotland, unfortunately, had succumbed to the dependency culture of socialism, a culture which had infected all levels of society from the churches to the media. This was a national illness which needed the curative medicine of Conservative individualism. The old order had gone: 'whereas in the past it might have been possible for the Conservatives to rely on a mixture of deference, traditionalism and paternalism to see them through, this was just no longer an option – and none the worse for that' (Thatcher, 1993: 619). That is the true voice of Thatcherite radicalism expressing a new vision of the entrepreneurial Conservative nation. However, 'deference, traditionalism and paternalism' (cf. Crick, 1990) were also aspects of the constitutional relationship between London and Edinburgh if not Cardiff, a relationship which might also be confused or subverted in the titanic battle between socialism and Thatcherite conservatism. More to the point, the Scots themselves might understand it as a struggle between Scottish traditions and an attempt to impose an alien 'English' policy.

Thus J. C. D. Clark has argued that the agenda of Conservative individualism (English influence) 'had never been in itself sufficient, over many centuries, to reconcile England's provinces, neighbours or colonies' (Clark, 1990: 42). It had been overlayed by other integrative doctrines such as liberal constitutionalism, imperial destiny and, latterly, social democracy. These integrative doctrines had now dissolved. It is this which has produced the current political tensions within the United Kingdom:

> from 1979 these aspirations were defined over against authoritarian individualism,
> the claim that the individual's interests and material prosperity were best
> advanced within a strong unitary state devoted to economic freedoms, the rule of
> law, and the individual's emancipation from intermediate powers whether trade
> unions, local government, or the threatened agencies of regional nationalism.
> (Clark, 1990: 42–3)

In the setting of the 1980s 'authoritarian individualism (which might, on the surface, be a culturally non-specific doctrine, exportable to all countries) can take on the air of an aspect of English cultural hegemony'. So it did in Scotland and, to a lesser extent, in Wales.

In her denial of this English cultural bias, Mrs Thatcher herself tended also to give some credence to it. In the conclusion to the chapter on Scotland in her memoirs she argued that part of the difficulty in Scotland was that 'the Tories are seen as an English party' and herself 'as a quintessentially English figure'. While Mrs Thatcher was proud of the second point, she denied the first. 'The Tory Party is not, of course, an English party but a Unionist one.' England, because of its population, just happens to dominate the Union. If the Scots want special treatment they have to persuade the rest of the United Kingdom, in particular the English, of its merits. 'It was understandable', conceded Mrs Thatcher, 'that when I come out with these kinds of hard truths many Scots should resent it' (Thatcher, 1993: 624); but that had nothing to do with her Englishness. On the other hand, as she herself admits, the Scots (collectively) were never persuaded of the merits of Conservative individualism even though many took the opportunity to profit personally by it. Ironically, the one major initiative undertaken for 'her people' in Scotland, the poll tax, became the very symbol of English political imposition (Mitchell, 1990: 113–18).

Part of the reason for Welsh and Scottish discontent lies in the weight given to the principle of parliamentary sovereignty. As Bulpitt argues persuasively, it was the intention of the Conservative government after 1979 to return to the practice of the 'dual polity', to re-establish that 'central autonomy' which the party felt had been lost under the 'overload' of social democracy in the 1960s and 1970s (Bulpitt, 1982: 148). However, this was not a Conservative leadership with a traditional governing perspective. It was a Conservative leadership with a programme to implement and a Prime Minister who wanted to change everything. A governing ideology originally designed to maintain continuity and to modulate differences in the interest of stability was now pressed into the service of a government determined on the regeneration of Britain.

The encounter of this absolute principle of sovereignty as a perceived weapon of English Conservative imposition and the dignity of the nations of the Kingdom is once again captured in Mrs Thatcher's fractious relationship with Scotland. The 'logic' of parliamentary sovereignty – the constitutional people – could provoke its equal and opposite reaction, the 'logic' of popular sovereignty, of national 'legitimacy'. Thus, as the Scottish Convention got under way in Edinburgh on 30 March 1989, there had been ten consecutive years of Conservative 'minority rule' in Scotland and the poll-tax crisis was coming to a head. In a provocative address to the Convention Canon Kenyon Wright asked, referring to Mrs Thatcher: 'What if that other single voice we all know so well responds by saying, "We say no, and we are the state"? Well, we say yes – and we are the people' (cited in Marr, 1992: 206). As it happened the Conservative government – although not Mrs Thatcher's government – did say no to devolution in Scotland; yet the substance of the problem has not disappeared.

Conclusion

Mrs Thatcher's successor, John Major, has rededicated the party to the unionist cause. Addressing prospective parliamentary candidates in Glasgow on 22 February 1992 he stated:

> I believe that we should stand for the historic union of the peoples of the United Kingdom. A union in which our nations work together but each sustains and develops its rich and varied traditions. Let me tell you why. Because England and Scotland, Wales and Northern Ireland together are far greater than the sum of their parts. (News Release JS/975/92)

What is it that is greater than the sum of the parts? It remains the familiar Conservative idea of the constitutional people, a people whose diverse traditions are formally united under the procedures of parliamentary democracy at Westminster.

In 1992 and subsequently, the Conservatives have proposed an old argument for England, Scotland and Wales which had currency at the time of the Irish Home Rule debates a century earlier. The argument, originally stated by Sir Edward Carson, holds that there is no halfway house between Union and separation. In Scotland it proved a reasonably successful cry which stemmed the depletion of the Scottish Conservative vote in the 1992 general election. In sum, the Conservative position on Scottish and Welsh self-government is this. They can have separation if they want it. In the meantime, they can have no self-determining influence over their form of government. In Northern Ireland, however, the Conservative position is that the people there do have the right to self-determination but only to remain formally part of the United Kingdom or to become formally part of a united Ireland. Like the peoples of Scotland and Wales they too have no right to determine their form of government. The difference is that Northern Ireland is to have a *prescribed* form of devolution/Irish dimension (there is a halfway house between Union and separation). As critics were quick to point out, the Conservative principles governing the Union of Great Britain and Northern Ireland and the Union of England, Scotland and Wales now seem to be dangerously inconsistent (see, e.g., Salmond, 1995: 50).

The self-confident assumption (perhaps, the often unthinking assumption) of most Conservative politicians has always been that the value of the United Kingdom is self-evident (Northern Ireland has always been something of a 'special case'). The apparent naturalness of the Conservative nation has tended to conceal the truth that its health has always depended upon will and conviction, upon the ability of the party to convince itself and others that the arrangement is valuable and desirable. Despite a decade-and-a-half of Conservative rule and regardless of the prominent unionism of both Margaret Thatcher and John Major, the Conservative nation is less certain of itself today than ever before. The Conservative leadership has recently staked a large political bet on the electoral appeal of unionist integrity in order to shake public confidence in the constitutional proposals and in the governing ability of Labour. As the Conservative Party has become less British and more English in popular support it has become more unionist in its popular appeal. It remains to be seen if the old union of Englishness, Britishness and constitutional patriotism can sustain and be sustained by the Conservative Party in the future.

CONCLUSION

Where to from here?

Philip Norton

The Conservative Party has a distinguished past. As we have seen, the twentieth century has been dubbed the *Conservative Century*; but does the party have a distinguished future?

There have been times when the party has been variously written off as a credible party of government, yet it has bounced back to dominate British politics. Various commentators wrote it off shortly before the 1992 general election. Even some leading figures in the party were worried about the outcome of the 1987 general election, yet the party remains in government. Is it not, then, in a strong position to dominate the politics of the new millennium?

On the face of it, there are clear grounds for answering yes. It is the party in government. It has been in government for a longer continuous period than any previous administration this century. It has emerged triumphant in four consecutive general elections. Despite internal divisions, it retains an instinct to unite when the political going gets especially tough or a general election is looming. It is led by a politician who, despite poor ratings in the opinion polls, has shown a capacity to fight when challenged, emerging triumphant – and ensuring that he will lead his party into the next election – in a leadership contest in 1995. It remains a party with an instinct for power and is regarded by its opponents as being willing to do whatever is necessary to retain power. Although unpopular during the lifetime of a Parliament, the government, as we have seen (Chapter 11), normally sees an increase in its popularity once an election is under way. Even in 1995, certain leading figures in the Labour Party were not certain that Labour would triumph in the next general election.

There are, however, also powerful grounds for giving an equivocal or even negative answer. Although the Conservative Party won four elections in a row after 1979, it did so with a lower share of the popular vote than it had achieved in previous election victories. It was notably unpopular between elections. The last time it retained a seat in a by-election (and then only just) was in February 1989. After the 1992 election, its popularity slumped. The party

234

plumbed unprecedented depths in the opinion polls, as did the party leader. The Conservative government was not regarded as competent in economic management (Chapter 11). Electors increasingly viewed the Labour Party, first under John Smith (1993–4) and then even more so under Tony Blair (1994 onwards), as more trustworthy and having better policies than the Conservative Party. The wide gap opened by the Labour Party in the opinion polls was maintained for a period unprecedented in polling history.

What is clear, then, is that the Conservative Party faces a situation that does not augur well for future success. That by itself does not consign the party to failure, but it does suggest the need for careful analysis in order to speculate about its future prospects. Why is the Conservative Party of the 1990s experiencing political seas that are so stormy and which, in the eyes of many commentators and, indeed, party members, threaten to swamp it? Are the problems faced by the party essentially superficial and short term or are they deeper and likely to prove lasting?

The problems faced by the Conservative Party can be grouped under three main headings. First, there are the problems faced by the Conservative government as a government: that is, problems that would be faced by any party in government. These are best described as deep and potentially lasting problems. Secondly, there are the problems that are specific to the Conservative Party. These are several in number, some potentially short term and others with long-term implications. Thirdly, there is the challenge posed by the Labour Party, which is now of a very different magnitude to that posed in earlier years. It is the combination of all three that puts the Conservative Party in an apparently perilous political situation in the 1990s.

The problems of government

There are two principal problems under this heading. The first is the increasing gap between expectations and resources. The second is the sheer scale of government responsibilities.

One of the criticisms of the adversarial nature of British politics is that it encourages each party to out-bid the other in election promises, the winning party then having difficulty in delivering on those promises. However, the problem that we identify here is of a different nature and is not confined to British politics. The argument is that popular expectations have changed, both qualitatively and quantitatively, and that the capacity of governments to meet those expectations is limited. The greater the gap, then the greater the popular exasperation with government.

As citizens face growing problems of unemployment, social disruption and uncertainty, the less able are national governments to deal with them. Power, both economic and political, has flowed upwards to multinational corporations and, in Western Europe, supranational institutions. Citizens look to national institutions to address problems that are no longer amenable to resolution at that level. The problem has been variously identified, including by Anthony King in a seminal essay entitled 'The Problem of Overload' in 1976, in which he focused on rising expectations and dependency relationships in a national context (King, 1976: 8–30), and more recently by a leading Conservative politician, William Waldegrave, who put the problem in its international context:

> . . . the malaise we face is, I think, to do with the fact that political systems designed to deliver rather limited objectives, mostly established in the nineteenth and early twentieth century, of a kind which could at least be partly successfully delivered within one's country borders, are now expected to influence decisions or control phenomena which are on a scale far outwith their national capacities to control. (Waldegrave, 1995: 175)

He notes that 40 per cent of Britain's manufacturing base is owned from overseas. Flows of money across the exchanges prevent any attempt at re-establishing more or less fixed currencies. Many problems, such as environmental problems, do not recognise national borders. Such developments invite an international political response. 'If we are to manage European fisheries or a European single market, we need European law. So we set it up' (Waldegrave, 1995: 175). This then generates further problems as national institutions come into conflict with limits to their sovereignty and start to lose allegiance, yet attempts to create international political institutions are insufficient to cope with global problems. 'There will certainly not be a Europe that can control international flows of money or information' (Waldegrave, 1995: 176); hence a growing gap between expectations and the capacity of politicians to do things.

One of the consequences of these developments is popular dissatisfaction with national government and leaders (see Butler, 1995). Thus, on this analysis, it does not matter which party is in government: there will be dissatisfaction with its capacity to deliver what electors expect of it. The actions of a particular government may make some difference, but arguably not enough to affect the basic dissatisfaction with government *qua* government.

The second problem of government is also not exclusive to British government but it is a distinctive feature of the British polity. It relates to the title of King's essay: 'The Problem of Overload'. The overload that we identify here however is not simply in terms of the capacity of governments *qua* governments to raise resources to meet commitments of public policy. It is also the overload on ministers individually.

The burden on ministers has increased significantly over the years. More and more time has to be devoted to a range of responsibilities – party, parliamentary, public and especially departmental – while, arguably, the power to do anything about them decreases. The growth of organised interests has resulted in far more groups making demands of government. Limited national resources means that groups fight harder for a share of those resources. Ministers are the target of such groups and have to spend time making choices. A greater willingness of groups to seek judicial review of ministerial actions means that ministers have to take especial care in reaching decisions. All this takes time. Membership of the European Union has added a particular burden in terms of time spent travelling to and from, and participating in, EU ministerial meetings.

The result is that ministers, especially senior ministers, have little time to relax or to stand back from what they are doing. One minister has recorded how a typical weekend did not begin until 4 o'clock on a Sunday. The process, he said, 'had become dangerously all-devouring. It pushed out everything else' (Fowler, 1991: 322). 'The pressure on Ministerial time', recorded another, 'is enormous. Ministers, with their apparent willingness to become involved in everything from what we eat to how we travel . . . have enormously increased the pressures on themselves' (Patten, 1995: 70). The consequence is ministers concerned almost exclusively with day to day administration and the immediate responsibilities of their departments.

This is significant for the party in government because it means that party leaders – those holding ministerial office – do not have time to stand back and think in strategic terms. There is little opportunity for reflection and forward planning. During the Conservative leadership contest in July 1995 one junior minister, questioned on *Channel 4 News* as to whether the contest was not detracting from the business of government, responded by saying that no, it was not and he had been at his desk at the Treasury all day. The answer reflected the culture of administration that pervades government. It could be argued that it would actually have been a good thing if the leadership contest had drawn ministers away from their desks and forced them to think about where the Conservative Party – and the Conservative government – was going. Both John Major and his challenger, John Redwood, issued manifestos during the contest. That was the closest the Conservative Party came to issuing a mid-term restatement of aims called for by former Cabinet minister, John Patten, in a major work on the future of the Conservative Party, *Things To Come*, published in May 1995. 'It is hard enough work to govern', he wrote. 'To think anew while governing is desperately difficult – but vital' (Patten, 1995: 2).

For the Conservative Party as the party in government there is the difficulty of finding the time to think ahead. Opposition parties have limited resources but nonetheless do have time to reflect and produce statements of principle and policy, rather in the way that the Conservative Party did in opposition in the late 1970s. By the mid-1990s, the Major government was following many of the policies of the Thatcher government. This could be seen not so much as a continuation of Thatcherite policies but simply as a continuation of what went before. Ministers have had little opportunity to reflect, individually and collectively. Cabinet ministers gathered at the Prime Minister's country residence for a one-day session in September 1995 to discuss future policy and the party's election manifesto. The event was notable for its rarity. It finished by early evening.

Hence the difficulty of being able to convey a sense of direction. Ministers spend too much time tending to the trees and have little or no time to stand back and contemplate the forest. What debate that does go on in government is no longer between alternative strategies derived from particular philosophies but rather an argument between carrying on with what has gone before or simply engaging in 'masterly inactivity' (that is, doing nothing). There is no fresh thinking.

Government, in short, is faced with more time-consuming tasks, tasks which it is increasingly unable to fulfil and which it has little time to think about. As John Patten put it, 'If Secretaries of State and Ministers in charge of Departments are to be steersmen, rather than oarsmen forgetfully pulling on the oars of administration, then they need help' (Patten, 1995: 72). The absence of such help works against the interests of the party in government; and that party since 1979 has been the Conservative Party.

The problems of the party

The party thus faces deep problems as the party in government. It also faces problems independent of its tenure of office. The erosion of the class–party nexus has undermined, although not destroyed, an established body of support for both main parties. Neither can take its class base of support as given, or at least not to the extent that it could during the immediate post-war decades. This does not mean that traditional supporters will necessarily switch allegiance, but it does mean that their allegiance cannot be taken for granted. 'The decline in the class basis of voting amounts to a weakening of constraints on volatility and self-expression and the consequence was to open the way to choice between parties on the basis of issue preference' (Franklin, 1985: 176). Each party thus has to work harder than before in order to maintain levels of support, producing policies that attract the support of a more volatile electorate. During the 1980s the Conservative Party had the advantage over the Labour Party in fashioning policies, or at least certain policies, that appeared electorally attractive. By the mid-1990s that advantage had disappeared (Chapter 11). To explain why we have to look not just at the problems facing a Conservative government as a government, but also at problems specific to the party.

There are several problems facing the party that are specific to it. They have been variously drawn out or touched upon in the preceding chapters. Here we draw them together under four headings: competence, issues, leaders and organisation. We can also consider a fifth element in this category: the longevity of the Conservative government.

Competence

In the Introduction, we noted that the capacity of the Conservative Party to convey the impression of being a competent party of government in economic affairs was a central element of the party's continued success. In the period between 1979 and 1992, the party pursued a number of policies that were unpopular, dramatically so in the case of the poll tax. The unpopularity of these particular policies did not appear to undermine the party's appeal as a safe pair of hands in economic affairs and did not act as a bar to the party's success in subsequent general elections. However, since the 1992 general election the party has adopted policies that have dented, indeed – according to some analyses – have destroyed, its appeal as a competent party of government. The party suffered a dramatic decline in political support following the United Kingdom's enforced withdrawal from the ERM in September 1992 (see Chapter 12). As David Sanders records:

> the Conservative lead on economic competence that was evident until mid 1992 had almost certainly been a crucial background resource that predisposed many voters to support the Conservatives electorally – particularly in times of economic uncertainty. From the time of the ERM crisis in September 1992, that resource seems to have dissolved. (Sanders, 1995: 162)

As Sanders goes on to point out, whether the ERM crisis provoked a change in perception or whether it triggered a change that, as a result of three years of recession, was waiting to happen is impossible to say. The important point for the purposes of this analysis is that it happened, and that it was compounded in subsequent years by continuing economic uncertainty and policies that fuelled popular dissatisfaction with the government's handling of economic affairs. The imposition of VAT on domestic fuel was especially unpopular (Chapter 3). Despite an appeal as the low tax party, the tax burden increased significantly during the period from 1992 to 1995. Continued uncertainty appeared to fuel a 'feel bad' factor, voters not being particularly optimistic about future prospects, for the economy generally as well as for themselves (Price and Sanders, 1995). However, even economic recovery was no longer seen as the guarantee it once was of a restoration of the party's electoral fortunes, since such recovery by itself would not necessarily restore the party's reputation for competence (Sanders, 1995: 167).

Issues

We treat issues as distinct from policy competence. The heading relates to disputes about the stance the party should adopt on particular issues. As we have seen in Chapters 4 and 5, the basic tenets and nature of the party offer the potential for clashes within the party, and at various points throughout the party's history that potential has been realised. That has been demonstrably so in recent decades. As Andrew Gamble has shown (Chapter 12), the economy was a notably divisive issue in the 1980s. The clash between 'wets' and 'dries' in the Cabinet in the early years of the decade were bitter and pronounced. The economy remains a divisive issue but has been overshadowed in the 1990s by that of European integration. This constitutes a notable fault line in Conservative politics. It is not a problem confined to the Conservative Party but as it is the party in government it is one that presents more severe problems than for its opponents.

The Conservative Party has been divided on the issue of European integration since the negotiation of the Treaties of Paris and Rome. Opponents of British membership made their voices heard within the party during the early 1960s and again in 1971 and 1972, voting against the European Communities Bill that provided the legal basis for entry (Norton, 1975, 1978). However, the split within the party has become more pronounced in recent years. Margaret Thatcher put the issue firmly back onto the political agenda during her tenure of the premiership, first by her combative stance in dealings with other EC heads of government and then, more significantly in terms of domestic party politics, by her Bruges speech in 1988, in effect delivering a clarion call against further moves towards political and economic union. Opposition to the European Communities (Amendment) Bill – to give effect to the Maastricht Treaty – in 1992 and 1993 maximised opposition on the back-benches, committed opponents of further European integration being joined by a growing body of traditionally loyal back-benchers worried about greater integration (see Chapters 5 and 13). The withdrawal of the whip from eight Conservative MPs in November 1994 for failing to vote for the EC Finance Bill (Chapter 3) emphasised the magnitude of the split and drew media attention to the whipless eight.

The split within the party has contributed to its electoral unpopularity. The issue appears less important than the fact that the party is demonstrably split over it. Electors do not reward divided parties and survey data in 1994 and 1995 showed that electors believed that the Conservative Party was a more divided party than the Labour Party. One MORI poll in November 1994 found that only 12 per cent of respondents believed that the party was the one that was 'most clear and united about what its policies should be', compared with 38 per cent giving the same response for the Labour Party (*British Public Opinion*, December 1994: 4).

Leaders

Margaret Thatcher was a strong leader – a warrior rather than a healer in politics – but her dominance, and especially her intransigence on a number of issues (particularly the poll tax and Europe), was seen as a liability by many Conservative MPs in 1990 (Norton, 1993): hence her replacement by a new leader. John Major, after leading his party to victory in the 1992 general election, is now seen by some Conservative MPs and party activists as a liability and his leadership has become a point of debate within the party. As we have seen (Chapter 9), this is not something peculiar to the Major leadership. However, the context is important.

John Major is a healer rather than a warrior, drawn from the party faithful rather than from a ideological faction within the party (Norton, 1990a, 1990b). He faces a situation where there are demands for both a healer and a warrior. The fact that he was a healer ensured his re-election as party leader in July 1995. Most Conservative MPs were not prepared to vote for a warrior (be it John Redwood or potential challengers in the form of Michael Heseltine, a supporter of greater European integration, or Michael Portillo, an opponent) who was likely to exacerbate splits within the party. However, the perceived need for more of a warrior as leader – someone prepared to take the lead and set the political agenda – appears to motivate back-bench disquiet. It is difficult to satisfy demands for a leader who is both healer and warrior. If the leader takes a strong stand on the issue of European integration, and especially on a single European currency (a must for supporters of European union, anathema to opponents), he is in danger of losing the support of a particular section of the party. If he tries to reach a compromise he allows others to set the political agenda and, potentially, satisfies nobody.

During the 1995 leadership contest some of those MPs and leader-writers demanding a change in leadership were blaming the party's poor showing in the opinion polls on John Major. They could point to the fact, drawn out by David Denver in Chapter 11, that John Major lagged notably behind Tony Blair in surveys as to who was the best person to be Prime Minister. Their view clearly was that the time had come for the leader to be pole-axed (see Chapter 9). For others the real problem was not so much the leader but rather the situation in which the leader found himself. From the point of view of the party's fortunes, the latter analysis could be argued to be the more depressing. The implication is that the party's fortunes cannot be restored by a simple fix – replacing the leader – but require longer-term actions. That analysis gains credence from the other factors that we have identified.

Organisation

As Philip Tether has shown in Chapter 7, the party is suffering from declining resources and membership. This, coupled with divisions over issues such as Europe, has undermined morale and prompted demands for reforms within the party. This decline may be seen as a consequence of the features we have outlined, although – as Philip Tether notes – it may be exacerbated by alternative means of absorbing political energies. A decline in organisational resources lessens the party's fighting capacity in a general election.

Indeed, there is the danger of a vicious circle. The lower the membership and morale, the less able is the party to campaign and get its message across. It therefore fares badly in local and European parliamentary elections and this contributes to a further decline in morale. Demands for changes within the party also contribute to tensions and may lead to some activists deciding to give up party activity if they do not achieve the changes they want. Declining membership may also allow some bodies within the party to be taken over by a particular ideological grouping. This happened in the early 1980s with the Federation of Conservative Students and similar claims have been made in the mid-1990s about the Young Conservatives.

The organisational capacity of the party remains substantial, but Philip Tether's analysis shows that it is far less than it was. The professional staff has been slimmed down. A further restructuring of the party's Central Office took place in the summer of 1995 under the new Party Chairman, Dr Brian Mawhinney. The party was getting ready for the next general election, but it was doing so with less staff than before, fewer party members and a massive overdraft.

Longevity

The length of time that the party has spent continuously in office is also seen by some as contributing to the party's problems. In part, this overlaps with the overload of government. Ministers have too much to do and no time to relax or to take an extended break. Fresh blood is variously brought in at times of reshuffles, but senior ministers are often in place for several years and there is no paradigmatic shift in composition. New ministers always form a small minority of the Cabinet. Ministers become physically and intellectually tired. The longer the period in office, the greater the danger of appearing tired – that is, as a government – and the greater the danger of voters thinking it is time for a change (see Patten, 1995: 2). The greater the danger of this happening, the greater the perceived need on the part of party leaders to engage in fresh thinking and produce new policies, but the less able they are to engage in such an exercise.

Under this heading falls also the argument that the longer the party is in office then the greater the arrogance, greed or laziness of leading party members. The 1980s and, more especially, the 1990s have been marked by Conservative MPs attracting media attention – and increasing media criticism and hostility – because of their acceptance of consultancy posts, taking well-paid posts in the City or in business after leaving ministerial office, having extra-marital affairs, taking ministerial decisions that have subsequently been overturned by the courts, or misleading Parliament. A Gallup Poll in 1985 found that 46 per cent of respondents believed that 'most MPs make a lot of money by using public office improperly'. In 1994 the percentage giving the same answer had risen to 64 per cent. As we saw in Chapter 8, one consequence – following stories concerning the acceptance of money by two Conservative MPs for tabling parliamentary questions – was the creation of the Committee on Standards in Public Life (the Nolan Committee) in 1994. Another was the Scott inquiry into ministerial decisions over the supply of weapon-making equipment to Iraq.

Most of the stories in the late 1980s and first half of the 1990s concerning the acceptance of money and gifts by Members of Parliament involved Conservative MPs. All those concerning ministerial decisions and the acceptance of well-paid posts by former ministers necessarily involved Conservatives. The result was that the Government and parliamentary party appeared tainted by what was dubbed 'sleaze'. The sleaze factor by itself was probably insufficient to destroy the party's electoral popularity, but in the 1990s its significance was in adding to the other variables that caused the party's unpopularity. It reinforced negative perceptions of the party in power.

Giving credence to the argument that longevity is significant is the fact that there appeared to be some parallel with the last years of the Conservative government of Harold Macmillan (see Chapter 2). After more than a decade in office the Conservative Party in the early 1960s was also beset by various scandals, including the Profumo affair (see, e.g., Irving *et al.*, 1963). The scandals appeared to contribute to a popular perception of a government that was tired and arrogant, and out of touch. Some argued that it was 'the natural fruit of a period of government when convenience was set above justice, loyalty above truth, and appearance above reality' (Young, 1963: 112). It undermined confidence in Macmillan's leadership and damaged the government; and, as in recent years (see Chapter 11), a traditionally friendly mass media became far less friendly or even hostile.

The challenge of Labour

As we saw in the Introduction, one explanation for Conservative success has been the capacity of the party's opponents to tear themselves apart at times beneficial to the Conservative Party. The most recent and obvious example was the Labour Party at the beginning of the 1980s, its internal disarray contributing to a massive Conservative victory in the 1983 general election. A negative perception of the Labour Party, especially its capacity to handle the economy, lingered into subsequent general elections.

The problem for the Conservative Party in the 1990s has been that negative perceptions of the Labour Party have largely disappeared. Under the leadership of Neil Kinnock from 1983 to 1992, the Labour Party started to shed its image as a left-wing party unready for government. It became increasingly seen as a serious challenger for office and came close to victory in the 1992 general election. Its image as a credible party of government was enhanced under the leadership of John Smith and even more so under Tony Blair, elected to lead the party in 1994. Survey data showed that electors took the view that Labour had better policies and leaders than the Conservative Party. We have already seen that electors prefer Tony Blair to John Major as the occupant of 10 Downing Street. In November 1994, 44 per cent of those questioned in a MORI poll thought that Labour had 'the best team of leaders to deal with the country's problems', compared with 22 per cent saying that the Conservatives had the best team. In March 1992, respondents had favoured the Conservatives by 40 per cent to 30 per cent. In the same poll in 1994, 42 per cent thought Labour had 'the best policies for the country', compared with 18 per cent giving the same response for the Conservatives. As shown in Chapter 11, Labour is judged the best party to handle economic affairs.

At the end of the nineteenth century the Marquess of Salisbury regarded Gladstone as the Conservatives' greatest asset. In 1983 Margaret Thatcher would have reason to regard the Labour leader, Michael Foot, in a similar light. John Major cannot look at Tony Blair in the same way.

Conclusion

The picture for the Conservative Party in the latter half of the 1990s is not a particularly rosy one. The party appears to have jeopardised its claim to be a party of governance, it is internally divided on issues such as and most notably European integration, it has difficulty thinking through a strategy and policies for the twenty-first century and it faces a revitalised opposition. Hence the Conservative dilemma of the 1990s.

To state the problems faced by the party is not to predict the future. The party has a long history and has proved politically resilient. It has bounced back from political low points before. To demonstrate that the party faces an uphill task if it is to remain office is not to prove that it will fail in scaling the hill. What we have done is to show the scale of the problem facing the party, the hill that it has to scale having grown over the years. In the 1983 general election the party faced an open field, indeed – to follow the analogy – one sloping downward in its favour. Just over a decade later, it faces a veritable mountain.

References

Abrams, M. and Rose, R. (1960) *Must Labour Lose?*, London: Penguin.

Adonis, A. (1994) 'The Transformation of the Conservative Party in the 1980s' in *A Conservative Revolution? The Thatcher–Reagan Decade in Perspective*, Adonis, A. and Hames, T. (eds) Manchester: Manchester University Press.

Allison, L. (1984) *Right Principles*, Oxford: Basil Blackwell.

Aspinall, A. (1926) 'English Party Organisation in the Early Nineteenth Century', *English Historical Review* **41** pp. 389–411.

Aspinall, A. (1952) *Three Early Nineteenth Century Diaries*, London: Williams & Norgate.

Aughey, A. (1981) 'Constituency Attitudes and Policy Formulation: The Role of the Conservative Political Centre', *Hull Papers in Politics No. 7*, Hull: Hull University Politics Department.

Aughey, A. (1989) *Under Seige: Ulster Unionism and the Anglo-Irish Agreement*, Belfast: Blackstaff Press.

Aughey, A. (1994a) 'A Conservative Party policy and Northern Ireland', in *The Northern Ireland Question: Perspectives and Policies*, Barton, B. and Roche, P. (eds) Aldershot: Avebury.

Aughey, A. (1994b) 'British Policy in Northern Ireland: Between Activism and Consolidation', in *Public Policy in Britain*, Savage, S., Atkinson, R. and Robins, L. (eds) London: Macmillan.

Baker, D., Gamble, A. and Ludlam, S. (1993a) 'Whips or Scorpions? The Maastricht Vote and the Conservative Party', *Parliamentary Affairs* **46** (3) pp. 151–66.

Baker, D., Gamble, A. and Ludlam, S. (1993b) '1846 . . . 1906 . . . 1996? Conservative Splits and European Integration', *Political Quarterly* **64** (4) pp. 420–34.

Baker, K. (1993) *The Turbulent Years: My Life in Politics*, London: Faber.

Ball, S. (1994a) 'The Conservative Party Since 1900: A Bibliography' in *Conservative Century*, Seldon, A. and Ball, S. (eds) Oxford: Oxford University Press.

Ball, S. (1994b) 'The National and Regional Party Structure' in *Conservative Century*, Seldon, A. and Ball, S. (eds) Oxford: Oxford University Press.

Ball, S. (1994c) 'Local Conservatism and the Evolution of the Party Organisation' in *Conservative Century*, Seldon, A. and Ball, S. (eds), Oxford: Oxford University Press.

Banks, Sir R. M. (1929) *The Conservative Outlook*, London: Chapman & Hall.

Barnes, J. (1994) 'Ideology and Faction' in *Conservative Century*, Seldon, A. and Ball, S. (eds) Oxford: Oxford University Press.

Beer, S. H. (1965) *Modern British Politics*, London: Faber. (Rev. edn 1969.)

Behrens, R. (1980) *The Conservative Party from Heath to Thatcher*, Farnborough: Saxon House.

Bellairs, C. (1977) *Conservative Social and Industrial Reform*, London: Conservative Political Centre.

Berkeley, H. (1978) *The Odyssey of Enoch: A Political Memoir*, London: Hamish Hamilton.

Berrington, H. (1961) 'Conservative Party: Revolts and Pressures 1955–61', *Political Quarterly* **32** pp. 363–73.

Bevins, R. (1965) *The Greasy Pole*, London: Hodder & Stoughton.

Biffen, J. (1961) 'The Party Conference and Party Policy', *Political Quarterly* **32** pp. 257–66.

Biggs-Davison, J. (1979) *Rock Firm for the Union*, Essex: Monkswood Press.

Blake, R. (1966) *Disraeli*, London: Methuen.

Blake, R. (1970) *The Conservative Party from Peel to Churchill*, London: Eyre & Spottiswoode.

Blake, R. (1976) 'A Changed Climate', in *The Conservative Opportunity*, Blake, Lord and Patten, J. (eds) London: Macmillan.

Blake, R. (1985) *The Conservative Party from Peel to Thatcher*, London: Methuen.

Blake, R. (1995) 'Why the Stupid Party usually Wins', *The Times* 7 September.

Block, G. (1964) *A Source Book of Conservatism*, London: Conservative Political Centre.

Bogdanor, V. (1980) 'Devolution' in *Conservative Party Politics*, Layton-Henry, Z. (ed.) London: Macmillan.

Bogdanor, V. (1994) 'The Selection of the Party Leader' in *Conservative Century*, Seldon, A. and Ball, S. (eds) Oxford: Oxford University Press.

Bolton Operatives Conservative Association (1836) *Report of the Proceedings at the Meeting of the Bolton Operatives Conservative Association*, Bolton Local Studies Library Catalogue, No. B 363 BOL.

Bow Group (1962) *Britain in Europe*, London: Conservative Political Centre.

Bown, F. A. C. S. (1990) 'The Shops Bill' in *Parliament and Pressure Politics*, Rush, M. (ed.) Oxford: Oxford University Press.

Boyce, G. (1988) *The Irish Question and British Politics 1886–1986*, London: Macmillan.

Brittan, S. (1964) *The Treasury under the Tories*, Harmondsworth: Penguin.

Bromhead, P. (1957) *The House of Lords and Contemporary Politics 1911–1957*, London: Routledge & Kegan Paul.

Bruce-Gardyne, J. (1974) *Whatever Happened to the Quiet Revolution?* London: Charles Knight.

Buck, P. W. (1975) *How Conservatives Think*, Harmondsworth: Penguin.

Bulmer-Thomas, I. (1953) *The Party System in Great Britain*, London: Phoenix House.

Bulmer-Thomas, H. (1967) *The Growth of the British Party System, Vol. 1: 1640–1923*, 2nd edn, London: John Baker.

Bulpitt, J. (1982) 'Conservatism, Unionism and Territorial Management' in *The Territorial Dimension in British Politics*, Madgwick, P. and Rose, R. (eds) London: Macmillan.

Bulpitt, J. (1986) 'The Discipline of the New Democracy: Mrs Thatcher's Domestic Statecraft', *Political Studies* **34** (1) pp. 19–39.

Bulpitt, J. (1991) 'The Conservative Party in Britain: A Preliminary Paradoxical Portrait', Paper presented to the Annual Conference of the Political Studies Association, University of Lancaster.

Bulpitt, J. (1992) 'Conservative Leaders and the 'Euro-Ratchet': Five Doses of Scepticism', *Political Quarterly* **63** (3) pp. 258–75.

Burch, M. (1980) 'Approaches to Leadership in Opposition: Edward Heath and Margaret Thatcher' in *Conservative Party Politics*, Layton-Henry, Z. (ed.) London: Macmillan.

Burch, M. and Holliday, I. (1992) 'The Conservative Party and Constitutional Reform: The Case of Devolution', *Parliamentary Affairs* **45** (3) pp. 386–98.

Burke, E. (1969) *Reflections on the Revolution in France*, O'Brien, C. C. (ed.), Harmondsworth: Penguin [first pub. 1790].

Butler, A. (1995) 'Unpopular Leaders: The British Case', *Political Studies* **43** (1) pp. 48–65.

Butler, D. (1955) *The British General Election of 1955*, London: Macmillan.

✓Butler, D. and Kavanagh, D. (1992) *The British General Election of 1992*, London: Macmillan.   1997   1997

Butler, D. and King, A. (1966) *The British General Election of 1966*, London: Macmillan.

Butler, D. and Pinto-Duschinsky, M. (1971) *The British General Election of 1970*, London: Macmillan.

Butler, D. and Stokes, D. (1969) *Political Change in Britain*, London: Macmillan.

Butler, D. and Stokes, D. (1974) *Political Change in Britain*, 2nd edn, London: Macmillan.

Byrd, P. (1987) 'Parties in a Changing Party System' in *Political Parties: Electoral Change and Structural Response*, Ware, A. (ed.) Oxford: Basil Blackwell.

Cambridge Monday Club (1965) 'A Europe of Nations', Cambridge: Cambridge Monday Club.

Campbell, J. (1994) *Edward Heath: A Biography*, London: Pimlico.

Cecil, Lord H. (1912) *Conservatism*, London: Williams & Norgate.

Charlton, M. (1983) *The Price of Victory*, London: BBC.

Churchill, R. S. (1959) *The Rise and Fall of Sir Anthony Eden*, London: MacGibbon & Kee.

Clark, A. (1994) *Diaries*, 2nd edn, London: Phoenix.

Clarke, D. (1973) *The Conservative Party*, London: Conservative Central Office.

Clark, J. C. D. (1990) 'The History of Britain: A Composite State in a *Europe des Patries*' in *Ideas and Politics in Modern Britain*, Clark, J. C. D. (ed.) London: Macmillan.

Coleman, B. (1988) *Conservatism and the Conservative Party in Nineteenth-Century Britain*, London: Edward Arnold.

Coleraine, Lord (1970) *For Conservatives Only*, London: Tom Stacey.

Coleridge, S. T. (1972) *The Constitution of Church and State, According to the Idea of Each*, London: Dent [first pub. 1830].

Committee on Standards in Public Life (1995) *First Report of the Committee on Standards in Public Life, Vol. 1: Report*, London: HMSO.

Conacher, J. B. (ed.) (1971) *The Emergence of British Parliamentary Democracy in the Nineteenth Century*, London: Wiley.

Conservative and Unionist Central Office (1933) *Handbook on Constituency Organisation*, London: Conservative Party.

Conservative Central Office (1962a) *Common Market Progress Report*, London: Conservative Central Office.

Conservative Central Office (1962b) *Weekend Talking Points, No. 391*, London: Conservative Central Office.

Conservative Central Office (1962c) *Weekend Talking Points, No. 392*, London: Conservative Central Office.

Conservative Central Office (1966) *Notes on Current Politics*, October, London: Conservative Central Office.

Conservative Party (1977) *The Campaign Guide 1977*, London: Conservative Central Office.

Conservative Party (1979) *The Conservative Manifesto 1979*, London: Conservative Party.

Conservative Party (1989–95) *Income and Expenditure Accounts*, London: Conservative Central Office.

Conservative Party (1993b) *The Funding of Political Parties: Memorandum of Evidence to the Select Committee on Home Affairs*, London: Conservative Central Office.

Conservative Research Department (1988) *Nine Years' Work*, London: Conservative Research Department.

Conservative Research Department (1994) *Politics Today* No. 1, London: Conservative Central Office.

Conservative Trade Unionists (undated) *Presenting the Conservative Trade Unionists*, London: Conservative Party.

Conservative Women's Organisation (1986) *Fair Comment*, London: Conservative Party.

Cowley, P. (1995) 'Parliament and the Poll Tax: A Case Study in Parliamentary Pressure', *Journal of Legislative Studies* **1** (1) pp. 94–114.

Craig, F. W. S. (1970) *British General Election Manifestos 1918–1966*, Chichester: Political Reference Publications.

Craig, F. W. S. (1982) *Conservative and Labour Party Conference Decisions 1948–81*, Chichester: Parliamentary Research Services.

Crewe, I. (1981) 'Why the Conservatives Won' in *Britain at the Polls 1979*, Penniman, H. (ed.) Washington DC: American Enterprise Institute.

✓ Crewe, I. (1985) 'How to win a landslide without really trying' in *Britain at the Polls 1983*, Ranney, A. (ed.) Washington DC: American Enterprise Institute.

Crewe, I. (1992a) 'The 1987 General Election' in *Issues and Controversies in British Electoral Behaviour*, Denver, D. and Hands, G. (eds) Hemel Hempstead: Harvester Wheatsheaf.

Crewe, I. (1992b) 'Why did Labour lose (yet again)?', *Politics Review* **2** (1) pp. 2–11.

Crewe, I., Day, N. and Fox, A. (1991) *The British Electorate 1963–87*, Cambridge: Cambridge University Press.

Crewe, I. and Searing, D. (1988) 'Ideological Change in the British Conservative Party', *American Political Science Review* **82** (2) pp. 361–84.

Crick, B. (1990) *Political Thought and Polemics*, Edinburgh: Edinburgh University Press.

Criddle, B. (1994) 'Members of Parliament' in *Conservative Century*, Seldon, A. and Ball, S. (eds) Oxford: Oxford University Press.

Critchley, J. (1973) 'Stresses and Strains in the Conservative Party', *Political Quarterly* **44** (4) pp. 401–10.

Critchley, J. (1994) *A Bag of Boiled Sweets: An Autobiography*, London: Faber.

Curtice, J. and Semetko, H. (1994) 'Does it Matter What the Papers Say?' in *Labour's Last Chance? The 1992 Election and Beyond*, Heath, A., Jowell, R. and Curtice, J. with Taylor, B. (eds) London: Dartmouth.

✓ Davies, A. J. (1995) *We The Nation: The Conservative Party and the Pursuit of Power*, London: Little, Brown.

Deedes, W. (1973) 'Conflicts within the Conservative Party', *Political Quarterly* **44** (4) pp. 391–400.

Denver, D. (1994) *Elections and Voting Behaviour in Britain*, Hemel Hempstead: Harvester Wheatsheaf.

Denver, D. and Hands, G. (1974) 'Marginality and Turnout in British General Elections', *British Journal of Political Science* **4** (1) pp. 17–35.

Denver, D. and Hands, G. (1985) 'Marginality and Turnout in British General Elections in the 1970s', *British Journal of Political Science* **15** (2) pp. 381–98.

Denver, D. and Hands, G. (1993) 'Measuring the Intensity and Effectiveness of Constituency Campaigning in the 1992 General Election' in *British Elections and Parties Yearbook 1993*, Denver, D., Norris, P., Broughton, D. and Rallings, C. (eds) Hemel Hempstead: Harvester Wheatsheaf.

Dickinson, G. Lowes (1955) *A Modern Symposium*, London: George Allen & Unwin [first pub. 1905].

Drewry, G. and Brock, J. (1993) 'Government Legislation: An Overview' in *The House of Lords at Work*, Shell, D. and Beamish, D. (eds) Oxford: Oxford University Press.

Eaves, J. (1958) *Emergency Powers and the Parliamentary Watchdog: Parliament and the Executive in Great Britain 1939–51*, London: Hansard Society.

Edelman, M. (1964) *The Minister*, Penguin: Harmondsworth.

Ewing, K. (1992) *Money, Politics and Law*, Oxford: Clarendon Press.

Feldman, B. and Conservative Central Office (1993) *Working Together to Build a Stronger Voluntary Party*, London: The Conservative Party.

Feuchtwanger, R. J. (1968) *Disraeli, Democracy and the Conservative Party*, Oxford: Oxford University Press.

Fisher, J. (1994a) 'Political Donations to the Conservative Party', *Parliamentary Affairs* **47** pp. 61–72.

Fisher, J. (1994b) 'Why Do Companies Make Donations to Political Parties?' *Political Studies* **42** (4) pp. 690–99.

Fisher, J. (1995) 'The Institutional Funding of British Political Parties' in *British Elections & Parties Yearbook 1994*, Broughton, D. *et al.* (eds) London: Frank Cass.

Fowler, N. (1991) *Ministers Decide*, London: Chapman.

Fowler, N. and Conservative Central Office (1993) *One Party: Reforming the Conservative Party Organisation*, London: Conservative Party.

Franklin, M. (1985) *The Decline of Class Voting in Britain*, Oxford: Oxford University Press.

Franklin, M., Baxter, A. and Jordan, M. (1986) 'Who Were the Rebels? Dissent in the House of Commons 1970–74', *Legislative Studies Quarterly* **11** (2) pp. 143–59.

Gamble, A. (1974) *The Conservative Nation*, London: Routledge & Kegan Paul.

Gamble, A. (1979) 'The Conservative Party' in *Multi-Party Britain*, Drucker, H. M. (ed.) London: Macmillan.

Gamble, A. (1988) *The Free Economy and the Strong State*, London: Macmillan.

Garrard, J. (1988) 'Parties, Members and Voters after 1867' in *Later Victorian Britain 1867–1900*, Gouvish, T. R. and O'Day, A. (eds) London: Macmillan.

Gash, N. (1977) 'From the Origins to Sir Robert Peel' in *The Conservatives*, Butler, Lord (ed.) London: George Allen & Unwin.

Gilmour, I. (1971) *The Body Politic*, revised edn, London: Hutchinson.

Gilmour, I. (1977) *Inside Right*, London: Hutchinson.

Gilmour, I. (1992) *Dancing With Dogma*, London: Simon & Schuster.

Goldthorpe, J. H., Lockwood, D., Bechhofer, F. and Platt, J. (1968) *The Affluent Worker*, 3 vols, Cambridge: Cambridge University Press.

Goodhart, P. (1973) *The 1922*, London: Macmillan.

Gorst, H. E. (1900) *The Earl of Beaconsfield*, London: Blackie.

Greenleaf, W. H. (1983) *The British Political Tradition, Vol. II: The Ideological Inheritance*, London: Methuen.

Greenwood, J. (1974) 'The Conservative Party and the Working Classes' *University of Warwick, Department of Politics, Working Paper No. 2*, Coventry: University of Warwick Politics Department.

Hanham, H. J. (1959) *Elections and Party Management: Politics in the Time of Disraeli and Gladstone*, London: Longman.

Harbour, W. R. (1982) *The Foundations of Conservative Thought*, Notre Dame, IN: University of Notre Dame Press.

Harris, N. (1972) *Competition and the Corporate Society*, London: Methuen.

Hart, C. (undated) *Your Party: A Campaign Guide*, London: Conservative Party.

Hayek, F. A. (1944) *The Road to Serfdom*, London: Routledge.

Hayek, F. A. (1960) *The Constitution of Liberty*, London: Routledge.

Hearnshaw, F. J. C. (1933) *Conservatism in England*, London: Macmillan.

Heath, A., Curtice, J., Jowell, R., Evans, R., Field, J. and Witherspoon, S. (1991) *Understanding Political Change*, London: Pergamon Press.

Heath, A., Jowell, R. and Curtice, K. J. with Taylor, B. (eds) (1994) *Labour's Last Chance? The 1992 Election and Beyond*, London: Dartmouth.

Heath, E. (1970) *Old World, New Horizons*, Oxford: Oxford University Press.

Hill, B. W. (ed.) (1975) *Edmund Burke: On Government, Politics and Society*, London: Fontana.

Hill, R. L. (1929) *Toryism and the People 1832–1846*, London: Constable [reprinted 1975, Philadelphia: Porcupine Press].

Hofferbert, R. I. and Budge, I. (1992) 'The Party Mandate and the Westminster Model: Election Programmes and Government Spending in Britain, 1945–85', *British Journal of Political Science* **22** (2) pp. 151–82.

Hogg, Q. (1947) *The Case for Conservatism*, London: Penguin.

Home Affairs, Select Committee on (1994) *Funding of Political Parties*, London: HMSO.

Honderich, T. (1991) *Conservatism*, London: Penguin Books.

Houghton Committee (1976) *Report of the Committee on Financial Aid to Political Parties*, Cmnd. 6601, London: HMSO.

Ingle, S. (1989) *The British Party System*, 2nd edn, Oxford: Basil Blackwell.

Irving, C., Hall, R. and Wallington, J. (1963) *Scandal '63*, London: Heinemann.

James, R. R. (ed.) (1967) *Chips: The Diaries of Sir Henry Channon*, London: Weidenfeld & Nicolson.

Jenkins, R. (1995) *Baldwin*, London: Macmillan Papermac.

Johnston, R. and Pattie, C. (1995) 'The Impact of Spending on Party Constituency Campaigns in Recent British General Elections', *Party Politics* **1** (2) pp. 261–73.

Jones, A. (1946) *The Pendulum of Politics*, London: Faber.

Jones, G. W. (1985) 'The Prime Minister's Aides' in *The British Prime Minister*, King, A. (ed.) London: Macmillan.

Joseph, K. (1976) *Stranded on the Middle Ground*, London: Centre for Policy Studies.

Kavanagh, D. (1976) 'The Deferential English: A Comparative Critique' in *Studies in British Politics*, 3rd edn, Rose, R. (ed.) London: Macmillan.

Kelly, R. N. (1989) *Conservative Party Conferences: The Hidden System*, Manchester: Manchester University Press.

Kelly, R. N. (1994) 'The Party Conferences' in *Conservative Century*, Seldon, A. and Ball, S. (eds) Oxford: Oxford University Press.

Kelly, R. N. (1995a) 'Power in the Tory Party: Developments since 1992', *Politics Review*, April pp. 11–14.

Kelly, R. N. (1995b) 'The Centralising of the Local Party', *Parliamentary Brief* May pp. 80–1.

King, A. (1976) 'The Problem of Overload' in *Why is Britain Becoming Harder to Govern?*, King, A. (ed.) London: BBC.

King, A. (1981) 'The Rise of the Career Politician in Britain – and its consequences', *British Journal of Political Science* **11** (3) pp. 249–85.

Kirk, R. (1953) *The Conservative Mind*, New York: Henry Regnery.

Laing, M. (1972) *Edward Heath: Prime Minister*, London: Sidgwick & Jackson.

Lawson, N. (1992) *The View From No. 11*, London: Bantam.

Letwin, S. (1992) *The Anatomy of Thatcherism*, London: Fontana.

Lindsay, T. M. and Harrington, M. (1979) *The Conservative Party 1918–1979*, 2nd edn, London: Macmillan.

Linton, M. (1994) *Money and Votes*, London: Institute of Public Policy Research.

Lowell, A. L. (1908) *The Government of England* Vol. 1, New York: Macmillan.

Lyttleton, O. (1962) *The Memoirs of Viscount Chandos*, London: Bodley Head.

McDowell, R. B. (1974) *British Conservatism 1832–1914*, London: Greenwood Press.

McKenzie, R. (1955) *British Political Parties*, London: Macmillan.

McKenzie, R. (1964) *British Political Parties*, 2nd revised edn, London: Heinemann.

McKenzie, R. and Silver, A. (1968) *Angels in Marble*, London: Heinemann.

Macleod, I. (1961) *Neville Chamberlain*, London: Muller.

Macmillan, H. (1938) *The Middle Way*, London: Macmillan.

Macmillan, H. (1969) *Tides of Fortune 1945–55*, London: Macmillan.

Macmillan, H. (1975) *The Past Masters*, London: Macmillan.

Mansfield, H. W. Jr (1987) 'Constitutional Government: The Soul of Modern Democracy', *Public Interest* **86** pp. 53–64.

Marr, A. (1992) *The Battle for Scotland*, Harmondsworth: Penguin Books.

Maude, A. (1963) 'The Conservative Crisis', *Spectator* 15 March pp. 319, 321.

Maxwell-Fyfe, D. (1964) *Political Adventure: the Memoirs of the Earl of Kilmuir*, London: Weidenfeld & Nicolson.

Miliband, R. (1973) *The State in Capitalist Society*, London: Quartet.

Miller, W. L. (1991) *Media and Voters*, Oxford: Clarendon Press.

Miller, W.L., Brand, J. and Jordan, M. (1981) 'Government without a Mandate: Its Causes and Consequences for the Conservative Party in Scotland', *Political Quarterly* **52** (2) pp. 203–13.

Miller, W. L., Clarke, H. D., Harrop, M., Leduc, L. and Whiteley, P. (1990) *How Voters Change*, Oxford: Clarendon Press.

Minkin, L. (1978) *The Labour Party Conference: A Study in the Politics of Intra Party Democracy*, London: Allen Lane.

Minkin, L. (1992) *The Contentious Alliance*, Edinburgh: Edinburgh University Press.

Minogue, K. (1992) 'Europe' in *Hubris: The Tempting of Modern Conservatism*, Anderson, D. (ed.) London: Centre for Policy Studies.

Mitchell, J. (1990) *Conservatives and the Union*, Edinburgh: Edinburgh University Press.

Montagu, V. (1970) *The Conservative Dilemma*, London: The Monday Club.

Moran, Lord (1966) *Winston Churchill : The Struggle for Survival 1940–1965*, London: Constable.

Mughan, A. (1993) 'Party Leaders and Presidentialism in the 1992 Election: A Postwar Perspective' in *British Elections and Parties Yearbook 1993*, Denver, D., Norris, P., Broughton, D. and Rallings, C. (eds) Hemel Hempstead: Harvester Wheatsheaf.

Nassmacher, K. H. (1993) 'Comparing Party and Campaign Finance in Western Democracies' in *Campaign and Party Finance in North America and Western Europe*, Gunlicks, A. B. (ed.) Boulder CO: Westview Press.

National Union of Conservative and Unionist Associations (NUCUA) (1961) *Conference Report*, London: Conservative Party.

National Union of Conservative and Unionist Associations (NUCUA) (1970) *Conference Report*, London: Conservative Party.

National Union of Conservative and Unionist Associations (NUCUA) (1972) *Report of the Review Committee to the Executive Committee* (the Chelmer Report), London: Conservative Party.

National Union of Conservative and Unionist Associations (NUCUA) (1993) *Model Rules for Constituency, Branch and European Constituency Councils*, London: Conservative Party.

National Union of Conservative and Unionist Associations (NUCUA) (1994) *Rules and Standing Orders of the National Union of Conservative and Unionist Associations*, London: Conservative Party.

National Union of Conservative and Unionist Associations, Yorkshire Area (1995) *Annual Report*, Leeds: Conservative Party.

Neustadt, R. E. (1960) *Presidential Power*, New York: Wiley.

Neustadt, R. E. (1990) *Presidential Power and the Modern Presidents*, New York: Free Press.

Newton, K. (1993) 'Economic voting in the 1992 general election' in *British Elections and Parties Yearbook 1993*, Denver, D., Norris, P., Broughton, D. and Rallings, C. (eds) Hemel Hempstead: Harvester Wheatsheaf.

Nicolson, N. (ed.) (1971) *Harold Nicolson: Diaries and Letters 1945–62*, London: Fontana.

Nordlinger, E. (1967) *Working-Class Tories*, London: MacGibbon & Kee.

Norpoth, H. (1992) *Confidence Regained: Economics, Mrs Thatcher and the British Voter*, Ann Arbor MI: University of Michigan Press.

Norton, P. (1975) *Dissension in the House of Commons 1945–74*, London: Macmillan.

Norton, P. (1978) *Conservative Dissidents*, London: Temple Smith.

Norton, P. (1979) 'The Organisation of Parliamentary Parties' in *The House of Commons in the Twentieth Century*, Walkland, S. A. (ed.) Oxford: Oxford University Press.

Norton, P. (1980) *Dissension in the House of Commons 1974–1979*, Oxford: Oxford University Press.

Norton, P. (1981) *The Commons in Perspective*, Oxford: Martin Robertson.

Norton, P. (1985) 'The House of Commons: Behavioural Changes' in *Parliament in the 1980s*, Norton, P. (ed.) Oxford: Basil Blackwell.

Norton, P. (1987a) *Parliament in Perspective*, Hull: Hull University Press.

Norton, P. (1987b) 'Prime Ministerial Power: A Framework for Analysis', *Teaching Politics* **16** (3) pp. 325–45.

Norton, P. (1987c) 'Parliament and Policy in Britain: The House of Commons as a Policy Influencer' in *Topics in British Politics 2*, Robins, L. (ed.) London: Political Education Press.

Norton, P. (1987d) 'Mrs Thatcher and the Conservative Party: Another Institution Handbagged?' in *Thatcher Personality and Politics*, Minogue, K. and Biddiss, M. (eds) London: Macmillan.

Norton, P. (1990a) ' "The Lady's Not For Turning": But What About the Rest? Margaret Thatcher and the Conservative Party 1979–89', *Parliamentary Affairs* **43** (1) pp. 41–58.

Norton, P. (1990b) 'Choosing a Leader: Margaret Thatcher and the Parliamentary Conservative Party 1989–90' *Parliamentary Affairs* **43** (3) pp. 249–59.

Norton, P. (1991) 'Parliament since 1945: A More Open Institution', *Contemporary Record* **5** (2) pp. 217–34.

Norton, P. (1993) 'The Conservative Party from Thatcher to Major' in *Britain at the Polls 1992*, King, A. (ed.) Chatham NJ: Chatham House, pp. 29–69.

Norton, P. (1994a) 'The Parliamentary Party and Party Committees' in *Conservative Century*, Seldon, A. and Ball, S. (eds) Oxford: Oxford University Press.

Norton, P. (1994b) 'Independence without Entrenchment: The British House of Commons in the Post-Thatcher Era', *Talking Politics* **6** (2) pp. 80–7.

Norton, P. (1994c) 'Factions and Tendencies in the Conservative Party' in *Turning Japanese: Britain with a Permanent Party of Government*, Margetts, H. and Smyth, G. (eds) London: Lawrence & Wishart.

Norton, P. (1995) 'Whipless MPs: Working without the Whip', *The House Magazine* **659** (20) 9 January pp. 10–11.

Norton, P. and Aughey, A. (1981) *Conservatives and Conservatism*, London: Temple Smith.

Norton, P. and Wood, D. (1993) *Back from Westminster*, Lexington KY: University Press of Kentucky.

Nossiter, T. J. (1975) *Influence, Opinion and Political Idioms in Reformed England*, Hassocks: Harvester Press.

Oakeshott, M. (1948) 'Contemporary British Politics', *Cambridge Journal* **1** (8) pp. 474–90.

Oakeshott, M. (1962) *Rationalism in Politics and Other Essays*, London: Methuen.

Oakley, R. (1980) 'Blue Chip and Guy Fawkes: Mrs Thatcher's Loyal Rebels', *Now!* 4 January pp. 44–5.

Ostrogorski, M. (1902) *Democracy and the Organisation of Political Parties* Vol. 1, *England*, London: Macmillan.

O'Sullivan, N. (1976) *Conservatism*, London: Dent.

Patten, C. (1980) 'Policy Making in Opposition' in *Conservative Party Politics*, Layton-Henry, Z. (ed.) London: Macmillan.

Patten, J. (1995) *Things to Come*, London: Sinclair-Stevenson.

Patterson, B. (1973) *The Character of Conservatism*, London: Conservative Political Centre.

Pattie, C. and Johnston, R. (1995) 'Paying Their Way: Constituency Organisations and Conservative Party Finance', Paper presented to the Annual Conference of the Political Studies Association, University of York.

Paul, W. (1838) *History of the Origin and Progress of Operative Conservative Societies*, Leeds: Paul.

Peele, G. (1976) 'The Conservative Dilemma' in *The Conservative Opportunity*, Blake, Lord and Patten, J. (eds) London: Macmillan.

Pinto-Duschinsky, M. (1972) 'Central Office and "Power" in the Conservative Party', *Political Studies* **20** (1) pp. 1–16.

Pinto-Duschinsky, M. (1981) *British Political Finance 1830–1980*, Washington DC: American Enterprise Institute.

Pinto-Duschinsky, M. (1985) 'Trends in British Party Funding 1979–1983', *Parliamentary Affairs* **38** (3) pp. 329–47.

Pinto-Duschinsky, M. (1989a) 'Trends in British Party Funding 1983–1987', *Parliamentary Affairs* **42** pp. 197–212.

Pinto-Duschinsky, M. (1989b) 'Financing the British General Election Campaign of 1987' in *Political Communications: The General Election Campaign of 1987*, Crewe, I. and Harrop, M. (eds) Cambridge: Cambridge University Press.

Powell, E. (1968) 'Conservatism and Social Problems', *Swinton Journal*, Autumn, pp. 8–16.

Price, S. and Sanders, D. (1995) 'Economic Expectations and Voting Intentions in the UK, 1979–87: A Pooled Cross-section Approach', *Political Studies* **43** (3) pp. 451–71.

Prior, J. (1986) *A Balance of Power*, London: Hamish Hamilton.

Pulzer, P. (1967) *Political Representation and Elections in Britain*, London: George Allen & Unwin.

Ramsden, J. (1980) *The Making of Conservative Party Policy*, London: Longman.

Regan, P. (1988) 'The 1986 Shops Bill', *Parliamentary Affairs* **41** (2) pp. 218–45.

Riddell, P. (1993) *Honest Opportunism*, London: Hamish Hamilton.

Ridley, J. (1992) 'The Unionist Opposition and the House of Lords 1906–1910', *Parliamentary History* **11** (2) pp. 235–53.

Roberts, A. (1994) *Eminent Churchillians*, London: Weidenfeld & Nicolson.

Rose, R. (1964) 'Parties, Factions and Tendencies in Britain', *Political Studies* **12** (1) pp. 33–46.

Rose, R. (1965) *Politics in England*, London: Faber.

Rose, R. (1974) 'Britain: Simple Abstractions and Complex Realities' in *Electoral Behaviour*, Rose, R. (ed.) New York: Free Press.

Rose, R. (1976) *The Problem of Party Government*, London: Pelican.

Rose, R. (1982) *Understanding the United Kingdom*, London: Longman.

Rose, R. and McAllister, I. (1990) *The Loyalties of Voters*, London: Sage.

Roth, A. (1972) *Heath and the Heathmen*, London: Routledge & Kegan Paul.

Runciman, W. G. (1966) *Relative Deprivation and Social Justice*, London: Routledge & Kegan Paul.

Rush, M. (1979) 'The Members of Parliament' in *The House of Commons in the Twentieth Century*, Walkland, S. A. (ed.) Oxford: Oxford University Press.

Rush, M. (ed.) (1990) *Parliament and Pressure Politics*, Oxford: Oxford University Press.

Russel, T. (1978) *The Tory Party*, Harmondsworth: Penguin.

Russell, R. (1962) 'The Value of Commonwealth Preference' in *Britain not Europe: The Commonwealth before the Common Market*, Corbet, H. (ed.) London: Anti Common Market League.

Rutherford, M. (1984) 'The Tories: Still Quite Happy', *Financial Times* 27 January.

Salmond, A. (1995), 'A Clean Break and an Amicable Divorce', *Parliamentary Brief* **3** (5) pp. 50–1.

✓Sanders, D. (1992) 'Why the Conservatives Won – Again', in *Britain at the Polls 1992*, King, A. (ed.) Chatham NJ: Chatham House.

Sanders, D. (1995) '"It's the Economy Stupid": The Economy and Support for the Conservative Party', *Talking Politics* **7** (3) pp. 158–67.

Sanders, D., Marsh, D. and Ward, H. (1987) 'Government Popularity and the Falklands War', *British Journal of Political Science* **17** (3) pp. 281–313.

Sanders, D., Marsh, D. and Ward, H. (1991) 'Macroeconomics, the Falklands War and the Popularity of the Thatcher Government: A Contrary View' in *Economics and Politics: The Calculus of Support*, Norpoth, H., Lewis-Beck, M. and Lafay, J.-D. (eds) Ann Arbor: MI, Michigan University Press.

Sanders, D., Marsh, D. and Ward, H. (1993) 'The Electoral Impact of Press Coverage of the British Economy 1979–87', *British Journal of Political Science* **23** (2) pp. 175–210.

Sarlvik, B. and Crewe, I. (1983) *Decade of Dealignment*, Cambridge: Cambridge University Press.

Schuettinger, R. L. (1969) 'Varieties of Conservatism (i)', *Swinton Journal* **15** (2) pp. 30–9.

Scruton, R. (1980) *The Meaning of Conservatism*, Harmondsworth: Penguin.

✓Seldon, A. and Ball, S. (eds) (1994) *Conservative Century*, Oxford: Oxford University Press.

Seyd, P. (1975) 'Democracy within the Conservative Party', *Government & Opposition* **10** (2) pp. 219–37.

Seyd, P. and Whiteley, P. (1992) *Labour's Grass Roots: The Politics of Party Membership*, Oxford: Clarendon Press.

Seyd, P. and Whiteley, P. (1994) 'A Message for Jeremy Hanley', *Parliamentary Brief* December pp. 28–9.

Seymour, C. (1970) *Electoral Reform in England and Wales*, Newton Abbot: David & Charles.

Southgate, D. (1977) 'From Disraeli to Law' in *The Conservative*, Butler, Lord (ed.) London: George Allen & Unwin.

Spicer, M. (1992) *A Treaty too Far: A New Policy for Europe*, London: Fourth Estate.

Stapleton, J. (1993) *Law and the State in English Political Thought since Dicey*, Durham Research Papers in Politics No. 5, Durham: University of Durham.

Stewart, M. (1977) *The Jekyll and Hyde Years*, London: Dent.

Stewart, R. (1989) *Party and Politics 1830–1852*, London, Macmillan.

Stuart, J. (1967) *Within the Fringe*, London: Bodley Head.

Sykes, R. A. (1982) *Popular Politics and Trade Unionism in South East Lancashire, 1829–1842*, unpublished PhD thesis, University of Manchester.

Szamuely, T. (1968) 'Intellectuals and Conservatism', *Swinton Journal* Spring pp. 5–15.

Tether, P. (1988) 'Conservative Clubs: A Neglected Aspect in Conservative Organisation', *Hull Papers in Politics No. 42*, Hull: Hull University Politics Department.

Tether, P. (1990) *Conservative Associations: Variations by Electoral Environment*, unpublished PhD thesis, University of Hull.

Tether, P. (1991a) 'Patrons' Clubs in the Conservative Party', *Political Quarterly* **62** (2) pp. 291–3.

Tether, P. (1991b) 'Membership Recruitment: A Changing Role for Central Office', *Parliamentary Affairs* **44** (1) pp. 20–32.

Tether, P. (1994) 'The Overseas Vote in British Politics', *Parliamentary Affairs* **47** (1) pp. 73–93.

Thatcher, M. (1972) *Education: A Framework for Expansion*, London: Department for Education and Science.

Thatcher, M. (1988) *Britain and Europe*, London: Conservative Political Centre.
Thatcher, M. (1993) *The Downing Street Years*, London: HarperCollins.
Thomson, G. M. (1980) *The Prime Ministers*, London: Secker & Warburg.
Times, The (1992) *The Times' Guide to the House of Commons 1992*, London: Times Books.
Timmins, N. (1995) *The Five Giants*, London: HarperCollins.
Utley, T. E. (1968) *Enoch Powell: The Man and his Thinking*, London: Kimber.
Vincent, A. (1990) *Disraeli*, Oxford: Oxford University Press.
Waldegrave, W. (1995) 'The Future of Parliamentary Government', *Journal of Legislative Studies* **1** (2) pp. 173–7.
Walker, P. (1962) 'The Challenge of the Commonwealth' in *Britain not Europe: The Commonwealth before the Common Market*, Corbet, H. (ed.) London: Anti Common Market League.
Wallace, W. (1994) 'Foreign Policy' in *The Major Effect*, Kavanagh, D. and Seldon, A. (eds) London: Macmillan.
Warrington Operative Conservative Association (1836) *Report of the Speeches at the Dinner of the Warrington Operative Association*, Warrington Local History Library and Record Office, Catalogue No. p 1363.
Whiteley, P. (1982) 'The Decline of Labour's Local Party Membership and Electoral Base, 1945–1979' in *The Politics of the Labour Party*, Kavanagh, D. (ed.) London: George Allen & Unwin.
Whiteley, P. (1983) *The Labour Party in Crisis*, London: Methuen.
Whiteley, P. and Seyd, P. (1992) 'The Labour Vote and Local Activism: The Impact of Local Constituency Campaigns', *Parliamentary Affairs* **45** (4) pp. 582–95.
Whiteley, P., Seyd, P. and Richardson, J. (1994) *True Blues: The Politics of Conservative Party Membership*, Oxford: Oxford University Press.
Williams, P. (1982) 'Changing Styles of Labour Leadership' in *The Politics of the Labour Party*, Kavanagh, D. (ed.) London: George Allen & Unwin.
Young, W. (1963) *The Profumo Affair: Aspects of Conservatism*, Harmondsworth: Penguin.

Select reading list

This list is designed to provide a guide to books, and some articles and book chapters, that are likely to be easily accessible to the student. The emphasis is therefore on books that have been published in recent years. Books that are no longer in print are mentioned if they have made significant contributions to an understanding of the Conservative Party and are still drawn on in contemporary writings.

History

There are few general historical works on the party. The most recent and substantial is *Conservative Century*, Anthony Seldon and Stuart Ball (eds) (Oxford: Oxford University Press, 1994), offering a wide range of chapters on different aspects of the party in the twentieth century.

Other works include Robert Blake's magisterial survey, first published as *The Conservative Party from Peel to Churchill* (London: Eyre & Spottiswoode, 1970) and updated and reissued in 1985 as *The Conservative Party from Peel to Thatcher* (London: Methuen, 1985), and *The Conservatives*, Lord Butler (ed.) (London: George Allen & Unwin, 1977). The Blake study is available in a paperback issue.

Beliefs and ideological strands

On Conservative thought there are a number of recent publications. These include *The Meaning of Conservatism*, Roger Scruton (Harmondsworth: Penguin, 1980), *Modern Conservatism*, David Willetts (London: Penguin, 1992) and *The Conservative Political Tradition in Britain and the United States*, Arthur Aughey, Greta Jones and W. T. M. Riches (London: Pinter, 1992). Also worth consulting is *Right Principles*, Lincoln Allison (Oxford: Basil Blackwell, 1984). *The British Political Tradition* Vol. II: *The Ideological Heritage*, W. H. Greenleaf (London: Methuen, 1983) traces political thought in this century.

There is a variety of publications that provide interpretations of Conservatism from a particular ideological stance within the party. These include *Dancing With Dogma*, Ian Gilmour (London: Simon & Schuster, 1992).

Competing views to those of Gilmour are to be found in memoirs that provide a distinctive philosophical argument, among them *'My Style of Government':
The Thatcher Years*, Nicholas Ridley (London: Hutchinson, 1991) and Nigel Lawson in his mammoth book, *The View from Number 11: Memoirs of a Tory Radical* (London: Bantam Press, 1992). A more recent and general overview of Conservatism, offered by a practising politician, is *Things To Come*, John Patten (London: Sinclair Stevenson, 1995).

Works on Thatcherism in Conservative thought are numerous. Foremost among them are *The Free Economy and the Strong State*, 2nd edn, Andrew Gamble (London: Macmillan, 1994) and *The Anatomy of Thatcherism*, Shirley Robin Letwin (London: Fontana, 1992). Also valuable are *Thatcherism: Personality and Politics*, Kenneth Minogue and Michael Biddiss (eds) (London: Macmillan, 1987), *Thatcherism and British Politics*, 2nd edn, Dennis Kavanagh (Oxford: Oxford University Press, 1990) and *A Conservative Revolution? The Thatcher–Reagan Decade in Perspective*, Andrew Adonis and Tim Hames (eds) (Manchester: Manchester University Press, 1994). For a critique from the left see *Thatcherism*, Bob Jessop, Kevin Bonnett, Simon Bromley and Tom Ling (eds) (Oxford: Polity Press, 1988).

Philip Norton (1990) '"The Lady's Not for Turning": But What About the Rest? Margaret Thatcher and the Conservative Party 1979–89' *Parliamentary Affairs* **43** (1) pp. 41–58, provides a detailed analysis of ideological groupings within the parliamentary party. *True Blues*, Paul Whiteley, Patrick Seyd and Jeremy Richardson (eds) (Oxford: Oxford University Press, 1994) analyses ideological leanings in the party membership. Recent divisions over the issue of Europe are to be found in Nigel Ashford, 'The Political Parties' in *Britain and the European Community: The Politics of Semi-Detachment*, Stephen George (ed.) (Oxford: Oxford University Press, 1992) and David Baker, Andrew Gamble and Steve Ludlam (1994) 'The Parliamentary Siege of Maastricht 1993' *Parliamentary Affairs* **47** (1) pp. 37–60.

Organisation and membership

There is no recent work devoted to the organisation of the Conservative Party. The classic work on the distribution of power within the Conservative Party is *British Political Parties*, Robert McKenzie, the last edition of which – the 2nd revised edn – was published by Heinemann in 1964. There have been various works focusing on particular parts of the organisation. *The Making of Conservative Party Policy*, John Ramsden (London: Longman, 1980) offers a good history of the Conservative Research Department. The party conference is covered in *Conservative Party Conferences: The Hidden System*, Richard Kelly (Manchester: Manchester University Press, 1989). The last book devoted to the organisation of the parliamentary party was *The 1922*, Philip Goodhart (London: Macmillan, 1972), with more recent coverage provided in chapters by Philip Norton in *The House of Commons in the Twentieth Century*, S. A.

Walkland (ed.) (Oxford: Oxford University Press, 1979) and the *Conservative Century* by A. Seldon and S. Ball (Oxford: Oxford University Press).

Membership of the party is analysed in some detail in *True Blues*, Whiteley *et al*. The composition of the parliamentary party is analysed by Byron Criddle in the Nuffield election volumes edited by David Butler and Dennis Kavanagh, the most recent being *The British General Election of 1992* (London: Macmillan, 1992). Party finance is covered in *British Political Finance 1830–1980*, Michael Pinto-Duschinsky (Washington DC: American Enterprise Institute, 1982) and *The Funding of Political Parties in Britain*, Keith Ewing (Cambridge: Cambridge University Press, 1987).

Leadership

There are numerous works on individual party leaders, especially Margaret Thatcher, but very few that provide a broad picture of party leaders. The most recent is *The Power Brokers: The Tory Party and its Leaders*, Robert Shepherd (London: Hutchinson, 1991). Before that there was *The Tory Leaders*, Sir Nigel Fisher (London: Weidenfeld & Nicolson, 1977). The latter was written shortly after Margaret Thatcher's election to the party leadership and the former in the immediate wake of her loss of it. The change of leadership from Thatcher to Major is covered in Philip Norton, 'The Conservative Party from Thatcher to Major', in *Britain at the Polls 1992*, Anthony King (ed.) (Chatham NJ: Chatham House, 1993).

Works on Margaret Thatcher's leadership and government are numerous. Foremost among them are *One of Us*, Hugo Young (London: Macmillan, 1989) and, in terms of the effect of her government, *The Thatcher Decade*, Peter Riddell (Oxford: Blackwell, 1989) and *The Thatcher Effect*, Dennis Kavanagh and Anthony Seldon (eds) (Oxford: Oxford University Press, 1989). Her leadership is also variously discussed in works by her former ministers – as, for example, *A Balance of Power*, Jim Prior (London: Hamish Hamilton, 1986), *The Turbulent Years*, Kenneth Baker (London: Faber, 1993) and *Conflict of Loyalty*, Geoffrey Howe (London: Macmillan, 1994) – and by Margaret Thatcher herself in her two volumes of memoirs, *The Downing Street Years* (London: HarperCollins, 1993) and *The Path to Power* (London: HarperCollins, 1995).

There is now a number of books on John Major. One of the earliest and best was *John Major*, Bruce Anderson (London: Fourth Estate, 1991). On the effects of his leadership, see *The Major Effect*, Dennis Kavanagh and Anthony Seldon (eds) (London: Macmillan, 1994).

Electoral support

Various classic works are cited in the text. Foremost among them is *Political Change in Britain*, David Butler and Donald Stokes, first published by

Penguin in 1970, with a second edition published by Macmillan in 1974. Among recent collections and analyses of electoral behaviour are *The Decline of Class Voting in Britain*, Mark Franklin (Oxford: Oxford University Press, 1985), *Voters Begin to Choose*, Richard Rose and Ian McAllister (London: Sage, 1986), *A Nation Dividing?* R. J. Johnston, C. J. Pattie and J. G. Allsopp (London: Longman, 1988), *Understanding Political Change*, Anthony Heath *et al.* (Oxford: Pergamon Press, 1992) *Issues and Controversies in British Electoral Behaviour*, David Denver and Gordon Hands (eds) (Hemel Hempstead: Harvester Wheatsheaf, 1992) and – for a useful overview – *Elections and Voting Behaviour in Britain*, David Denver (Hemel Hempstead: Harvester Wheatsheaf, 1994). See also David Sanders, 'Why the Conservative Party Won – Again', in *Britain at the Polls 1992*, A. King (ed.) Chatham NJ: Chatham House, and, by the same author, '"It's the Economy Stupid": The Economy and Support for the Conservative Party' *Talking Politics* **7** (3), 1995, pp. 158–67.

Policies

The best sources on policy are the party's election manifestos and, more substantially, *The Campaign Guide* compiled by the Conservative Research Department and published regularly by Conservative Central Office: the most recent edition, edited by Alistair B. Cooke, is *The Campaign Guide 1994* (London: Conservative Central Office, 1994). The pamphlets published regularly by the Conservative Research Department – under the generic title of *Politics Today* – and by the Conservative Political Centre (usually the texts of speeches by leading party figures) also offer valuable source material.

Various works analyse the effect of conservative administrations on particular sectors of policy, including *The Thatcher Effect* and *The Major Effect*, Kavanagh and Seldon, *The Thatcher Decade*, Riddell, and *A Conservative Revolution?* A. Adonis and T. Hames (eds) (Manchester: Manchester University Press). A wide-ranging review is to be found in *Public Policy Under Thatcher*, Stephen P. Savage and Lynton Robins (eds) (London: Macmillan, 1990). Books written from a critical perspective include *Beyond Thatcherism*, Phillip Brown and Richard Sparks (eds) (Milton Keynes: Open University Press, 1989) and *After Thatcher*, Paul Hirst (London: Collins, 1989).

Updates

For those wishing to keep up to date on recent developments in the Conservative Party in terms of organisation, leadership, policies, and analyses of electoral support, useful articles appear regularly in *Talking Politics*, published by the Politics Association, and *Politics Review*, published by Philip Allan.

Index